BETWEEN EXPERIENCE AND INTERPRETATION

Luke Timothy Johnson

BETWEEN EXPERIENCE AND INTERPRETATION

Engaging the Writings of the New Testament

Edited by **MARY F. FOSKETT**
and **O. WESLEY ALLEN JR.**

Abingdon Press
Nashville

BETWEEN EXPERIENCE AND INTERPRETATION
ENGAGING THE WRITINGS OF THE NEW TESTAMENT

Copyright © 2008 by Abingdon Press

All rights reserved.

No part of this work may be reproduced or transmitted in any form or by any means, electronic or mechanical, including photocopying and recording, or by any information storage or retrieval system, except as may be expressly permitted by the 1976 Copyright Act or in writing from the publisher. Requests for permission should be addressed to Abingdon Press, P.O. Box 801, 201 Eighth Avenue South, Nashville, TN 37202-0801.

This book is printed on acid-free paper.

Library of Congress Cataloging-in-Publication Data

Between experience and interpretation : engaging the writings of the New Testament / edited by Mary F. Foskett and O. Wesley Allen, Jr.
   p. cm.
Festschrift for Luke Timothy Johnson.
Select bibliography of works by Luke Timothy Johnson—P.
Includes bibliographical references (p.   ).
ISBN 978-0-687-64739-2 (binding: pbk. with lay-flat binding : alk. paper)
1. Bible. N.T.—Criticism, interpretation, etc.   2. Johnson, Luke Timothy.   I. Foskett, Mary F., 1961- II. Allen, O. Wesley, 1965-   III. Johnson, Luke Timothy.
   BS2393.B48   2008
   225.6—dc22

2008028763

Scripture quotations unless otherwise noted are taken from the New Revised Standard Version of the Bible, copyrighted 1989, Division of Christian Education of the National Council of the Churches of Christ in the United States of America. Used by permission. All rights reserved.

Scripture marked NIV taken from the Holy Bible, NEW INTERNATIONAL VERSION®. Copyright © 1973, 1978, 1984 by International Bible Society. All rights reserved throughout the world. Used by permission of International Bible Society.

08 09 10 11 12 13 14 15 16 17—10 9 8 7 6 5 4 3 2 1

MANUFACTURED IN THE UNITED STATES OF AMERICA

To
Luke Timothy Johnson,
teacher, scholar, colleague, and brother in Christ,
in honor of his sixty-fifth birthday

CONTENTS

Introduction ix

Contributors xv

Part One
Religious Experience and the New Testament

Religious Experience in the New Testament 3
   James D. G. Dunn

Spiritual Sacrifices in Early Christianity 17
   Daniel J. Harrington, S.J.

"Speaking the Very Words of God": New Testament Perspectives
   on the Characteristics of Christian Speech 35
   Donald Senior, C.P.

"For the Glory of God": Theology and Experience in Paul's Letter
   to the Romans 53
   Beverly Roberts Gaventa

Ecstasy and *Exousia*: Religious Experience and the Negotiation
   of Social Power in Paul's Letter to the Galatians 67
   Sze-kar Wan

The Beatitudes: Jesus' Recipe for Happiness? 83
   Carl R. Holladay

Part Two
Theological Appropriation of the New Testament

Kerygma and Midrash: A Conversation with Luke Timothy
   Johnson and C. H. Dodd 105
   Richard B. Hays

Jesus Made Real in Music: *La Pasión según San Marcos* and
    Luke Timothy Johnson's Experience/Interpretation Model 127
  Gail R. O'Day

"Watch How You Hear": The Healing of *kōphoi* ["Deaf-mute"]
    Persons in Luke 147
  Dennis Hamm, S.J.

From the Servant in Isaiah to Jesus and the Apostles in Luke–Acts
    to Christians Today: Spirit-Filled Witness to the Ends of
    the Earth 175
  William S. Kurz, S.J.

Swallowing Jonah: Scripture and Identity in Early Christianity 195
  Wayne A. Meeks

Notes 217

Select Bibliography of Works by Luke Timothy Johnson 253

INTRODUCTION

Luke Timothy Johnson is a generalist in the best sense of that word. In a day when most biblical scholars focus on a very specialized area of the discipline, Johnson has refused to stay put. He has roamed through the expanse of New Testament studies and sometimes even wandered beyond its boundaries. He does not linger long in the Gospels before moving over to the Epistles, and once there he willingly takes up the role of tour guide through Pauline, pastoral, and catholic writings alike. Similarly, he crosses over historical periods—the historical Jesus, the first century, the early church, all the way to contemporary theological debates—with greater ease than most of us switch buses, trains, or planes. In a word, Luke Timothy Johnson is a scholar for the church and the academy whose work has spanned the New Testament canon and addressed critical issues in literary interpretation of the NT texts, biblical scholarship, NT theology, the social and cultural dimensions of the earliest Christian communities, and current challenges and concerns facing the contemporary church. (See the bibliography included at the end of the book.) Among the most respected and prolific New Testament scholars of his generation, he is also well known by a vast audience of lay readers for his popular writing and frequent contributions to periodicals such as *The Christian Century* and *Commonweal*.

No single volume can do justice to all of Johnson's scholarly and theological commitments. Instead, this volume seeks to honor Johnson by addressing, as its title suggests, a key intersection of his interests that enlivens much of Johnson's work, namely, the relationship between religious experience, the writings of the New Testament, and their interpretation and theological appropriation.

Johnson articulated the significance of the relationship between religious experience and interpretation as well as its formative role in the composition of the New Testament texts and the traditions they recount in his influential and widely read introductory textbook, *The Writings of the New Testament: An Interpretation.* Writing in 1984, Johnson emphasized what he called "the dialectic between experience and interpretation" in the New Testament. He developed his position further in the 1998 foreword to the revised edition of *Writings of the New Testament:*

> This dialectic of experience and interpretation is the basic model I am proposing for the understanding of the writings of the NT. It allows us to answer the fundamental questions of origin and shape: why the documents were written and why they look the way they do. . . . It allows us to ask about the experience that generated, indeed necessitated, the process of interpretation. And it enables us to read each of the writings of the NT as specific *modes* of interpretation: the reshaping of the symbols of Judaism in light of the experience of a crucified and raised messiah.[1]

Thus one of Johnson's most important contributions to NT scholarship has been his insistence on placing the religious experience of the earliest Christians at the very center of NT interpretation.

The consistency of this theme over the span of his career is most obviously evidenced by the 1998 publication of *Religious Experience in Earliest Christianity: A Missing Dimension in New Testament Studies,* where Johnson argued for a phenomenological approach to the study of earliest Christianity that goes beyond the historical and theological paradigms of historical criticism and NT theology to engage the specifically religious dimension of the New Testament texts. However, much of Johnson's work has addressed either explicitly or implicitly the matter of religious experience. A number of his most well-known books (*Faith's Freedom: A Classic Spirituality for Contemporary Christians; The Real Jesus: The Misguided Quest for the Historical Jesus and the Truth of the Traditional Gospels; Scripture and Discernment: Decision-Making in the Church; Living Jesus: Learning the Heart of the Gospels; The Future of Catholic Biblical Scholarship: A Constructive Conversation* (with William S. Kurz, S.J., a contributor to this volume), as well as several of his essays ("Fragments of

Introduction

an Untidy Conversation: Theology and the Literary Diversity of the New Testament;" "Imagining the World Scripture Imagines," "Glossolalia and the Embarassments of Experience," "The Humanity of Jesus: What's at Stake in the Quest for the Historical Jesus"), posit the religious claims and experience of the earliest Christians as a key point of entry for the study of early Christian literature. The point for Johnson is that "Christianity came to birth because certain people were convinced that they had experienced God's transforming power through the resurrection of Jesus" (*Religious Experience*, 185). Interest in the power of this experience—in terms of its ability to impact the symbolic worlds of the followers of Jesus and the way in which religious language and symbol facilitate the very capacity to perceive and interpret experience in the first place—persists throughout Johnson's career.

The scholars whose essays constitute this volume answer Johnson's call for sustained attention to the role and power of religious experience in early Christian writing, even as they move examination of such experience in new directions. Part One of the volume, Religious Experience and the New Testament, opens with James D. G. Dunn's essay, "Religious Experience in the New Testament." As he considers how NT references to the activity of the Spirit speak to an "experiential concept" rooted in Judaism as well as "fresh experiences of the Spirit," Dunn affirms the collective experience that early Christian communities valued, as well as the language and symbols that shaped their perception of experience. After arguing that the Spirit of God functions as "a concept which gains its connotation and resonance from experience," Dunn explores the problematics of claims to experience and the means that Paul promoted for evaluating them.

In his essay, "Spiritual Sacrifices in Early Christianity," Daniel J. Harrington, S.J., focuses on a religious experience that went largely unpracticed in earliest Christianity, namely, the offering of material sacrifice. Arguing that the NT writers "used it creatively as a powerful metaphor to express important aspects of Christian theology and practice," Harrington demonstrates how a common religious experience, or rather its absence, could be harnessed as a device for articulating a distinct religious identity and vision.

Donald Senior, C. P., amplifies Johnson's examination of speech in the Letter of James in his essay on "New Testament Perspectives on the Characteristics of Christian Speech." Using James as a starting point, Senior surveys reflections on speech in the Synoptic Gospels, Colossians, Ephesians, 1 Peter, and the Pastorals and shows readers how "the fundamental basis for the quality of Christian speech is found in the very being of the Christian that has been transformed by his or her renewed life in Christ." For the NT writers, speech evidenced the transformational impact of religious experience.

In their essays, Beverly Roberts Gaventa and Sze-kar Wan delve into the role of religious experience specifically in Pauline literature. Recalling Johnson's image of the back versus the front of an American Catholic church, Gaventa explores how Romans "reflects the move from theology to experience, particularly by the movement from critical reflection to doxology." In " 'For the Glory of God': Theology and Experience in Paul's Letter to the Romans," Gaventa demonstrates that the letter aims not only to "engage in the praise of God," but to "elicit thanksgiving and praise from those who hear it." Wan moves in a different direction in his essay, "Ecstasy and *Exousia:* Religious Experience and the Negotiation of Social Power in Paul's Letter to the Galatians." Here Wan considers the role of ecstatic experience and how the claim of such experience relates to the leveraging of social power in Paul's letter to the Galatians. Thus Gaventa and Wan each ask new questions of Romans and Galatians to unveil previously unexamined dimensions of the letters.

With Carl R. Holladay's reading of the Beatitudes in Matthew and Luke, Part One closes with a fresh look at material that Johnson examined early in his career. Holladay explicates Matt 5:1-13 and Luke 6:20-26 in the context of a conference on ancient attitudes about the human experience of happiness.

Introduction

Part Two, Theological Appropriation of the New Testament, highlights in various ways the significance of religious experience for the theological interpretation and appropriation of scripture. In the opening essay, "Kerygma and Midrash: A Conversation with Luke Timothy Johnson and C. H. Dodd," Richard B. Hays examines "the hermeneutical implications of Johnson's treatment of the New Testament's interpretation of the Old" through a detailed side-by-side analysis of Johnson's *Septuagintal Midrash in the Speeches of Acts* and Dodd's influential *According to the Scriptures*. As he explicates Johnson's work, Hays identifies how Johnson's study taps into the theme of this volume, namely that "the NT writings are fundamentally to be understood as efforts to interpret religious experience."

Gail R. O'Day's essay, "Jesus Made Real in Music: *La Pasión según San Marcos* and Luke Timothy Johnson's Experience/Interpretation Model," illustrates the potential of Johnson's model to serve as a "hermeneutical lens for looking at explorations of the meaning and present experience of Jesus for contemporary life that are not conventionally ecclesial." As she explores Ozvaldo Golijov's setting of the Markan passion narrative, O'Day finds in the composition "an occasion for fresh access to Jesus as a living presence."

The essays by Dennis Hamm, S.J. ("'Watch How You Hear': The Healing of *kōphoi* ['Deaf-mute'] Persons in Luke") and William S. Kurz, S.J. ("From the Servant in Isaiah to Jesus and the Apostles in Luke-Acts to Christians Today: Spirit-Filled Witnesses to the Ends of the Earth") honor Johnson's work in Luke-Acts by examining narrative and intertextual aspects of the two-volume work to arrive at the theological implications of specific Lukan images. Whereas Hamm explores the pastoral and theological resonances of the Lukan theme of "heart-hearing," or "deep listening," Kurz argues for a specifically Catholic appropriation of the Lukan "servant witness." In this manner, both essays take seriously the relevance of NT interpretation for contemporary communities of faith that Johnson has repeatedly emphasized and demonstrated.

Introduction

In the volume's closing essay, "Swallowing Jonah: Scripture and Identity in Early Christianity," Wayne A. Meeks illustrates a particular form of "deep listening." His examination of the Jonah cycle in early Christian art and the commentaries on Jonah that Theodore of Mopsuestia and Jerome produced reveal the degree to which Christians read Jonah, and all of scripture, as a Christian "history of salvation, neatly illuminated against its shadow side, the *Unheilsgeschichte* of the Jews, the history of their sin and rejection." Thus Meeks takes ancient interpretation of Jonah as an opportunity to interrogate the theological and ethical challenges of scriptural interpretation and discernment. While affirming Johnson's focus on the dialectic "between 'the texts of human lives' and the multiple and malleable texts of scripture," Meeks faces head-on "the risk of reading texts that count as sacred" and the ethical imperative to let "complicated hearing happen."

Together these essays honor and develop new arguments for the importance of attending to religious experience when examining the New Testament and its interpretation and appropriation. In the interpretation of these writings that Johnson has described as "fully *human* productions," there is always complexity and always theological potential. Our thanks to these contributors and especially to Luke Timothy Johnson for helping so many students and scholars of the New Testament see that in the interpretation of sacred texts there are riches both human and divine. *Gloria dei homo vivens.*

CONTRIBUTORS

O. Wesley Allen, Jr.,
  Associate Professor of Homiletics and Worship
  Lexington Theological Seminary

James D. G. Dunn
  Emeritus Lightfoot Professor of Divinity
  University of Durham

Mary F. Foskett
  Associate Professor of Religion
  Wake Forest University

Beverly Roberts Gaventa
  Helen H.P. Manson Professor of New Testament Interpretation
    and Exegesis
  Princeton Theological Seminary

Dennis Hamm, S.J.
  Professor of New Testament
  Creighton University

Daniel J. Harrington, S.J.
  Professor of New Testament
  Weston Jesuit School of Theology

Richard B. Hays
  George Washington Ivey Professor of New Testament
  Duke Divinity School, Duke University

Carl R. Holladay
  Charles Howard Candler Professor of New Testament Studies
  Candler School of Theology, Emory University

William S. Kurz, S.J.
  Professor of New Testament
  Marquette University

Contributors

Wayne A. Meeks
Woolsey Professor Emeritus of Religious Studies
Yale University

Gail R. O'Day
Associate Dean of Faculty and Academic Affairs and
A. H. Shatford Professor of Preaching and New Testament
Candler School of Theology, Emory University

Donald Senior, C.P.
President and Professor of New Testament Studies
Catholic Theological Union

Sze-kar Wan
Professor of New Testament
Perkins School of Theology, Southern Methodist University

PART ONE
RELIGIOUS EXPERIENCE IN THE NEW TESTAMENT

RELIGIOUS EXPERIENCE IN THE NEW TESTAMENT

JAMES D. G. DUNN

One of the many services that Luke Timothy Johnson has done for New Testament scholarship, and Christian reflection at large, has been to draw attention to the importance of religious experience in the beginnings of Christianity.[1] This is "a missing dimension in New Testament studies"—the subtitle of his book on the subject. As one who shares the concerns he expressed in that book,[2] it is perhaps appropriate to add my further pennyworth on the subject, both to express my appreciation to Johnson (Happy Birthday, Luke), and to further underline the importance of the missing dimension. I do so as one who came from a rather cerebral Presbyterian tradition and who found that John Wesley's experience of the "heart strangely warmed" spoke to something that had been lacking in his own pilgrimage.

The point was illustrated for me early on by the contrast between Calvin and Wesley on the witness of the Spirit (Rom 8:15-16). For Calvin the witness of the Spirit was the conviction of the truth of scripture.[3] For Wesley, on the other hand, "the testimony of the Spirit is an inward impression on the soul, whereby the Spirit of God directly witnesses to my spirit, that I am a child of God; that Jesus Christ hath loved me, and given himself for me; and that all my sins are blotted out, and I, even I, am reconciled to God".[4] Despite my continuing respect for Calvin, I could not but conclude that Wesley's was a much superior grasp of Romans 8:15-16. My increasing familiarity with the hymns of Charles Wesley reinforced for me how important was the theme of assurance—that is, not the *doctrine* of assurance, but the *experience* of assurance—for the early Methodists.[5] And my growing appreciation of the religious experience attested by the New Testament brought home to me how similar were the beginnings of Christianity and the beginnings of Methodism in this respect.

Equally illuminating for me in my early days of research was the recognition that the tension between the Apollonic and the Dionysiac is a constant in religions generally, and how the balance between the rational and the experiential has fluctuated in our own western European history, with the Enlightenment and the Romantic revival marking two of the most prominent swings of the pendulum. It was certainly a step forward when the History of Religions movement re-emphasized the importance of religious experience over against an understanding of Christianity as doctrine, as Johnson points out, though his criticism of the movement for being diverted into looking for precedents for Christian beliefs and practices is valid.[6] What struck me forty years ago was the fact, missed by most theologians, that at about the same time as the History of Religions school began to dominate studies of earliest Christianity, nineteen centuries later Pentecostalism was beginning to emerge as a third force in western Christianity, emphasizing and winning its steadily increasing support precisely in that it gave primary place to the experience of the Spirit.[7] The point is even more obvious today, given that Pentecostal and the similarly charismatic new churches seem to be becoming an ever stronger expression within world Christianity.

So perhaps it is appropriate to reinforce Johnson's plea to highlight the "missing dimension" in NT studies, since it may be a dimension that needs to be rediscovered yet again in traditional contemporary Christianity.

The fundamental point for me is that the Spirit of God is *an experiential concept*. By that I mean that "Spirit" has been the term used from the beginning of Judaeo-Christianity to speak of the experience of God; the Spirit of God is God insofar as mere human beings can experience God.

The point has been made repeatedly in New Testament studies since Hermann Gunkel's break with the concept of the spirit in idealism: "The theology of the great apostle [Paul] is an expression of his experience, not of his reading. . . . Paul believes in the divine Spirit, because he has experienced it/him."[8] Eduard Schweizer in the opening words of the New Testament section of his famous Kittel article on *pneuma* echoed the same point: "Long before the Spirit was a theme of doctrine, He was a fact in the experience of the community."[9] Highly appropriate, then, is the title Gordon Fee gives to his thoroughgoing analysis of the references to the Holy Spirit in the letters of Paul—*God's Empowering Presence*.[10] I assume Johnson is on the same tack when he writes, "the symbol 'Holy Spirit' serves as the linguistic expression of the experience of power."[11]

The very word first used, *ruach*, remains a vital key. Its range of reference is noteworthy: (1) "wind"—an invisible, mysterious but powerful force experienced by humankind,[12] regularly with the notion of strength or violence;[13] (2) "breath" (or "spirit")—the same mysterious force understood as the life and vitality of humans (and beasts),[14] a force which can be disturbed or activated,[15] diminished or revived;[16] (3) divine power—when *ruach* possesses an early charismatic leader[17] or inspires a prophet.[18]

It is not that these are distinct meanings or references, for they overlap, most strikingly in Ezekiel's famous vision of the dry bones (Ezek 37:9-10),[19] and in the equally famous word play in Jesus' dialogue with Nicodemus (John 3:8).[20]

What seems to unite these different strands is the experience of energy, of *vitality*. We could almost use *ruach* to describe the life force, the mystery of the experience of living. In Hebrew thought this was closely linked with the experience of God, God experienced as life-giving power. Hence the interconnected thought from Genesis 2:7, through Ezekiel 37:9, to John 20:22—the divine breath as that which breathes life into what was otherwise inert and lifeless. So too the early understanding of the human spirit as an extension of God's Spirit—as in Genesis 6:3: "My spirit shall not abide in mortals forever"; and Psalm 104:29-30: "When you take away their breath, they die and return to their dust. When you send forth your spirit they are created." From which, no doubt, derives the degree of confusion evident in the New Testament as to which *pneuma* is being referred to—human or divine?[21] It is no accident or coincidence, then, that the New Testament knows the Spirit particularly as the "life-giver."[22] A vital, living relation with God is the work of the Spirit, and the Spirit is characteristically manifested in the experience of life, of that living relationship.

It also needs to be stressed afresh that the beginnings of Christianity are forever tied to fresh experiences of the Spirit. The Gospels are united in their presentation of Jesus' mission as beginning with his anointing by the Spirit (Mark 1:10-11). That should not be reduced to the equivalent of some ritual act, independent of Jesus' own experience. The naming of the event as "the baptism of Jesus" is regrettable since it allows the event to be understood as a sacrament which conveys grace whether the baptizand experiences anything or not. But the central feature of the event, as described by the Evangelists, is not the baptism itself, but the descent of the Spirit following the baptism.[23] And although all of the Evangelists do not tell the story as an experience of Jesus, in the earliest version of it the descent of the Spirit and the heavenly voice is described as a personal encounter which Jesus experienced (Mark 1:10-11). Moreover, it would appear that Jesus himself referred to the event as an anointing by the Spirit, entailing a strong sense of commission in the spirit of Isaiah 61:1-2.[24] And one of the earliest narrations of the event apart from the Gospels likewise speaks of Jesus being anointed with the Spirit and power (Acts 10:38).

Similarly it is evident that Christianity began as a fresh experience of God, of God's Spirit. We are not dependent solely on the account of the first Christian Pentecost in Acts, vivid as that is, in terms of the group of the first disciples being filled with the Spirit and with ecstatic praise (Acts 2:1-11). Such a revivalist launch of Christianity is embarrassing to more sober-minded Christians of subsequent generations, and it would be easy to discount the Acts testimony as a solitary voice within the New Testament canon. But in fact the experiential character of the first Christians coming to faith is strongly emphasized elsewhere in the New Testament, particularly in the other two dominant contributors to the New Testament, Paul and John. Paul takes it for granted that all believers have been "baptized by one Spirit into one body . . . and we were all given of the one Spirit to drink" (1 Cor 12:13 NIV) once again an experience of Spirit which is not simply to be reduced to undergoing the rite of baptism. He recalls his Galatian converts to their experience of receiving the Spirit, as something they could readily remember (Gal 3:2-5). He speaks of the love of God "poured out" (the Pentecost word) in their hearts through the Holy Spirit given to them (Rom 5:5). The nearest he comes to defining a Christian is in terms of the Spirit indwelling believers, again obviously referring to their experience of the new life given them (Rom 8:9). And the witness of the Spirit, the Spirit bearing witness with our spirits that we are children of God by crying "Abba, Father" (Rom 8:15-16; Gal 4:6-7), uses intense language (*krazein*) which can hardly be divorced from experience. Likewise John uses the vivid imagery of the Spirit as a well of life-giving water welling up in their inner beings (John 4:10, 14), a powerfully experiential image. Similarly the Spirit is depicted as a river of living water bringing life to the one who comes and believes (7:37-39). And in 1 John 3:24 and 4:13 the presence of the Spirit is one of John's "tests of life."

A point that should be given particular emphasis is the fact that the great, the amazing breakthrough of taking the gospel to uncircumcised Gentiles, is attributed in our texts entirely to the work and experience of the Spirit. For all Peter's loyalty to traditional Jewish practices and attitudes, it was the manifest fact that the Spirit had been poured out on Cornelius and his friends which convinced Peter that God had accepted them, and that they should be baptized forthwith (Acts 10:44-48). And the proof of the Spirit was so strong that it convinced even traditionalist James of Jerusalem (11:3-18; 15:14-18). Paul's account of the breakthrough is to similar effect. When at the Jerusalem conference, the pillar-apostles, James, Peter, and John, saw that the grace of God had been so fully and freely given to Gentiles through the mission of Paul and Barnabas, they agreed that God no longer required Gentile believers to be circumcised (Gal 2:6-9)—a hitherto unheard of step.[25] The terms of Paul's report of his evangelistic success are indicated in his questions to his Gentile Galatian converts: "How did you receive the Spirit? By works of the law, or by hearing with faith?" (Gal 3:2). In both versions of the great breakthrough, the key factor is the same. In both accounts it was the experience of the Spirit, the manifest fact that non-Jews were receiving the Spirit of God without becoming proselytes, that convinced even traditional Jewish believers in Jesus that it was now God's will to dispense with the scriptural requirement of circumcision.

The point is worth reflecting on further. For what the joint testimony of Acts and Paul tells us is that without the Spirit being experienced as it was, the new messianic sect of the Nazarene might never have reached far beyond the confines of the Judaism of its time. The point is not to be reduced to another paragraph in the doctrine of the Spirit. The point is that Gentiles experienced something which they had not experienced elsewhere. The experience presumably included a sense of forgiveness and acceptance, an experience of joy, enthusiastic or ecstatic rejoicing in many cases, no doubt. But an experience understood as an experience of the Spirit of God, of God as proclaimed by Peter and Paul. And it was this experience that proved decisive—not (just) their confessing belief or undergoing baptism, but (primarily) their experience of the Spirit. At this point the comment of Lesslie Newbigin in regard to Paul's encounter with the twelve disciples in Ephesus (Acts 19:1-7) is apropos:

> The apostle asked the converts of Apollos one question: "Did ye receive the Holy Spirit when you believed?" and got a plain answer. His modern successors are more inclined to ask either "Did you believe exactly what we teach?" or "Were the hands that were laid on you our hands?" and—if the answer is satisfactory—to assure the converts that they have

received the Holy Spirit even if they don't know it. There is a world of difference between these two attitudes.[26]

There is indeed!

The testimony of the New Testament is also important at this point, since it includes directions on how the abuse of spiritual experience, the experience of the Spirit, may and should be guarded against. Luke's account of Christianity's beginnings encourages a strong emphasis on the experience of the Spirit and on the importance of what may loosely be described as "charismatic phenomena." One need think only of the experiences of glossolalia and inspired speech which evidently manifested the Spirit's coming at Pentecost (Acts 2:1-11), implied at the conversion of the Samaritans (ch. 8), and evidently crucial in the breakthrough to the Gentiles in Caesarea (10:44-48) and in the drawing in of the twelve "disciples" in Ephesus (19:1-7). But also to be noted are the accounts of extraordinary miracles (e.g. 5:15-16; 19:11-12), and the reports of decision-shaping visions (9:10; 10:3-6, 10-16; 16:9-10; 18:9; 22:17-18), two of them explicitly described as "ecstatic" (10:10; 11:5; 22:17). So it is no wonder that the Book of Acts has provided such encouragement to subsequent revivalist movements within Christianity or that it serves as the primary textbook for contemporary Pentecostalism. The problem is, however, that Luke himself seems to share the uncritical attitude to such phenomena which is so often a feature of "enthusiasm" (*Schwärmerei*). In this, we may say, he provides an authentic reflection of the enthusiastic character of earliest Christianity—again a matter of some embarrassment to subsequent more formal and strait-laced generations of Christian. What Acts does not provide, regrettably, is clearer guidelines on how such enthusiasm can be prevented from going to extremes.[27]

It is Paul in particular who shows awareness that checks and balances are necessary in regard to spiritual experience. He himself can hardly be regarded as strait-laced: he counsels his converts to be "led by the Spirit" (Rom 8:13-14; Gal 5:16-18, 25); and he does not hesitate to give thanks to God that he speaks in tongues more than all the Corinthians (1 Cor 14:18)! Nevertheless, the church at Corinth showed Paul clearly how quickly spiritual enthusiasm can get out of hand (see 1 Cor 14:12, 23), and he takes care to warn against that possibility and to provide guidelines for the scope to be granted to enthusiastic phenomena in the gathered assembly.

Here we may express a word of gratitude to the Corinthian church, or at least be grateful for the facts both that there was such a church within the first generation of Christianity, and that Paul was required to address problems which have re-emerged periodically in subsequent generations. For he showed that the way to avoid or deal with excesses of experience-oriented Christianity is not to exclude experience from the definition of Christianity or to disparage experience as inevitably dangerous to good order, but to treat its vitality maturely, as a parent treats the sometimes excessive energy of a child. The advice with which he ends what was probably his earliest letter sums up a balance he evidently sought to maintain throughout his ministry: "Do not quench the Spirit. Do not despise the words of prophets, but test everything; hold fast to what is good; abstain from every form of evil" (1 Thess 5:19-22).

The checks and balances, the tests that Paul uses in dealing with the charismatic enthusiasms in Corinth, are of particular interest.[28] In describing various gifts of the Spirit (charisms) he makes a point of linking some together (1 Cor 12:8-10). The most obvious example is the way "interpretation of tongues" is evidently linked to "various kinds of tongues" (12:10). For Paul's subsequent discussion of tongues makes it clear that for Paul the function of "interpretation of tongues" was, in large part at least, to provide some control over the potential excesses of glossolalia being allowed too much prominence; summed up in the brusque rule that unless speaking in tongues is accompanied by interpretation, glossolalia should be forbidden in the assembly (14:27-28). What is sometimes missed, however, is that the two preceding charisms, prophecy and discernment of spirits (12:10), stand in the same relationship to each other, so far as Paul was concerned. The rules governing the use of glossolalia in the assembly are closely matched by the rules governing the freedom to prophesy (14:29-31). As a contribution to the assembly in a strange tongue must be accompanied by an interpretation (or translation?), so a prophecy must be accompanied by a process of discernment and evaluation. This will be what Paul meant in 1 Thessalonians 5:21: "test everything." Noteworthy is the fact that in 1 Corinthians 14:29 the responsibility to evaluate the prophecy is laid upon the others, that is, probably, the other prophets;[29] but in 1 Thessalonians 5:21 the responsibility is laid on the congregation as a whole (the "brothers" of 5:12, 14).[30] Perhaps it was more important for Paul that prophecy should be tested rather than who it should be tested by.

A second criterion Paul uses should not escape notice—what we might call some preference for the rational when it became at odds with the spiritual, or simply "common sense." I am thinking of the arguments he uses in 1 Corinthians 14:6-25 in regarding prophecy more highly than speaking in tongues. The common sense aspect is most obvious in 14:6-12. The parallels with glossolalia which he draws are indistinct sounds played on the flute or harp, or confused trumpet calls when what is required is a clear trumpet summons to battle. The disparagement is a matter of common sense. Equally silly for Paul is the thought of a language that no one can understand—evidently a contradiction in terms. Paul can even refer to people who are (over)attracted to glossolalia as "immature" or even "infantile" (*nēpios*) (14:20), where it is precisely engagement at the level of the mind that is being taken as the mark of maturity. And 14:13-19 make it equally clear that for Paul it was important that the mind should be engaged in worship. Speaking in tongues leaves the mind "unproductive, unfruitful" (*akarpos*); much to be preferred is prayer and praise "with the mind also" (14:14-15).

The same point can be made with reference to prophecy itself. The fact that prophecy engages the mind does not mean that inspired speaking in a known language is always to be given free rein. In one of those passages where the distinction between (divine) Spirit and (human) spirit becomes blurred, Paul can even say that "the spirits of prophets are subject to the prophets" (14:32). The situation envisaged is where more than one prophet wished to speak/prophesy. The advice given by Paul is that one prophet should be willing to give way to another, even if (the implication is) the first still has something to say under inspiration (14:29-30). Here again the advice is a matter of common sense: either the assumption that the Spirit would not be inspiring two different prophets to speak at the same time; or that as a matter of good order one who has already spoken should give way to the other (14:31, 40). In all this there is obviously an understanding of spirituality as involving the whole person, of the mind equally engaged in understanding and exercising critical appraisal of the phenomena of religious experience which is notably lacking in Luke's account of such phenomena.

A prominent criterion in 1 Corinthians 14 is *oikodomē*, "building up, edifying". The word appears in this chapter four times, and the verb *oikodomeō*, "build (up)", a further three times. He who prophesies speaks upbuilding and encouragement and consolation to those addressed (14:3); the speaker in tongues builds up himself, but he who prophesies builds up the church (14:4-5, 17); the charisms to be most sought are those which function for the building up of the church (14:12, 26). An important aspect of this concern is that the worship of the assembled congregation should be corporate worship; it is important that the others present in the gathering should be able to express their agreement with or assent to what is said, to say "Amen" (14:16). The logic is that of Paul's understanding of the gathered congregation as the body of Christ; the charisms are the functions (*praxeis*) of the body (Rom 12:4), so the charisms function for the benefit of the body as a whole (1 Cor 12:7, 14-26).

A further important aspect, however, should not be ignored. That is the impression made not simply on believing members of the congregation, but also on non-believers and visitors to the assembly. The point is made by posing two extreme cases, where the contrast is still between speaking in tongues and prophesying. In the one case Paul envisages the whole congregation speaking in tongues all at once, giving outsiders the impression that they are all mad. In the other case, all prophesy, speaking intelligible words which penetrate the hearts of the outsider (Acts 14:23-25). The extremes simply illustrate more vividly the basic point: that a spirituality which is intensively focused on oneself, or makes sense only to a very limited number within a congregation, or which is off-putting to the visitor is counterproductive to the church's mission and witness; whereas a spirituality which speaks to the actual condition of outsiders is one which wins others to faith and worship for themselves.

A more profound criterion can be discerned in the background—the criterion of conformity to Christ. In 1 Corinthians 14 it is implied in the opening appeal to *agapē*, "love" (14:1), since the epitome of love for Paul was always the love expressed in Christ's self-giving on the cross (as in Rom 5:8; 8:31-39; 14:15; 1 Cor 8:1; Gal 2:20). It is implied also in the earlier test of the Spirit given in 1 Corinthians 12:3: the mark of the Spirit is the confession (s)he inspires, "Jesus is Lord." But it is implied also in the very fact of Paul's describing the Christian congregation as "the body of Christ" (most strikingly in 1 Corinthians 12). For Paul the "body" is the means by which an individual can live in the world and by which different individuals can be in relationship to each other.[31] So the implication is evidently that the Christian congregation is the means by which Christ relates to the world, and the mutual relations of the members of the congregation are means by which Christ relates to the different members of his body. The phenomena of spiritual experience that he designates as "charisms" Paul thinks of as the functions of the body (Rom 12:4 again). That is to say, the Spirit inspiring various expressions of grace (charisms)[32] is how Christ functions in and through his church. So Christ is the measure of all such spirituality.

Elsewhere Paul describes this in terms of the Spirit as the Spirit of Christ. It is no coincidence that in what is one of the most experientially loaded references to the Spirit—the Spirit crying "Abba, Father!"—it is precisely the Spirit of the Son who inspires the utterance. The cry attests the fact that the worshiper is sharing in the sonship of Jesus, whose own prayers were characterized by the distinctive "Abba" prayer, the fact that the worshiper is a joint-heir with Christ (Rom 8:15-16; Gal 4:6-7).

Similarly significant is the fact that for Paul the goal and norm for the transforming work of the Spirit in the believer's life is conformity to Christ, to the divine image which the eschatological Adam bears (Rom 8:29; 2 Cor 3:18; Col 3:10); the key proof of the Spirit's presence and activity in a life is that the person becomes more like Jesus! And that includes a sharing in Christ's sufferings and becoming like Jesus in his death (Rom 8:17; 2 Cor 1:5; 4:10-12; Phil 3:10-11).[33] The mark of the Spirit for Paul is not charismatic ecstasy or powerful feelings of joy or love, but cruciformity.[34] A *theologia gloriae* without a *theologia crucis* may have characterized the spirituality of many in the church of Corinth, as it has characterized many over-enthusiastic Christian sects in the centuries since. But it does not characterize Paul's spirituality or his understanding either of the Spirit or of how Christ continues to manifest his presence in and through his churches.

I remain persuaded therefore, with Luke Johnson, that religious experience is a core factor in a vital spirituality, and that to reduce the significance of religious experience by confusing the psychological mechanisms and the social forces involved with such experience itself is a fundamental mistake. All academic disciplines are instinctively imperialistic in their attempts to explain as much of perceived reality in the terms distinctive to their own discipline; that is simply a fact of academic life; for centuries Theology was the principal example of the trait. But a mark of the maturity of a discipline is when its practitioners move on to a post-imperialist phase by fully recognizing both that there are other disciplines which quite legitimately and satisfactorily explain the phenomena being studied in their own terms, and that there are aspects of all phenomena which escape the analysis of the tools of one's own discipline. An explanation of religious experience that does not give place to or make room for religious factors is never going to be satisfactory or persuasive.

My point has been simply to reinforce Johnson's argument by underlining the fact that when Christians refer to the Spirit of God they are referring to an experiential concept, a concept which gains its connotation and resonance from experience. "Spirit" is the word that was coined to indicate and express the aweful mysteriousness of experiences of otherly power and vitality from the beginning. Such experiences have always been at the heart of the Judaeo-Christian religion, and go much of the way to explain the sustained vitality and periodical renewals of both Judaism and Christianity. Any attempt to speak coherently of the Spirit of God cannot avoid speaking of religious experience. And any attempt to speak coherently of religious experience in a Christian context cannot avoid speaking of the Spirit of God. As "spirit" denotes that dimension of human being which is other than body and mind, so "Spirit" is the term which grows from the experiential awareness that the same dimension transcends the individual, is wholly "other" and resonates with deity.

A mark of post-imperialistic maturity is recognition of the need for and readiness to engage in self-criticism. One of the chief lessons to emerge from Israel's experience of prophecy was the danger of false prophecy and the importance of being able to test the spirit of prophecy. The canonical prophets, we may say, are those prophets whose prophecies passed that test. And for Paul in particular the discernment of spirits and the evaluation of prophecy (and other charisms) was itself one of the chief gifts that a congregation needed to have and to exercise. Such tests were obviously important in the early generations of Christianity (1 John 4:1-6; Didache 11.1-2; Hermas, *Mand.* 11). And the checks which Paul came up with continue to be relevant today: the necessity not to accept any phenomena of spiritual experience simply at face value; the importance of common sense in evaluating the role and prominence given to religious experience; the priority to be given to what builds up the congregations over the edification of any individual; and the primacy of a corporate life which expresses the character of Christ, the crucified as well as the risen Christ, most fully and clearly.

SPIRITUAL SACRIFICES IN EARLY CHRISTIANITY

DANIEL J. HARRINGTON, S.J.

Sacrifice has been a prominent feature in many religions throughout the centuries.[1] Early Christianity developed out of a sacrificial religion (Judaism) and was surrounded by various Greek and Roman cults in which sacrifice was a central phenomenon. In fact, one of the most peculiar and controversial characteristics of early Christianity was that its adherents did not have temples and did not offer material sacrifices to God, and refused to participate in the sacrificial rituals incumbent on citizens and other inhabitants of the Roman Empire.[2] However, the New Testament writers did not neglect the idea of sacrifice entirely. Rather, they used it creatively as a powerful metaphor to express important aspects of Christian theology and practice.

When I first read Luke Timothy Johnson's volume on the religious experiences of early Christians, I was impressed by its methodological soundness and ability to make come alive some of the central experiential features of early Christianity.[3] This essay honoring Professor Johnson explores what early Christians made out of a common religious experience that they did not share with their ancient neighbors: the offering of material sacrifices to God. After supplying background information about sacrifice in general and in the New Testament world in particular, it explores how in the New Testament the imagery of sacrifices appears in three important theological contexts: ethical (Rom 12:1), ecclesiological (1 Pet 2:5), and christological (Heb 13:15-16). It concludes with a brief reflection on the contributions that these texts can make to our understanding of Christian religious experience in antiquity and today.

My principal personal contact with Luke Johnson came in my capacity as editor of the New Testament commentary series Sacra Pagina. When I was organizing the project, I identified Luke Johnson as the appropriate person to do the volume on Luke's Gospel. I found that he was willing to do Luke only if he could also do the volume on Acts. That was an easy decision to make. The result was two early and fine contributions to the series that are still widely used and quoted by scholars, teachers, and students almost twenty years after their first publication.[4] He also helped me articulate the purpose of the series and to explain in what senses it tries to be "catholic." I have not forgotten his generosity, wise advice, and encouragement.

SACRIFICES IN THE NEW TESTAMENT WORLD

The origin and meaning of sacrifice are shrouded in mystery. Few of its ancient practitioners bothered to comment on these topics. Plato in *Euthyphro* 14c offers the basic definition of sacrifice as a gift to the gods. From this starting point ancient and modern writers have added some specifications that build on Plato's insight. They include the following: a way of feeding the god; providing appropriate food for the temple as the household of the god; giving something precious to the god in the hope of getting something even better in return (*do ut des*); a means toward developing a personal relationship of communion with the god; a vehicle for warding off the anger of the gods; a way of atoning or expiating for offenses committed against the gods or other humans; a ritual enactment of communal violence visited upon a scapegoat; imitating the generosity of God the creator of all things; and attracting and maintaining the divine presence.[5] Every one of these explanations explains something, but no one of them explains everything about sacrifice.

Sacrifice was a central practice in both Greek and Roman religions.[6] The earliest extant texts, such as the *Iliad* and *Odyssey*, contain many references to sacrifice, and take for granted that the readers are familiar with the custom. The offerings consisted of fruits, vegetables, cereals, wine, oil, incense, cakes, and meat from animals and birds. The meat offered to the deities was carefully selected and burned on an altar. In many cases the worshipers and priests shared in the cooked flesh of the animals, thus developing a kind of communion with the gods. In other cases the flesh was totally consumed by the fire, usually as a way of propitiating the deity for some sin and making purification on behalf of those offering the sacrifice. While there are a few references to humans being sacrificed (the most prominent being Iphigeneia at Aulis) in Greek and Roman literature, there is no evidence that the Greeks or the Romans practiced human sacrifice with any regularity.

To an observer retrojected from the twenty-first century into antiquity, the sacrificial system practiced in ancient Israel would not look radically different from the systems at work in other Near Eastern and Mediterranean religions. The materials being offered, the kinds of sacrifices (communion, thanksgiving, expiatory, and so on), the roles of the priests, and the rituals themselves would appear similar at least to the untrained eye.

The most comprehensive presentation of sacrifices in ancient Israel appears in Leviticus 1–7.[7] It describes the rituals associated with the burnt offerings or holocausts, the grain offerings, the guilt offerings, and the sacrifices of well being or communion (see Lev 7:37). Leviticus 16 gives a detailed description of the rituals undertaken on the Day of Atonement (Yom Kippur), on which the high priest entered the Holy of Holies and atoned for his sins and the sins of the people with the sprinkling of blood. What distinguishes Israel's regimen of sacrifices, according to Leviticus 7:38, is the insistence that Israel was to offer sacrifices only to YHWH and only at the tabernacle (and then in the Jerusalem temple as its permanent replacement). Of course, there is abundant evidence throughout the Hebrew Bible that some in Israel offered sacrifices to other gods and at other places. In the view of the redactors of the Torah, however, such conduct was idolatry, the worst sin and the root of all other sins.

The biblical prophets are frequently critical of those in Israel who were neglecting their more basic covenantal obligations (such as justice) or those who presumptuously regarded the temple worship as an absolute guarantee of Israel's security. But no canonical prophet proposes that temple worship and its sacrifices should be abolished. Their goal was the reformation of God's people, including the temple and its sacrificial system. It is in that context that prophetic statements like the one in Hosea 6:6 ("For I desire steadfast love and not sacrifice, the knowledge of God rather than burnt offerings") should be read.

There is, however, a strand in early Jewish apocalyptic that is negative about or even dismissive of the Second Temple built after the return from the Babylonian exile as inferior and unworthy of the one true God. Some apocalyptists hoped for a new and better temple as part of the fullness of God's kingdom. In the "Apocalypse of Weeks" in *1 Enoch* the scenario for the eighth week (concerning Israel's eschatological future) is typical of this sentiment: "A house shall be built for the Great King [= God] in glory for ever more" (91:13).

The Dead Sea scrolls display a variety of attitudes toward the Jerusalem temple and the sacrifices offered there.[8] The central section (B) in the work known as MMT (*Miqsat Ma'ase ha-Torah*) seems to be a list of suggestions about how the sacrifices and related cultic matters should be practiced at the temple, presumably in contrast to how they were actually being practiced under the Maccabean priests who had control of the temple. This impression is confirmed in the concluding exhortation (C) that claims that the calendar in section A and the list of cultic practices in section B were sent for the purpose of correcting certain errors regarding temple worship. The relatively irenic tone adopted in MMT may well reflect an early stage in the Qumran community's split from the Maccabean movement.

The Qumran *Pesher on Habakkuk* reflects a later phase in which the Wicked Priest (who is usually identified as Jonathan or Simon Maccabeus) is accused of pursuing and persecuting the figure known as the Teacher of Righteousness. Some scholars speculate that the Teacher may have been the legitimate high priest. When the Teacher assumed leadership in the Qumran community, it is likely that the members began to regard themselves as a kind of spiritual temple whose prayers constituted acceptable sacrifices to God (as opposed to those being offered improperly in the Jerusalem temple). The shift may well reflect the community's own self-identification as expressed in the *Rule of the Community* as "a House of Holiness for Israel, an Assembly of Supreme Holiness for Aaron . . . a Most Holy Dwelling for Aaron" (8:5-9). This claim in turn seems to underlie the notion that the community's worship constitutes a sacrifice of praise or spiritual sacrifice: "In their seasons I will bless Him with the offering of the lips" (10:6).

Other manuscripts found at Qumran such as the *Temple Scroll* and the *New Jerusalem* texts envision a much larger and more perfect temple city where the sacrifices will be carried out in strict accordance with the divine plan. The work known as the *Songs of the Sabbath Sacrifice* contains poems that were theoretically to accompany the worship services taking place in the (perfect) heavenly sanctuary. The implication is that community members in their worship services on earth were in a kind of mystical union with the angelic host.

From the bulk of the sectarian Dead Sea scrolls one gets the impression that the hope of the Qumran community was that in the blessed future the proper worship would be restored at the Jerusalem temple, and that they would be in charge of it and would carry it out as it should be done. Their apocalyptic expectations very likely included the restoration of a legitimate high priest and a legitimate order of worship, including the proper material sacrifices at the Jerusalem temple. Their documents, however, show how a Jewish group could carry on (at least on a temporary basis) a spirituality of sacrifice without offering material sacrifices.

Several Gospel passages assume that Jesus participated in the sacrificial rites at the Jerusalem temple. According to Luke, when Jesus' parents presented him as an infant in the temple, they "offered a sacrifice according to what is stated in the law of the Lord" (Luke 2:24; see Lev 12:6-8). In the Sermon on the Mount Jesus stresses the need for personal reconciliation with others prior to offering sacrifices at the altar (Matt 5:23-24). And in Matthew 8:4 Jesus instructs a healed leper to "show yourself to the priest, and offer the gift that Moses commanded, as a testimony to them."

However, in the days preceding his death Jesus appears in Jerusalem as a critic of the operation of the temple (if not the temple itself) and as the champion of an alternative approach to "temple Judaism" that can be termed "kingdom Judaism."[9] His prophetic action in "cleansing" the temple (Mark 11:15-19) and his prophecy about the temple's imminent destruction (Mark 13:2) were used against him at his trial before the Jewish leaders (Mark 14:58). On the historical level, they were undoubtedly major factors in the condemnation and execution of Jesus under Pontius Pilate (see Mark 15:29).

There are some indications in the Gospels that Jesus viewed his own death in sacrificial terms. According to Mark 10:45, Jesus as the Son of Man came "to give his life [as] a ransom for many." Likewise, Jesus' words and actions at the Last Supper suggest a sacrificial interpretation of his death. Especially striking in this regard is his saying over the cup: "This is my blood of the covenant, which is poured out for many" (Mark 14:24; see Exod 24:8; Isa 53:11-12). The very early Christian interpretation of Jesus' death as "for us" and "for our sins" implies a sacrificial background. This understanding appears in several pre-Pauline formulas (see 1 Cor 11:24; 15:3; Rom 3:25-26) and in Paul's letters (Rom 5:6; 14:15; 2 Cor 5:14, 21; Gal 1:4; 3:13), that is, in the earliest extant writings in the New Testament.

The material sacrifices associated with pagan rituals caused crises of conscience for some early Christians. In 1 Corinthians 8–10 Paul tried to mediate a dispute between the "weak" and the "strong" about whether Christians can eat meat and other foods connected somehow with sacrifices offered in pagan temples.¹⁰ In Revelation, John the seer encouraged Christians in western Asia Minor to stand firm in their refusal to offer sacrifices to the emperor as a god and to the goddess Roma as a symbol of the Roman Empire. Whereas Paul was flexible and pastorally sensitive in the crisis at Corinth, the author of Revelation was strongly and even rigidly opposed to any participation by Christians in pagan sacrifices in the cities of western Asia Minor.

Two of the six divisions in the Mishnah, the earliest and most authoritative of the rabbinic writings, supply a large amount of information about the temple and the sacrifices offered there. The division known as "Appointed Times" (Mo'ed) deals primarily with the proper celebration of Jewish festivals such as the Sabbath, Passover, the Day of Atonement, and so on, while the division called "Holy Things" (Qodashim) treats sacrifices to be offered in the temple.¹¹

The topic of sacrifices appears sporadically in the other four divisions of the Mishnah, and it is clear that the rabbis who shaped the Mishnah regarded sacrifices as very important, despite the fact that they had not been offered at the Jerusalem temple for a very long time (about 130 years!). The temple had been destroyed and the sacrificial rituals were interrupted in 70 C.E. It is generally held that the Mishnah was compiled by Rabbi Judah the Prince around 200 C.E.

Why then were the rabbis of around 200 C.E. so interested in sacrifices and the temple? One theory suggests that in the Mishnah the rabbis sought to preserve an accurate historical record of the ritual practices carried out in the last days of the Second Temple. Another approach says that the rabbis were planning for the (hoped for) Third Temple, and so wanted to work out an ideal plan for the sacrifices and other rituals that would be performed in the new temple. This would be a case of the phenomenon of "map without territory" in which religious idealists put their time and energy into getting the "map" correct when they no longer have the territory (the temple) itself.¹² A variation on these two approaches says that the rabbis wanted the Third Temple to mirror exactly what the

Second Temple had been.[13] These theories, of course, are not mutually exclusive, and some combination of them appears likely.

SPIRITUAL SACRIFICES IN THE NEW TESTAMENT LETTERS

While the Gospels portray Jesus as visiting and participating in the rituals of the Jerusalem temple (see Luke 2 and John 1–12), several texts in the New Testament letters—Romans 12:1; 1 Peter 2:5; and Hebrews 13:15-16—put forward the concept of "spiritual sacrifices." This development is often described as the "spiritualization" of sacrifice, and the relevant texts are interpreted as rationales for the fact that early Christians were not offering material sacrifices.

Those characterizations are not incorrect, at least from a history-of-religions perspective. However, they are too facile and often dismissive, and neglect the theological profundities that a reading of each of these passages in its context will reveal. The three texts provide ethical, ecclesiological, and christological explanations, respectively, for why early Christians did not offer material sacrifices. They also invoke essential elements in Christian theology and practice. Thus they provide a positive glimpse into the religious experiences and expressions of the early Christians with regard to a religious phenomenon (material sacrifices) with which they were certainly familiar but chose not to practice. How they explained that choice theologically is the subject of what follows.

THE ETHICAL APPROACH: ROMANS 12:1

The earliest New Testament reference to spiritual sacrifices appears in Paul's Letter to the Romans.[14] Whereas the other six undisputed Pauline letters (1 and 2 Corinthians, Galatians, Philippians, 1 Thessalonians, and Philemon) are addressed to communities that Paul himself had founded, Christianity at Rome apparently arose within the Jewish community there some time before Paul wrote his letter around 56 or 57 B.C.E. Paul wrote to the Romans primarily to request their hospitality as he made his way to begin (as he hoped) a new mission in Spain (see Rom 15:22-29).

The Roman Christians would have been familiar with the practice of material sacrifices. The Jews among them may have had first-hand experience of sacrifices in the Jerusalem temple from their youth or as they traveled back and forth between Italy and Palestine. The Gentiles among them had very likely observed and practiced material sacrifices as part of their former pagan religious regimens. Both Jews and Gentiles at Rome would have found themselves in daily contact with temples and shrines all around them in which offerings were being sacrificed to various deities. Thus the concept of material sacrifices must have been commonplace to the first recipients of Paul's Letter to the Romans.

The principal theme of Paul's Letter to the Romans is "the gospel," that is, the good news of Jesus Christ, especially with reference to his death and resurrection, and its implications for believers. After defining the gospel (1:1-17) and establishing the universal need for the gospel (1:18–3:20), Paul relates the gospel to faith (3:21–4:25), freedom (5:1–7:25), life in the Spirit (8:1-39), and God's plan (9:1–11:36), respectively. His mention of spiritual sacrifices in 12:1 comes at the beginning of his general treatment of Christian life (12:1–13:14). What follows are pieces of practical advice about a community conflict (14:1–15:13) and about ways of promoting the gospel (15:14–16:27).

At the beginning of the section devoted to the gospel and Christian life (12:1–13:14), Paul offers the following advice: "I appeal to you therefore, brothers and sisters, by the mercies of God, to present your bodies as a living sacrifice, holy and acceptable to God, which is your spiritual worship" (Rom 12:1; NRSV).[15] As is usually the case in the "ethical" or paraenetic sections of his letters, Paul adopts the stance of one who encourages and exhorts (*parakaleō*), not one who commands or gives orders.

Most of the language in Romans 12:1 would have been familiar to those who knew material sacrifices from their personal experience: "to present . . . a sacrifice, holy and acceptable to God, which is your . . . worship."

But there are some surprises connected with the expressions "your bodies" (*ta sōmata hymon*), "living" (*zosan*), and "spiritual" (*logike*). In the sacrifices familiar to Paul's first readers the offerings would have been animals or other material entities, the offerings (especially the animals) would have been killed and not left alive, and the form of worship would have been regarded as obviously material and not spiritual or rational.

In Paul's letters the word *sōma* ("body") often refers to persons in relationship. By using the plural *sōmata* to describe what is to be sacrificed, Paul suggests that the worship of the Christian that is holy and acceptable to God involves the whole human person in every aspect of life, not animals or other material offerings sacrificed in a temple ritual at one point in time. The holy and acceptable sacrifice of the Christian flows from the "life" of Christ and bears witness to "life" in the Spirit. It proceeds from the divine life and issues in still greater life for the believer and other persons.

The translation "spiritual" for *logike* seems a bit weak and vague, though "rational" and "logical" present their own problems for English-speakers today. Paul's point, however, is clear. The worship that embraces all of Christian life is not materialistic as are the sacrifices offered by pagans and Jews in their temples. Rather, it is spiritual or rational as opposed to materialistic.

Paul employs these references to presenting one's body as a living sacrifice in the form of spiritual worship as a way of introducing the "ethical" sections of his Letter to the Romans. The Pauline ethical ideal is "faith working through love" (Gal 5:6), that is, good works flow from whomever one has become in and through Christ. This Pauline dynamic is often described in terms of the indicative (who one now is in Christ) and the imperative (what one must do to live out and express that identity).

In the context of Romans, Paul evokes the notion of spiritual sacrifices in 12:1 as the first part in his treatment of the foundations of Christian ethics, along with the concepts of realized or anticipated eschatology (12:2), the community as the body of Christ (12:3-5), and the charisms

(12:6-8). Having laid this foundation, Paul moves on to treat love toward others (12:9-21), attitudes toward the Roman Empire (13:1-7), love as fulfilling the Law (13:8-10), and the significance of the coming day of the Lord for Christian conduct (13:11-14).

Besides its ethical dimension, the Pauline concept of Christian life as a living spiritual sacrifice suggests that worship properly understood must involve all aspects of life and should take place at all times and in all places. It is not confined to an hour or so on a special day in a temple (or in a church on a Sunday morning). Rather, formal Christian worship should be viewed as one part in a life in which worship occurs always and everywhere. Formal liturgical worship for the Christian makes sense only in the wider context of the whole of Christian life as a living spiritual sacrifice. It serves as a focusing, encouraging, and energizing moment in a much larger order of authentic Christian worship.

THE ECCLESIOLOGICAL APPROACH: 1 PETER 2:5

The New Testament letter known as 1 Peter is addressed to "the exiles of the Dispersion in Pontus, Galatia, Cappadocia, Asia, and Bithynia" (1:1). It was apparently intended as an encyclical letter to be circulated among Christian communities in various places in northern Asia Minor (present-day Turkey). It was sent from Rome, which is identified by the code name "your sister church in Babylon" (5:13). While some scholars defend its direct Petrine authorship, most associate it with some kind of Petrine circle in Rome around 80 C.E.[16]

The original addressees of 1 Peter seem to have been Gentile Christians for the most part. The author reminds them of "the desires that you formerly had in ignorance" (1:14) and how they "were ransomed from the futile ways inherited from your ancestors" (1:18). These are not statements that would have been made so facilely about Jewish Christians. Their identity as Gentiles is further clarified by the reminder that "once you were not a people but now you are God's people" (2:10). The several references to their "exile" (1:17) and their status as "aliens and exiles" (2:11) have led some scholars to suppose that these Gentile Christians may have been some sort of migrant workers.[17] At any rate, they were at least suffering social ostracism because their new faith and new way of life made them different from their neighbors (4:4, 16). However, despite the obvious Gentile origins of those addressed in 1 Peter, the author writes to them as if they are part of the historic people of Israel. By using the term "dispersion" (*diaspora*) in 1:1 he establishes this identity at the outset, and in 2:12 he even urges them to "conduct yourselves honorably among the Gentiles."

There is much baptismal language in 1 Peter, with particular attention to the new identity that these people have obtained through "the precious blood of Christ" (1:19). The rhetorical and theological high point of the letter comes in 2:9 when the author describes his (Gentile Christian) readers as "a chosen race, a royal priesthood, a holy nation, God's own people." Thus he attributes to them the salvation-historical privileges bestowed on ancient Israel at Mount Sinai (see Exod 19:6).

The theme of spiritual sacrifices appears in 1 Peter 2:5: "like living stones, let yourselves be built into a spiritual house, to be a holy priesthood, to offer spiritual sacrifices (*pneumatikas thysias*) acceptable to God through Jesus Christ." This verse follows an appeal in 2:4 to the Gentile Christians to "come to him [Christ], a living stone, though rejected by mortals yet chosen and precious in God's sight." Such an appeal was appropriate for people who because of their new faith found themselves rejected by and alienated from their neighbors. At several other points the addressees are urged to look to the sufferings of Christ as a source of encouragement and perseverance in the midst of their sufferings (see 2:21, 24; 4:13).

The appeals in 1 Peter 2:4-5 are followed in 2:6-8 by a chain or catena of biblical quotations that leads up to the climax in 2:9-10. The catena in 2:6-8 is structured around three OT passages containing the word "stone" (*lithos* in Greek): "see I am laying in Zion a stone" (Isa 28:16); "the stone that the builders rejected has become the very head of the corner"

(Ps 118[117]:22); and "a stone that makes them stumble, and a rock that makes them fall" (Isa 8:14). The implication is that each text really refers to Christ (or has reached its "fuller meaning" in him) as the "stone." These same texts appear elsewhere in the NT (see Matt 21:41; Rom 9:33), suggesting that the catena used here was already traditional.[18] Similar collections of biblical quotations have been found among the Qumran scrolls and are called florilegia (anthologies) by modern scholars. The "stone" catena may well reflect a play on the Hebrew words *'eben* ("stone") and *ben* ("son"), that is, the Son (Jesus) is the "stone."

All this provides the context for the mention of "spiritual sacrifices" in 1 Pet 2:5. In their sufferings the Christians of northern Asia Minor understood themselves to be imitating the example of Christ, the living stone rejected by others but precious before God. Through their baptism and incorporation into Christ they formed a spiritual temple or "house," and functioned as a corporate or collective "holy priesthood." Instead of the Jerusalem temple, the Christian community made up of Jews and Gentiles became the place where God was understood to be especially present. Rather than relying on priests designated to offer sacrifices, these Christians formed a priesthood that was understood to be capable of offering the sacrifices that were truly acceptable to God.

These "aliens and exiles" did not have temples or permanent houses of worship, nor did they offer material sacrifices to God and Christ. However, as those called by God "out of darkness into his marvelous light" (2:9), and as the church of Jesus Christ, they functioned as the people of God. As ones constituting the true temple and the true priesthood, they offered the true sacrifices.

Their spiritual sacrifices were most likely their prayers and hymns offered to God. The occasion for these spiritual sacrifices was most likely the community assembly at which the Lord's Supper was celebrated.[19] However, there are no indications that the Eucharist itself was yet being equated with the "spiritual sacrifices," though Jesus' words over the cup about "the blood of the covenant, which is poured out for many" (Mark 14:24) might suggest such an equation. Rather, the use of the expression "spiritual sacrifices" in 1 Peter is better described as ecclesiological than as sacramental.

THE CHRISTOLOGICAL APPROACH: HEBREWS 13:15-16

The only reference to spiritual sacrifices in the Letter to the Hebrews comes in the final chapter amidst what looks like a scramble to conclude a long sermon ("word of exhortation," 13:22). As the author moves rapidly from topic to topic, he takes up the kind of "sacrifices" that Christians may and should offer to God: "Through him [Jesus Christ], then, let us continually offer a sacrifice of praise to God, that is, the fruit of lips that confess his name. Do not neglect to do good and to share what you have, for such sacrifices are pleasing to God" (13:15-16).

According to the author of Hebrews, true worship for Christians is not to be expressed in the material sacrifices of the old covenant. Rather, the sacrifices that are now acceptable to God are preeminently the praise of God ("the fruit of lips") and good deeds ("to do good and to share what you have"). The extent to which the sacrifice of praise alludes to the Eucharist is uncertain (though dubious). More likely, it refers simply to the prayers and hymns offered to God as in the Qumran *Rule of the Community* 10:6 and 1 Peter 2:5.

Elsewhere in Hebrews the focus has been on the material sacrifices of the old covenant and the perfect sacrifice of the new covenant in the death of Jesus. Nevertheless, the insistence on spiritual sacrifices offered by Christians is related closely to the central concern of the letter as a whole. In fact, it flows logically and theologically from the rest of the work.

What is traditionally called the Letter to the Hebrews is better understood as an early Christian sermon. The description of it as "a word of exhortation" in 13:22 is a more accurate categorization. In fact, it is arguably the greatest Christian sermon ever written down. Throughout the text the author does what a good Christian preacher should do by combining biblical interpretation and pastoral advice.[20]

The historical origin of Hebrews remains mysterious.[21] The Church

Father Origen observed that only God knows who wrote Hebrews. There is some connection with Italy (see 13:24), and perhaps it was sent to (or from) Rome. Some scholars date it early (in the 60s C.E.), while others assign it a later date (up to 100 C.E.). The scenario that interprets Hebrews as a sermon written before 70 C.E. for a Jewish Christian community at Rome that had become discouraged with their new Christian faith and were contemplating a return to Judaism is attractive but cannot be proved definitively.[22]

What is clear are the author's theological convictions that Christ is the key to interpreting the Scriptures (1:1–4:13) and that Jesus' death on the cross was the perfect and acceptable sacrifice for sins (4:14–10:18). Thus Hebrews is an extended meditation on the early Christian confession of faith that "Christ died for our sins in accordance with the scriptures" (1 Cor 15:3). What the author adds to the early Christian tradition is the idea that because Jesus willingly offered himself as a sacrifice for sins, he can therefore be regarded as the great high priest. Since priests offer sacrifices and since Christ willingly offered himself, he must have been a priest even though he did not come from a Jewish priestly family (see 7:13-14).[23]

In the central section of Hebrews (4:14–10:18), the author explains first that Christ possessed the qualifications for being a compassionate high priest, and how he became "the source of eternal salvation for all who obey him" (5:9). In chapter 7 he argues (somewhat artificially, to put it mildly) that the priesthood of Melchizedek (see Gen 14:17-20; Ps 110:4) was superior to that of Aaron and Levi, and that the one perfect sacrifice of himself offered by Christ rendered obsolete the sacrifices offered by the Jewish Levitical priests (7:27). He regards the furnishings of the tabernacle (and by extension, of the temple) as only a "sketch and shadow" (8:5) of the heavenly sanctuary where Christ the true high priest now presides. The better priesthood of Christ is based on "a better covenant, which has been enacted through better promises" (8:6). This is the priesthood of the new covenant.

On the Day of Atonement (see Lev 16), the Jewish high priest offered animal sacrifice (the scapegoat) and sprinkled blood in the Holy of Holies. The purpose of these annual rituals was to atone (*kipper* in Hebrew) on behalf of his own sins and those of the people. For the author of Hebrews, the very fact that he did so every year was proof of the ineffectiveness of the material sacrifices offered in the tabernacle and the temple. These material sacrifices were at best "a shadow of the good things to come" (10:1). What Christ did on the cross was to offer the only truly effective sacrifice for sins and thus to achieve the goal that the material sacrifices foreshadowed. The author describes Christ's sacrifice with an emphasis on its absolute efficacy: "we have been sanctified through the offering of the body of Jesus Christ once for all" (10:10); and "Christ . . . offered for all time a single sacrifice for sins" (10:12).

The central section of Hebrews provides a christological foundation for the spiritual sacrifices mentioned only near the end, in 13:15-16. In the author's perspective, Christ in his death on the cross brought about what the material sacrifices of the Levitical priests pointed toward but could never fully and permanently achieve: forgiveness of sins, genuine communion with God, and access to the throne of grace. His lengthy reflection on Christ as both the perfect (in the sense of fulfilling its goal or *telos*) sacrifice and the great high priest (who willingly offered himself) provided the christological rationale for early Christians not to offer material sacrifices and not to revert to Judaism and its sacrificial system of material offerings.

CONCLUSION

In the world in which early Christianity took shape, material sacrifice was a common religious phenomenon. Jewish Christians knew about sacrifice from direct experience at the Jerusalem temple or at least from the relevant biblical passages. Gentile Christians (like Diaspora Jews) who lived in the major cities of the Roman Empire were in constant contact with the sacrifices being offered in various pagan temples and homes. In this context early Christians stood out because they did not offer material sacrifices. Some of them even had scruples about eating the meat sold in the markets on the grounds that it had been contaminated by association with pagan temple rituals (see 1 Cor 8–10).

Why exactly the earliest Christians did not offer material sacrifices is not entirely clear. Perhaps it was for pragmatic reasons—because there were so few of them, and they did not have the numbers or financial resources to support a temple and its sacrificial system. Perhaps it was because they were familiar with and influenced by the practices of the Jewish synagogues, where worship consisted of Scripture readings, prayers, and hymns, and did not include material sacrifices. Perhaps it was because the "kingdom" emphasis (as opposed to the "temple" emphasis) taken over from Jesus had already relativized the importance of material sacrifices and temples.

What we do know from the New Testament letters is that early Christians soon explained their neglect of material sacrifices in various theological ways. They did so in the context of ethics (Rom 12:1), ecclesiology (1 Pet 2:5), and Christology (Heb 13:15-16). Taken together and in reverse order, these three rationales offer a profound vision of Christian faith and life. The passage from Hebrews insists on the absolute efficacy of Jesus' death on the cross for the forgiveness of sins and for right relationship with God. The text from 1 Peter stresses the new identity that Christians enjoy as God's people in Christ. The challenge in Romans to regard all of Christian life as an opportunity to worship God provides a solid foundation for Christian existence and the practice of what we call ethics.

In some Christian circles in the second and third centuries C.E. it became common to understand the Eucharist as a sacrifice and its presider as a priest (*hiereus*).[24] This is not the place to trace that complicated and controversial development. However, those who stand and worship in this tradition (as I do) should draw two conclusions from the New Testament evidence. First, the primary analogue here is not the material sacrifices so widely practiced in antiquity. Rather, it is the paschal mystery, that is, Jesus' life, death, and resurrection, and its saving significance. Second, the understanding of the Eucharist as a sacrifice demands that we regard it as a participation in the one and only effective sacrifice of Christ (Hebrews), that our identity as God's people in Christ demands that we view ourselves in continuity with Israel as the historic people of God (1 Peter), and that we try earnestly to make all that we do into "a living sacrifice, holy and acceptable to God" (Romans).

"SPEAKING THE VERY WORDS OF GOD": NEW TESTAMENT PERSPECTIVES ON THE CHARACTERISTICS OF CHRISTIAN SPEECH

DONALD SENIOR, C.P.

During the last presidential campaign I was invited by a local Chicago parish to speak on the issue of "speech" from a New Testament perspective. The invitation and the topic were triggered by a then-raging debate about the crude level of political discourse that was characteristic of so many political ads, speeches, and commentaries. Name-calling, false accusations, outright lies, and an abundance of distortions seemed to be the reigning norm, and the parish education committee wondered if the Bible had anything to say about this.

This was not a biblical topic I had ever really explored in any serious way. To my surprise, I found that there was relatively little written on this subject, particularly from a scholarly perspective, while at the same time there were significant references to the manner of Christian speech in various New Testament books. One exception to the relative scholarly neglect of this topic is the honoree of this Festschrift. In his commentary on the Letter of James and in several independent studies related to the letter, Luke Timothy Johnson has taken up this issue of speech. He has treated the topic with his usual acute awareness of the wider cultural setting of the New Testament writings and with equal sensitivity to the theological and pastoral significance of these texts.[1]

My goal in this brief study is to amplify Johnson's study of the pertinent texts in James, explore some similar exhortations in other select New Testament texts, and conclude with a reflection on some of the theological and pastoral implications of this material.

THE LETTER OF JAMES

The reflection on the "tongue" and its dangers in James 3:1-12 is undoubtedly the most extensive treatment of this topic in all of the New Testament. The passage in chapter 3 is not isolated within the body of the letter but is prepared for in 1:26 ("If any think they are religious, and do not bridle their tongues but deceive their hearts, their religion is worthless"). In fact, the topic of speech and its impact is close to the surface of several passages in the letter, including the climatic exhortation of 5:9-20.

As Johnson points out in his Anchor Bible commentary on the letter, James draws on some typical Greco-Roman rhetorical devices in his exhortation in chapter 3.[2] The concern that teachers use their powers of speech in a thoughtful way (3:1), the notion that one's speech should be deliberate or "slow" (1:19), the comparisons of the power of the tongue to the bit in the mouth of a horse (3:2-3), or to the rudder of a great ship (3:4-5), or to the force of a raging fire (3:5-6) are typical metaphors and images that find parallels in classical Greco-Roman and Jewish reflections on proper speech. Brevity and conciseness in speech were also considered virtues by many classical authors, while loquaciousness, or careless speech, was deemed a sign of senility or a lack of discipline.[3]

Although there are some parallels with other ancient writings, James's treatment of speech is ultimately quite distinctive. First of all, as Johnson notes, James appears to be much more pessimistic about the possibility of controlling the tongue than most classical authors. While James affirms that "Anyone who makes no mistakes in speaking is perfect" (3:2), the author goes on to say, "No one can tame the tongue—a restless evil, full of deadly poison" (3:8). Such pessimism is predicated on the characteristic theological perspective that James brings to the subject of speech, and it is here that his treatment differs substantially from classical reflections.

Although James begins his treatment of the tongue and its dangers with a focus on the responsibility of the teacher (3:1), it soon becomes clear that his exhortation is also directed to all of the members of the community, whatever their roles might be. Because teachers have such authority and responsibility, particularly within the Christian community, and because speech is the primary tool of the teaching profession, they are the most vulnerable to the dangers of the tongue. In fact, James discourages his readers from becoming teachers in view of this danger (3:1). Presumably in view of their role and its impact on the community, teachers with an unbridled tongue will face a more severe judgment. James's tactic of discouraging one from becoming a teacher is presumably a rhetorical one—not really trying to limit the number of teachers but attempting to alert would-be teachers to the serious responsibilities of their profession and the power they hold in the Christian community.

Yet as James continues his reflection on the tongue and speech, it is clear that he has a broader application in mind. Towards the end of this brief passage in chapter 3, the author notes that from the same tongue can come both "blessing and cursing" (3:9-10). The brethren whom he warns about such "double-mindedness" (see 1:8; 4:8 *dipsuchos*) appear to include a wider circle than teachers and extend to all the members of the community in their relationships to each other. The opportunity to "bless" or "curse" is not limited to or necessarily characteristic of the teaching role. This wider application is also the case in the opening section of the letter (see 1:19, 26), as well as in the sweeping exhortations that conclude the letter (see 5:9-20)—both of which are directed to all of the recipients within the community who would engage James's message.

Even though some of James's exhortations extend to the whole community, nevertheless, the grave responsibility borne by teachers and the severe judgment they might face for misuse of the tongue manifest the profound and multi-faceted theological perspective underlying James's concerns. The harm caused by vicious or false speech has its ultimate origin in the demonic. It represents the "world of iniquity" (3:6) and its harmful impact on the body can be traced to the fire of Gehenna (3:6b).[4] This iniquity expressed by the abusive tongue leads to a state of "double-mindedness" (*dipsuchos*; see 1:8; 4:8) that is a fundamental concern of James. The Christian has to be firmly rooted in friendship with God and cannot succumb to the spirit of the "world," which is saturated with evil (see 3:13-18; 4:4-10). Those who are animated by friendship with God express God's wisdom in their lives, namely, they are "pure, then peaceable, gentle, willing to yield, full of mercy and good fruits, without a trace of partiality or hypocrisy" (3:17). By contrast, those who are imbued with a "friendship with the world" (4:4) lead lives tainted by a whole series of vices ("bitter envy," "selfish ambition," "disorder," "wickedness of every kind"; see 3:16). From such friendship with the world come the cravings that lead humans astray, even to acts of violence (see 4:1-4; the author lists "disputes," "conflicts," even "murder").

Such "double-mindedness" or split allegiance between God and evil results in the same human instrument—the tongue—expressing both "blessing" and "cursing." James's words express the inherent scandal of this—with the same tongue one blesses "the Lord and Father" and then curses "those who are made in the likeness of God" (3:9). As the author exclaims: "My brothers and sisters, this ought not to be so" (3:10).

At stake, therefore, is a fundamental integrity that must be present within the being of the Christian. Made "in the likeness of God" and committed to "friendship with God," Christian speech must be in harmony with this overriding reality. The content and manner of one's speech should come from within the depths of one's being as a creation of God and one made in God's own likeness. This perspective underlies virtually all of James's exhortations about the quality of relationship and speech that should pass between members of the community. The Christians should "humble (them)selves before the Lord" (4:9) and "not speak evil against one another" (4:11). Echoing the saying of Jesus in Matthew 5:37, the word of the Christian needs no external oath to ensure its honesty, but a "yes" is a "yes" and a "no" is a "no" (see James 5:12-13).

In his commentary on chapter 5 of James, Johnson also fits the concluding exhortation of the letter into this overall perspective. While most of James's exhortations warn about the dangers of contentious and deceitful speech, the letter's final exhortations can be seen as a word portrait of speech that is truly expressive of the Christian spirit imbued with God's friendship. Thus those who suffer should "pray" (5:13); those who are cheerful should "sing songs of praise" (5:13); those who are sick should be prayed over by other members of the community (5:14-15); those who have committed sins should "confess" to one another (5:16) while others pray on their behalf for forgiveness and healing (5:16); and those who wander from the truth should be admonished and brought back (5:19-20).

Implicit in all of James's reflections on the qualities of Christian speech is the abiding biblical conviction about the power of the word, particularly the creative word of God. The letter alludes to this in its opening lines, where the author notes that God "gave us birth by the word of truth, so that we would become a kind of first fruits of his creatures" (1:18). One thinks of the famous text of Isaiah 55:10-11, itself influenced by wisdom and creation motifs:

> For as the rain and the snow come down from heaven, and do not return there until they have watered the earth, making it bring forth and sprout, giving seed to the sower and bread to the eater, so shall my word be that goes out from my mouth; it shall not return to me empty, but it shall accomplish that which I purpose, and succeed in the thing for which I sent it.

As Johnson concludes about the characteristic theology of James, "Speech is evaluated in relational, indeed, covenantal terms; human speech and action should be normed by the speech and action of the God who has involved himself with humans."[5]

OTHER NEW TESTAMENT TEXTS

While the Letter to James contains the most extensive reflections on proper Christian speech and its theological foundation, there are other significant New Testament texts worth considering.

Within the Gospel literature, for example, there are two sets of dominical sayings that in fact may have echoes in James. The dispute about washing of hands in Mark 7:1-23 and its parallel in Matthew 15:1-20 offers at least a remote parallel to James's emphasis on fundamental integrity in speech. In both of these Synoptic Gospels, the originating concern is about ritual purity. The Pharisees protest that Jesus' disciples eat with "unwashed hands," which leads in turn to Jesus' counter question about violating God's commands for the sake of human traditions. The finale comes with Jesus' statement that it is not that which goes into the mouth that defiles but that which comes out of the mouth and originates from the human heart. (Mark's Gospel draws the sweeping conclusion that Jesus thus declared "all foods clean" [Mark 7:19], a claim not made by Matthew's version). The list of "evil intentions" (*dialogismoi hoi kakoi*) that proceed from the human heart and come out of the mouth include among other vices, such evils of the tongue as "deceit" (*dolos*) and "blasphemy" (*blasphēmia*); Matthew adds to Mark's list "false witness" (*pseudomarturiai*; see Matt 15:19). Jesus' point in both versions is that these evils that appear through the mouth have their origin in a perverted human heart and thus cause true impurity, unlike the ingestion of impure food or eating with unwashed hands that causes physical impurity to enter the mouth only to proceed to the stomach and ultimately wind up in the sewer.

The application to abusive speech is reaffirmed in Matthew 12:36-37, where Jesus warns the Pharisees of the judgment that awaits "every careless word" (*pan rēma argon*)—the adjective *argon* or "careless" has the connotation of words that are without effect or meaningless. Jesus concludes: "for by your words you will be justified, and by your words you will be condemned" (12:36).

More to the point, as noted above, is the saying found in Matthew's Sermon on the Mount (see 5:33-37), which prohibits the taking of oaths in favor of plain and honest speech. The disciples' speech is to be "yes, yes" and "no, no," with no need of ratification by an oath. Jesus goes on to say, "anything more than this comes from the evil one" (Matt 5:37b), an intriguing link to James's assertion that false speech is ultimately an expression of the demonic (cf. James 3:6, 15).[6]

Likewise Matthew 5:21-26 deals with the severe consequences of anger against a community member that leads to insult and abusive speech. To call a brother *"raka"* (found only here in the New Testament and probably derived from an Aramaic word implying "fool") makes one liable to judgment before the council; to call a brother *mōre* (a more common word but also meaning "fool" or "idiot"), one is subject to the "fires of Gehenna" (Matt 5:22; compare James 3:6). Perhaps the most challenging and eloquent command about speech is found in a saying of Jesus that is recognized as the characteristic if not absolutely unique formulation of his teaching: "Love your enemies and pray for those who persecute you, so that you may be children of your father in heaven; for he makes his sun rise on the evil and on the good and sends rain on the righteous and on the unrighteous" (Matt 5:44-45). As noted in the final exhortations of the Letter of James and will be repeated in other New Testament examples, among the supreme expressions of Christian speech are words of forgiveness to others and words of praise for God.

More examples of pertinent texts are found in the deutero-Pauline and other New Testament letters, particularly in the exhortational sections of these texts. It is noteworthy that while in the major, undisputed letters Paul on occasion warns against false teaching and is concerned that the charism of speaking in tongues should be for the "building up of the church" (see 1 Cor 14), he makes in fact few explicit exhortations about honest or gracious speech.[7] Most of these are found in the later, deutero-Pauline materials; this may in fact reflect the increase of doctrinal and other factional disputes within the community—leading to more contentious speech.

COLOSSIANS

In the concluding portion of this letter, the author turns to exhortation.[8] The theological foundation for Christian conduct is similar to that described in James: through the resurrection of Christ, the Christians are "to set (their) minds on things that are above, not on things that are on earth" (Col 3:2). This entails "putting to death" such earthly things and avoiding those practices symptomatic of one who lives an "earthly" life such as "anger (*orgēn*), wrath (*thumon*), malice (*kakian*), slander (*blasphēmian*), and abusive language from your mouth" (*aischrologian ek tou stomatos humōn*—probably obscene or scurrilous speech; 3:8). The community members are also urged to "not lie to one another" (3:9). By contrast, those who have "clothed (them) selves with the new self" (3:10) exemplify "compassion (*splanchna*), kindness (*oktirmou*), humility (*chrēstotēta*), meekness (*tapeinophrosunēn*), and patience (*makrothumian*)" (3:12). They are to "bear with one another" and "if anyone has a complaint against another, forgive each other; just as the Lord has forgiven you, so you also must forgive" (3:13). They are to let "the word of Christ dwell in you richly" and therefore "teach and admonish one another in all wisdom; and with gratitude in your hearts sing psalms, hymns, and spiritual songs to God. And whatever you do, in word or deed, do everything in the name of the Lord Jesus, giving thanks to God the Father through him" (3:16-17). Noteworthy is the emphasis on the quality of Christian discourse, which is not to give way to anger or inappropriate (i.e., "abusive") speech but takes on the specific Christian hues of forgiveness, gratitude, and even liturgical expression.

A similar saying punctuates the letter but extends the exhortation of gracious speech to dealings with those outside the community: "Let your speech always be gracious (*pantote en chariti*), seasoned with salt, so that you may know how you ought to answer everyone" (4:6). Here the author employs a conventional metaphor "seasoned with salt" (*halati ērtumenos*), which implies speech that is pleasing and appropriate.[9] The Christian is to be ready to answer the questions and challenges of those outside the community but to do it in a manner that reflects the same values that should characterize speech within the community.

EPHESIANS

As in Colossians, the exhortations to proper speech in Ephesians come as illustrations of the new way of life that expresses the Christians' state before God. The author reminds the Christians that they had been taught "to put away your former way of life, your old self, corrupt and deluded by its lusts, and to be renewed in the spirit of your minds, and to clothe yourselves with the new self; created according to the likeness of God in true righteousness and holiness" (Eph 4:22-24). This entails "putting away falsehood" so that the Christians would "speak the truth to our neighbors, for we are members of one another" (4:25). This echoes the exhortation in Colossians 3:9 which also prohibits "falsehood" (*pseudos*). Some authors see a possible allusion to Zechariah 8:16, although the prohibition against lying is typical of Jewish ethical tradition.[10] The phrase "for we are members of one another" makes clear that the author has in mind discourse within the Christian community, whose unity is a strong motif of Ephesians.

As in the other texts we are considering, uncontrolled anger is included in the list of behaviors unbecoming a Christian. The Christians are exhorted to "be angry but do not sin; do not let the sun go down on your anger, and do not make room for the devil" (4:26-27). Likewise, "Let no evil talk come out of your mouths, but only what is useful for building up, as there is need, so that your words may give grace to those who hear" (4:29). The adjective "evil" (*sapros*) literally means "rotten" or "putrid"—something that has gone bad. In Matthew 7:17-20 Jesus refers to a "bad" or "rotten" tree that produces "rotten" fruit. In the context of

Ephesians 4:29, "evil" or "rotten" words are contrasted with speech that builds up the community and confers "grace" (*charin*) on those who receive it. Both the notion of building up the unity of the community and the conferral of "grace" of salvation are key concepts for this letter.¹¹

The author continues (4:31) with similar exhortations that illustrate Christian conduct that flows from a life renewed in Christ, with several of the vices repeating the list of Colossians 3:8: they are to "put away ... all bitterness (*pikria*) and wrath (*thumos*, as in Col 3:8) and anger (*orgē*, cf. Col 3:8) and wrangling (*kraugē*) and slander (*blasphēmia*, cf. Col 3:8), together with all malice" (*pasē kakia*, cf. Col 3:8). By contrast they should be "kind (*chrēstoi*) to one another, tenderhearted (*eusplanchnoi*), forgiving (*chariszomenoi*) one another, as God in Christ has forgiven you" (4:32).

Chapter 5 of the letter has a profusion of such exhortations, with a strong emphasis on appropriate discourse. In a sentence that ends with some alliteration (Eph 5:4) the Christians are warned that speech that is "obscene" (*aischrotēs*, see Col 3:8), "silly" (*mōrologia*), or "vulgar" (*eutrapelia*) is entirely out of place; instead, Christian speech should be characterized by "thanksgiving" (*eucharistia*). Christians should not be deceived by "empty words" (*kenois logois*) and therefore avoid those who are "disobedient" (5:6).

As in James and Colossians, characteristic Christian discourse that is prompted by the Spirit should be marked by singing "psalms and hymns and spiritual songs, singing and making melody to the Lord in your hearts, giving thanks to God the Father at all times and for everything in the name of our Lord Jesus Christ" (5:19-20).

1 PETER

The First Letter of Peter has similar exhortations to proper Christian speech, but the overall context of the letter and its theology give it a somewhat different tone from that of Colossians and Ephesians. As in the previous letters, the author is concerned about the cohesion of the Christian community and the proper relationship among the members rooted in the new reality of their Christian existence. But there is also a strong "witness" dimension to the theology of this letter; the author is aware that the communities he addresses lead a somewhat precarious existence as "aliens" and "exiles" in their own land and face mounting misunderstanding and even hostility on the part of the surrounding dominant culture.[12] How they act toward each other and toward their neighbors is a part of a "mission strategy" to present the Christian community in a positive light to the wider community.

This is evident, for example, in the exhortations of 1 Peter 3:8-13. The members of the community are urged to have "unity of spirit, sympathy, love for one another, a tender heart (*eusplanchnoi*, as in Eph 4:31b; see also Col 3:12), and a humble mind" (3:8 *tapeinophrones*). They should not "repay evil for evil or abuse for abuse (*loidorias*); but, on the contrary, repay with a blessing" (3:9). Presumably the evil and abuse foreseen here is from those outside the community, just as the slaves and wives married to non-Christian husbands had experienced such suffering but were urged to respond in a manner consistent with their faith and the example of the suffering Christ (see 1 Pet 2:18–3:6).

The author goes on to cite Psalm 34:13-17 and here introduces more explicitly the notion of proper speech. Those "who desire life" are to "keep their tongues from evil and their lips from speaking deceit" (1 Pet 3:10). The Christians should stand ready even in the face of suffering and abuse to give a witness to those outside the community "for the hope that is in (them)" (v. 15) but do it with "gentleness (*prautētos*) and reverence (*phobou*)" (v.16). The connotation of *prautētos* here is that of humility, not being puffed up with one's importance and therefore "gentle" or courteous. "Reverence" (*phobos*), on the other hand, implies in the context of 1 Peter not an attitude of fear or deference to the outsider but an attitude of reverence toward God that stems from the faith of the Christian who recognizes God's sovereignty and providence (see, for example, 1 Pet 1:17, 3:2). The Christian is not "to fear what the pagans fear" (see 3:14) but to found their allegiance on God alone.[13]

A final exhortation concerning proper speech is found in 1 Peter 4:10-11 and it echoes the conclusions of the other letters we have considered where a lyrical description of Christian discourse is given:

> Like good stewards of the manifold grace of God, serve one another with whatever gift each of you has received. Whoever speaks must do so as one speaking the very words of God; whoever serves must do so with the strength that God supplies, so that God may be glorified in all things through Jesus Christ. To him belong the glory and the power forever and ever. Amen.

Although the term for "speak" is quite generic here (*lalein*), it is possible that the author has in mind a more formal role of "speaking" such as that exercised by the teachers or leaders of the community. The only functions singled out are "speaking" and "serving" (*diakonein*). Yet by extension, speaking as if one were speaking the very words of God is surely meant as a fundamental principle for all Christian speech and harmonizes with a theological motif of conformity between the manner of God and Christian conduct that has run through virtually all of the New Testament that we have considered.

THE PASTORAL LETTERS

In considering the quality of Christian discourse, the Pastoral Letters focus much more explicitly on the role of the teacher within the community than do Colossians, Ephesians, or 1 Peter.

In 1 Timothy the overriding literary convention of the letter is the purported author Paul's address to Timothy who serves as a "teacher" of the communities under his care and as an example and instructor to others who teach within the community (see 1 Tim 1:1-3). There is a pervasive concern with false teaching and with those who oppose the truth.

"Paul" urges Timothy to counsel teachers not to be embroiled in "myths and endless genealogies" (1:4) or to engage in "meaningless talk

... without understanding either what they are saying or the things about which they make assertions" (1:6-7). Rather, the aim of Christian instruction should be "love that comes from a pure heart, a good conscience, and sincere faith" (1 Tim 1:5). The author returns to this theme at the conclusion of the letter. Those whose teaching is not in accord with the words of Jesus Christ and godliness (*eusebeian*) crave "controversy and disputes" (*zēteseis kai logomachias*), from which come "envy, dissension, slander, base suspicions, and wrangling" (6:4). Leaders and members of the community (3:3) should not be "angry" (*orgē*; cf. Col 3:8) or "quarrelsome" (*dialogismos* 2:8), nor should the *episkopos* or leader be a "bully" (*plēkēn*, see also 5:1). Deacons, likewise, are not to be "double-tongued" (*dilogos*), most probably a reference to deceitful speech.[14]

Timothy himself should set an example in "speech" (*logō*), as well as in other aspects of his conduct (4:12). He should not speak "harshly" or in an overbearing manner (*epiplēssō*) to his elders but "in all purity as if speaking to a father or as younger men to their brothers" (5:1). As a "man of God" he should exemplify "godliness, faith, love, endurance, gentleness" (6:11).

Similarly in 2 Timothy, the author exhorts Timothy to remind teachers to "avoid wrangling over words (*logomachein*; 2 Tim 2:14; cf. 1 Tim 6:3-4) which does no good" and leads to catastrophe for the listeners. Idle talk spreads "like gangrene" (2 Tim 2:17). All "stupid" (*mōras*) and "senseless" (*apaideutous*) talk is to be avoided because it only breeds quarrels (*machas*; 2:23; see James 4:1). The truly Christian teacher, by contrast, is "kindly to everyone," "patient," "correcting opponents with gentleness" (2 Tim 2:24-25)—the latter phrase emphasizing the quality of "gentleness" (*en prautēti*) even in dealing with those who are "in opposition" (*antidiathemenous*).[15]

In somewhat sharper tones, the Letter to Titus warns of the need to silence "rebellious people" who are "idle talkers" (*mataiologoi*) and "deceivers" (*phrenapatai*) who belong to the "circumcision" group (Titus 1:10).

Titus is to urge "younger men" to be models of good works and exemplify sound teaching (2:6-8). In a final exhortation (3:1-8) that gathers several of the virtues deemed characteristic of Christian speech, the author exhorts the whole community to be "ready for every good work" (3:1), which is demonstrated by not speaking evil of anyone (*blasphēmein*; 3:2, cf. Col 3:8), avoiding quarrels (*amachous*; 3:2 cf. James 4:2; 1 Tim 3:3; 2 Tim 2:24), being gracious (*epieikeis*; 3:2; 1 Tim 3:3; James 3:17; 1 Pet 2:18), and showing gentleness (*prautēta*; cf. Eph 4:2; Col 3:12; 2 Tim 2:25; James 1:21; 3:13; 1 Pet 3:15) to every person.

THE FOUNDATION AND CHARACTER OF CHRISTIAN SPEECH

Although the contexts, literary style, and overall theological perspective of the New Testament texts we have considered each have their own distinctiveness, an overall profile of what is considered a "Christian" manner of speech and its theological basis or rationale is detectable.

1. As elaborated most explicitly and extensively in the Letter of James, the fundamental basis for the quality of Christian speech is found in the very being of the Christian that has been transformed by his or her renewed life in Christ. Christians who have been "recreated" or "renewed" by God are no longer to live as they may have in their previous way of life. A variety of transformative metaphors are used, but each refers to the fundamental conversion of being and behavior that must now characterize Christians in comparison with their former ways of life. They are, in the terminology of James, no longer in friendship with the world but now are to exemplify friendship with God. Or, in the terminology of 1 Peter, they have been "reborn" and can no longer live the life they once lived when they were pagans but now must live a new life in Christ. Similarly, Ephesians speaks of the Christian's "new self" that is no longer compatible with the corrupt and immoral ways of their former life. Colossians reminds the Christian that they are to put their minds on the

things "that are above" and no longer on the "things that are below" or of this earth.

One of the characteristic expressions of this new way of living or transformed life is the manner of one's speech, first and foremost with other Christians, but also with those outside the community. Throughout these exhortations we have been examining is the underlying assumption that speech expresses the inner being of the human person. This conviction has deep roots within the biblical tradition and is not an alien thought to classical Greco-Roman reflection. But for the New Testament it is an overriding conviction that also has roots in the teaching of Jesus. "What comes out of the mouth proceeds from the heart" (Matt 15:18) is a fundamental anthropological and theological principle that underlies much of the New Testament teaching about speech. For the Letter of James this principle is driven to its most profound level. Evil and destructive speech is ultimately traced to the cosmic power of the demonic, which holds sway over the human heart and stands over against friendship with God. For both blessing and cursing of another human being and child of God to come from the same mouth is a fundamental contradiction, a "double-mindness" that is incompatible with the Christian life because it betrays a compromised allegiance to God and Christ.

Thus proper speech takes on a profoundly serious quality in this brand of New Testament reflection. The character of one's speech must ultimately reflect the character of one's being before God. Thus in the climactic antithesis of the Sermon on the Mount, the disciple is commanded to love the enemy and to pray for one's persecutors, which imitates God's own benevolence towards the bad and the good, the just and the unjust (see Matt 5:44-45). Or quite simply, as the Letter of 1 Peter puts it, "whoever speaks must do so as one speaking the very words of God" (1 Pet 4:11).

2. There is also a broad commonality in naming those qualities or virtues which should characterize Christian speech. While again these are not completely distinct from the list of the qualities that should

characterize proper speech found in the popular moral teaching of the Greco-Roman world and Judaism itself, cumulatively these lists of virtues (and the list of their opposing or contrasting vices) reflect the characteristic virtues of the Christian life, including those rooted deeply in the Gospel traditions of Jesus' teaching, such as that found in the Sermon on the Mount. Thus Christian speech is not contentious or "bullying" or arrogant but "gentle" and "humble." Christian speech, reflective of Christian life itself, is aimed at building up the community and is therefore loving and forgiving rather than confrontative and destructive. It must be truthful and honest—unadorned and not elaborate or artificial. Certain manners of human speech that are destructive of community relationships are typically avoided: unbridled expressions of anger, slander, quarrels, abusive or obscene speech, useless or idle speech, lying and deceptive speech. Even when it is necessary to be corrective, the Christian is urged to do so with "gentleness" and "compassion." Proper relationships within the community must be maintained by thoughtful and respectful speech; thus leaders should not speak in an overbearing manner; speaking with one's elders should been respectful and considerate.

Particularly revealing and uniquely characteristic of these exhortations to proper speech are those that call for the singing of hymns and words of liturgical praise. Given the assumptions about the nature of speech as expression of one's transformed being before God, it is entirely logical that the ultimate expression of Christian speech would be that of prayer and praise of God.

It should be noted that the emphasis on the generally irenic character of Christian speech in these New Testament texts is not incompatible with other more forceful and confrontative rhetoric. Standing within the biblical tradition of prophetic speech and accustomed to polemical forms of debate within the wider Greco-Roman and Jewish cultural contexts of the time, these authors did not hesitate to sharply criticize opponents or to vigorously correct those they had judged to have gone astray. The same could be said, of course, about Jesus' own sayings reflected in the Gospel traditions of his encounters with his opponents. Despite this, however, the overall thrust of those texts where these New Testament authors give explicit counsel about the use of speech places the emphasis on moderation and constructive forms of discourse.

3. Throughout most of these texts there is particular concern with the role of the teacher. This, too, reveals some of the characteristic concerns of the biblical and specifically New Testament traditions. The traditional biblical conviction about the power of the "word" stems ultimately from the power of God's own word that created the world and has the power to both sustain and destroy human life. This conviction is amplified and even intensified in the Christian tradition, which associated its own fundamental message with the proclamation of the "Word of God," reaching perhaps its ultimate expression in the Johannine tradition which identifies Jesus as the eternal and incarnate Word of God.

All of this gives an added dimension to the role of the teacher within the Christian community. The teacher represented a culturally respected profession in the ancient world, whose central activity was that of informed and influential speech. In the Christian community that revered role took on even greater status and responsibility in that the word of the teacher was to hand on and communicate the word of God. As James warns, therefore, teachers within the Christian community face greater accountability because of their role and awesome responsibility. Such a perspective also is expressed in the advice that Paul the (most likely fictive) author of the Pastoral Letters gives to Timothy and Titus—urging them to teach in the proper manner and warning the community about false and deceitful teachers who use their influence in a destructive manner.

The Scottish historian and theologian John Coffey has written a provocative and interesting essay on what he entitled "The Myth of Secular Tolerance."[16] His point was to challenge the growing number of aggressively atheistic and secularist assertions about the destructive and violent nature of religion and religious belief that has made its appearance particularly in England in the writings of such authors as Richard Dawkins and A. N. Wilson. Such authors, Coffey notes, accuse religion of being the source of contention and violence in society and attribute a pacifying and irenic role to the tolerance advocated by secular rationalists and those who keep religion in check. He notes such thinking identifies intolerance with religious conviction and credits the Enlightenment with the notion of tolerance and moderation. Coffey observes that attributing such a benign role to secular rationalism is naïve and conveniently overlooks the kind of atavistic violence generated by the French revolutionaries or the excesses of the Communist world, not to mention the world wars of the twentieth century. While there is no denying the violence that has been a result of religious conflicts, one can also find strong traditions of moderation and the need for reconciliation and mutual respect within religious traditions.

Such is the case, I think, with the remarkably consistent traditions about gracious speech within the early Christian communities. While the early Christians were no strangers to conflict, both among factions within their communities and with opposing forces outside the communities, nevertheless the exhortations of their normative literature was to use speech that was tolerant, respectful, compassionate, and forgiving. The Christians were, in fact, urged to speak like the God revealed through Jesus Christ.

"FOR THE GLORY OF GOD": THEOLOGY AND EXPERIENCE IN PAUL'S LETTER TO THE ROMANS

BEVERLY ROBERTS GAVENTA

In the opening of his book on religious experience in early Christianity, Luke Timothy Johnson contrasts the back and the front of an American Catholic church. The altar and the pulpit are concerned with carefully reasoned words and imagery that correctly reflect "doctrine, morality, authority, procedure."[1] By contrast, in the vestibule the notice boards spill over with announcements about pilgrimages, charismatic prayer, and healing services; here the discourse is that of "the experience of transforming power in any available form."[2] With his customary vividness, Johnson writes: "The issue is not whether St. Philomena lived but whether prayer to her cures cancer, not whether Mary's latest declarations in the presence of a harried housewife square with papal decrees but whether pilgrimage to the place of Mary's appearance might transform this family."[3]

The genius of Catholicism, Johnson goes on to observe, lies in its ability to hold the front of the church and the back of the church together in a creative tension. The academic study of Christianity, he avers, has concerned itself almost entirely with matters of theology and institutional history (the "front" of the church), while ignoring, sometimes willfully, questions of religious experience (the "back" of the church).

Although Paul's Letter to the Romans is not absent from the pages of *Religious Experience in Earliest Christianity*, neither does it figure prominently in the book, and for understandable reasons. Because Paul has not yet been to Rome, he cannot comment on the Romans' reception of the Spirit or their practices of worship as he does in Galatians or 1 Corinthians, for example. The three activities that provide the test cases for Johnson's study—initiation, glossolalia, and meals—barely make an appearance in Romans. Baptism briefly enters the discussion in Romans 6, when Paul depicts baptism as being buried with Christ (6:1-5). It is at least possible that chapter 8 offers an oblique reference to glossolalia (8:15, 26). The discussion of dietary practices in chapter 14 probably arises from conflicts over the communal meal, since it is in the context of the gathered community that what various groups eat and refuse to eat becomes a problem,[4] but we do not find the direct instruction about the meal that appears in 1 Corinthians 11.

Given this relative silence on questions of practice, we might conclude, as Johnson does in the introduction to his Romans commentary, that the letter "moves beyond prayer into critical thought," beyond "celebration to cerebration," as Paul "reflects on what the meaning of his mission might be for the salvation of humanity."[5] Johnson characterizes the letter in this way in response to Stanley Stowers's argument that Romans is moral exhortation, against which claim Johnson defends a reading of the letter as a work of Christian theology. Yet in the process of delineating in what sense he uses the term "theology" he—probably unwittingly—separates the two things he elsewhere endeavors to hold together, theology and religious experience ("beyond prayer into critical thought," and from "celebration to cerebration"). In this essay, I contend that Romans is not to be characterized solely by the movement "beyond" prayer or celebration, but that the letter also reflects the move from theology to experience, particularly by the movement from critical reflection to doxology. Not only does the letter itself engage in the praise of God, but its reading in the several house churches of Rome is designed to elicit thanksgiving and praise from those who hear it.

Given the vast quantity of publications on Romans, any claim that a topic is underrepresented in the literature is suspect, but there is relatively less attention to the language of thanksgiving and praise than one might expect. A few commentaries make observations in passing, as when Leander Keck comments that the concluding doxology (which he regards as a later addition) "invites the reader to read Romans again, and again—as an act of praise,"[6] or when Robert Jewett writes that Romans promotes Paul's "missionary project," which involves "restoring the proper stance of humans in glorifying God."[7] Numerous articles treat individual doxologies, although most focus on the text critical questions regarding 16:25-27.[8] This relative neglect should come as no surprise, standing as it does as a corollary to the long-standing scholarly preoccupation with questions such as Paul's treatment of the law and the standing of Israel, as well as the purpose and occasion of the letter. However significant those questions are, reference to thanksgiving and praise also runs through the letter and it merits our attention as well.

"THEY REFUSED TO GIVE GOD THANKS AND PRAISE"

Following the opening of the letter, which explains that Paul wants to preach the gospel in Rome and announces the salvific power of God that is apocalyptically revealed in that gospel, Paul undertakes to expose the captivity of humanity to the powers of Sin and Death. Importantly, he opens the exposition with the claim that humans are "without excuse," because they knew God but did not "glorify God or give him thanks" (vv. 20-21). Idolatry provides the most forceful example (v. 23), and verse 25 restates the claim that "they worshiped and served the creation rather than the creator."[9] The charge is reinforced in v. 28 with the assertion that they "did not see fit to recognize God." Although Paul adduces a range of behavior as evidence for his conclusion that God handed them over to Sin and Death (in the form of their own desires),[10] the proximate cause of the handing over appears to be humanity's refusal to acknowledge God properly through acts of praise and thanksgiving. Scholarly preoccupation with the *religionsgeschichtliche* background to Paul's comments and with his attitudes toward sexuality ought not obscure the logic of the argument. It is humanity's withholding of praise and thanksgiving that prompts God to hand humanity over, which in turn results in sexual misconduct and the other activities enumerated in the vice list of verses 29-31. As Paul Minear has written, for Paul ingratitude is "the deepest, most stubborn root of sin, the root from which all sinning springs."[11]

Given the often noted parallels between this passage and Jewish polemics about Gentile sin, it is possible to read 1:18-32 as having to do only with the behavior of Gentiles.[12] Even if that is the case, the argument that follows makes clear that it is not only Gentiles who have been "handed over," since both Jew and Greek are "under the power of Sin" (3:9). The catena of biblical quotations (3:10-18) that brings this long indictment to its conclusion leaves no room for the notion that Jews are exempted from the declaration of God's wrath in 1:18. Jews are indeed the beneficiaries of God's Scripture (the "oracles" of God in 3:2), but a carefully chosen set of those same oracles indicts all humanity with the refrain, "no one" and "there is no":

No one is righteous (v.10);
no one understands, no one seeks God (v.11);
no one does the good (v. 12);
there is no fear of God before their eyes (v. 18).

Although Paul does not here woodenly repeat the charge of 1:21 that "they did not glorify God or give God thanks," the connection in substance between the two passages seems undeniable. Those who do not glorify or praise God (1:18-32) are the very ones who do not fear God (3:10-18), and "they" include all of humanity. At the beginning of this indictment, Paul identifies the failure to recognize God with glory and thanksgiving as the reason for God's "handing over" of humanity to Sin; at the end, a leading characteristic of humanity "under Sin" is its refusal to honor God. It is consistent with this observation that verses 13-14 focus on the corruption of human speech and that verse 19 concludes that the law speaks so that "every mouth" might be shut.[13]

To be sure, Paul will later write that Abraham did not doubt God's promise or God's power, and specifically that Abraham "gave glory to God" (4:20),[14] which could support the familiar charge that Paul is simply inconsistent.[15] Yet Paul is not claiming that no individual human being ever utters words of thanksgiving to God or that no individual human being ever praises God (just as Rom 1:29 does not mean that everyone is guilty of murder). As Ernst Käsemann has observed, however, for Paul the individual is inseparable from "his world," and that world is "governed by the primal sin of rebellion against God."[16]

"TOGETHER WITH ONE VOICE"

Given this emphasis on human ingratitude and refusal to glorify God, it should not be surprising to find that, when the letter turns to the consequences of the Christ event, it also turns to expressions of praise and thanksgiving. To be sure, Paul does not announce this shift directly (along the lines of "Now that we are baptized into Christ, we know how to praise and thank God rightly"), but it may be inferred from statements at a number of important junctures in the letter. The first such statement comes toward the conclusion of Paul's explication of the transfer of humanity from the reign of Sin to that of God, here identified by the terms "grace" and "righteousness."

> Thanks be to God that you, who were slaves of Sin, have now become genuinely obedient to the type of teaching to which you were handed over, having been freed from Sin, you have become slaves of righteousness (6:17-18).[17]

No mere emotional outburst, this expression of thanks epitomizes the argument of 5:12–6:23. The obedience of Christ (5:19) has freed humanity from the rule of Sin and Death, resulting in new life through baptism (6:1-11) and the paradoxically life-giving enslavement to righteousness (6:12-23).

The second expression of thanksgiving appears at 7:25. The problems posed by the second half of this verse are notorious, but none of the solutions cancels the force of verse 25a: "Thanks be to God through Jesus Christ our Lord!" At the very bottom of what Leander Keck has aptly termed the "spiral" of the human condition in Romans,[18] even as Paul admits that Sin is powerful over the holy and righteous and good law of God, he declares the even greater power of the deliverance brought about by Jesus Christ.[19]

To be sure, the importance of these exclamations can be minimized, as when Jewett describes 6:17 as a "conventional expression of gratitude for divine benefaction."[20] The possibility that these are more than literary conventions emerges when we see the motif of thanksgiving and praise return forcefully in chapters 14 and 15. At the outset of the discussion of disputes about food, Paul describes the conflicts between the omnivores (those who eat "everything," 14:2) and the vegans (those who eat only "vegetables," 14:2). He insists that they are both household slaves of the same Lord and that it is that Lord who upholds them both (v. 4). For that reason, they may not judge one another:

> The one who eats [everything], eats in the Lord, for he gives thanks to God; and the one who does not eat anything does so in the Lord, and he also gives thanks to God (14:6).

Whatever differences of conviction or practice may separate these believers from one another, Paul seems certain that they have common ground in their act of thanksgiving.

This point is reinforced at the culmination of this discussion in 15:6, when the prayer wish ends with the prayer that "together with one mouth you may glorify the God and Father of our Lord Jesus Christ." Moving toward 15:6, Paul underscores the importance of the community itself. Even though he agrees with the "strong," he advises that they should exercise restraint by way of seeking "peace" and "upbuilding" within the community (14:19). No freedom of practice for the individual is more important than protecting the brother or sister (14:21). The prayer-wish of 15:5-6 seeks from God their unity of mind and of voice. Yet that unity is not an end in itself: even the goal of upbuilding yields to the ultimate goal of glorifying God.[21]

FOR THE GLORY OF GOD

That emphasis on glorifying God is reinforced in 15:7-13, a passage some identify as the culmination of the major themes of Romans.[22] Although the passage begins with the exhortation "Welcome one another," what is at stake here is more than the reconciliation of "strong" and "weak," since Paul repeatedly refers to praise and thanksgiving:[23]

> Christ welcomed you *for the glory* [*doxa*] of God. (v. 7)
> and in order that the Gentiles might *glorify* [*doxasai*] God for God's mercies... (v. 9)[24]
> For this reason I will *praise you* [*exomologēsomai*] among the Gentiles
> and *sing praise* [*psalō*] to your name. (v. 9)
> *Rejoice* [*euphranēte*] Gentiles, together with his people (v. 10)
> *Praise the Lord* [*aineite*], all the nations,
> and let all the peoples *praise* [*epainesatōsan*] him (v. 11)

This is not simply "an exhortation concerning tolerance in community life"[25] or the ending of ethnic conflict.[26] That is not at all to diminish the significance of those achievements of the gospel, but to locate them properly in the praise of God. If Richard Hays is correct in arguing that the psalms here are understood to be placed in the mouth of Christ,[27] then the *arrabōn* of this eschatological choir is Christ himself, in whom humanity finally comes to see what it means to give glory to God (v. 7).

BLESSINGS AND DOXOLOGIES

Alongside this motif of praise and thanksgiving offered within the letter (6:17; 7:25) and by Jew and Gentile together (14:1–15:13), it is revealing to see that the number of blessings and doxologies found in Romans is significant when compared with the rest of the Pauline corpus. Twice in 2 Corinthians Paul includes an ascription of blessing to God. The first ("Blessed be the God and father of our Lord Jesus Christ") appears at the opening of the letter, in place of the customary thanksgiving. The second occurs in 11:31 as a parenthesis to Paul's insistence that he is not lying concerning his own experience of hardship and suffering ("The God and father of our Lord Jesus —knows—who is blessed forever!—that I am not lying"). These two passages, together with the two in Romans, are the only blessings that appear in Paul's undisputed letters. Similarly, doxologies appear in Galatians 1:5; 6:18; Philippians 4:20; and 1 Thessalonians 3:13, but Romans contains at least two (11:36; 15:33) and perhaps three, if 16:25-27 is considered part of the original letter.

The blessings and doxologies differ from one another slightly in form,[28] but all of them conclude with the word "amen," and here they are discussed together. The first comes at 1:25 where, following Paul's accusation that "they served the creation rather than the one who created," he adds "who is blessed forever. Amen!" Joseph Fitzmyer comments that "Paul betrays his native background in spontaneously uttering in Jewish fashion a doxology at the mention of God the creator," but none of the texts he adduces actually refer to God's work in creation (1 Sam 25:32; 2 Sam 18:28; 1 Kgs 1:48; 8:15; Ps 41:14; although see Gen 14:19-20).[29] In the New Testament, comparable blessings of God appear outside the Pauline corpus only at 1 Peter 1:3 and Ephesians 1:3. These considerations make the inclusion of a blessing at this point in the letter a little unusual. James D. G. Dunn comments that the inclusion reflects Paul's aversion to what he has just said,[30] and, while surely Paul is deeply offended by the stance of rebelliousness toward God limned in these verses, there are other statements in Romans to which Paul would also have an aversion, and an apotropaic motive does not account for the other "amen" statements in Romans. It seems more likely, and more in keeping with the other "amen" statements in Romans, to see this one as underscoring the positive assertion Paul is making about God as the creator of all things. (See below, where I return to suggest an additional function of the "amen.")

The second and third statements of blessing or doxology stand at either end of Romans 9–11. At 9:5, just following the introductory statement of Paul's own grief and his listing of the gifts that have been bestowed on Israelites (sonship, glory, the covenants, the giving of the law, service to God, the promises, the fathers, and the Messiah), he concludes with a statement that may be rendered as "May God be blessed forever. Amen." The disputes about the translation and the theological implications of this verse are ancient and intense.[31] For my purposes at present, however, resolving that debate is less urgent than simply noting the presence of another blessing, one that follows immediately on the statement that God (or Christ) is "over all."

It is in no way surprising to find that Paul opens the discussion of God's dealings with Israel (and the Gentiles) in Romans 9–11 with a statement that God is "over all," since that phrase might well stand as a summary of Paul's resolution to the quandary that provokes these chapters.[32] How is it possible that Israel, called by God from the day of God's promise to Abraham, does not recognize Jesus as God's Christ? And how is it possible that Gentiles do recognize Jesus as God's Christ? Do these developments mean that God has rejected God's own people, that God has been proven faithless? The resounding "no" offered in Romans 9–11 to any such absurdity comes to its logical conclusion with 11:32, "God has imprisoned all in disobedience so that [God] might have mercy on all." But the argument does not end at 11:32; instead, it continues in a hymn to the inscrutability of God's knowledge and judgments, the inability of human beings to advise or counsel God, culminating in the statement that "from him and through him and unto him are all things. To him be glory forever. Amen" (11:36). The assertion of 9:5 that God is "over all" is here enlarged; everything is from and through God; everything has its goal, its end, in God. It is to this all-encompassing conclusion that Paul offers his "amen." Although the context of these two "amen" statements differs significantly from that of the indictment in chapter 1, they share this insistence on God's power, whether reflected in creation or in the less specific claim that God is "over" all.

The fourth "amen" statement appears at the end of chapter 15. Paul has returned to his opening comments about his hope now to travel to Rome and has placed that hope in the context of his upcoming trip to Jerusalem and eventual mission to Spain. In verses 30-32 he asks that the congregations at Rome join him in prayer that his service for believers in Jerusalem (the collection, see vv. 26-27) will be well-received, so that he may continue on his way to Rome. Having sought prayer for his own labors, he in turn asks God's peace on the Romans, "May the God of peace be with all of you. Amen."[33]

The final "amen" statement appears in the concluding doxology 16:25-27, which takes us into a veritable thicket of text critical problems. Space does not permit a discussion of these problems, except to observe that the fact that this doxology appears in varying places in various manuscripts and that some manuscripts omit it altogether has prompted many scholars to conclude that it does not belong in the letter at all, although that judgment is by no means "virtually unanimous."[34] If 16:25-27 belongs to the original letter, it amply underscores my point about the importance of doxology of this letter. If it comes from a later hand, the person or persons who composed and inserted it "as a more stately conclusion for public reading"[35] understood rightly the importance of doxology in this letter.

THE READING OF THE LETTER

To this point, we have gathered together what may seem to be disparate strands of the letter to observe that Romans reflects considerable interest in thanksgiving and praise directed toward God. The human action (or inaction) that prompts God to hand humanity over to the powers of Sin and Death is characterized in the first instance as ingratitude; in the realm of grace and righteousness, however, the new human is capable of giving thanks. Paul himself embodies this thanksgiving in his own expressions of gratitude at 6:17 and 7:25. He utters blessings of God's name as he recalls all of God's benefits to Israel (9:5) and ascribes glory to God for his saving power and knowledge (11:36). He understands the coming together of Jew and Gentile as an occasion of praise and thanksgiving to God (14:6; 15:6, 9-13). All of this might be subsumed under Johnson's pithy phrase: in Romans Paul "moves beyond prayer into critical thought," beyond "celebration to cerebration."

It seems to me that something remains to be said about thanksgiving and praise in Romans, which is that Paul hopes that *the letter itself will generate thanksgiving*. Importantly, Paul does not do this by what I have come to think of as "oughting" it; Paul does not tell the Romans that they "ought" or "should" or "must" be thankful to God and give God praise. The exhortations of 12:1–13:14 do not include exhortations to gratitude, although the appeal to the "mercies of God" in 12:1-2 assumes that those who present themselves (their "bodies") to God are grateful people. Instead of exhorting the Romans to be grateful, as we have seen, Paul himself utters words of thanksgiving and praise. And in 14:6 he appears to acknowledge that the Roman congregations do give God thanks, even if they find fault with one another on other grounds. And in 15:7-13, he hymns the goal of the gospel itself in the coming together of Israel and the Gentiles in praise of God.

This thread of thanksgiving reinforces my own contention that one of the purposes of the letter is to enlarge the understanding of the gospel operative at Rome.[36] When Paul writes in 1:15 that he is obliged to "preach the gospel" in Rome, he does so because he does not regard the Romans as having understood the full extent of the gospel. These Gentile house-churches at Rome have come to see the gospel as their way of gaining access to a place among the people of Israel; indeed, some may claim that they now *replace* Jews as God's own people (11:17). Paul agrees that the gospel means that Gentiles are now brought into God's people on an equal footing with Jews, but the gospel he proclaims involves an entire creation enslaved to the powers of Sin and Death and threatened by a host of anti-God powers. One goal of this letter, then, is to enlarge their understanding of the gospel.

But a review of the language of thanksgiving and praise in Romans suggests that Paul's desire is not simply that the Romans have a better grasp of the gospel's content. There are also hints that *Paul anticipates that the reading of the letter itself will generate thanksgiving and praise.* We may see this in Paul's outpourings of praise in 6:17 and 7:25 and especially in his climactic move in 15:7-13. Perhaps more important, we see hints in the appearance of the several "amen" statements. In the Old Testament, the word *ʾmn'* is usually found in contexts that are corporate (as in Num 5:22; Deut 27:15-26), and often corporate *liturgical* settings (1 Chron 16:36; Neh 5:13; 8:6; Ps 41:13; 72:19; 89:52; 106:48).[37] Similarly in the Dead Sea Scrolls, the word *ʾmn'* is associated with corporate acts of worship (as in e.g., 1QS 1.20; 2.10; 2.18; 4Q286 7.ii.1; 7.ii.5; 7.ii.10). In 1 Corinthians 14:16, Paul assumes that the community follows this same practice of confirming thanksgiving with the word "amen" (see also 2 Cor 1:20; and notice also Rev 5:14; 7:12; 22:20).

But it is noteworthy that, while the term "amen" occurs only six times in all of the undisputed epistles *outside Romans* (1 Cor 14:16; 2 Cor 1:20; Gal 1:5; 6:18; Phil 4:20; 1 Thess 3:13), it occurs four (possibly five) times in this letter alone. Understanding why that might be the case requires us to reflect on the native habitat of the "amen" in corporate worship.

As Phoebe gathers with various house-churches in Rome and reads this letter,[38] as a matter of course she reads the various "amens." When she does so, those gathered to hear her are invited, not simply to concur with Paul's arguments, to assent intellectually to his interpretation of the gospel, but to join both Phoebe and Paul in praise and thanksgiving.[39] If they join their own amens to that of the letter, then the letter becomes an occasion of praise. It is at this point that we have returned to Luke Timothy Johnson's insistence that the "back" and the "front" of the church belong together, since the "cerebration" that characterizes

Romans becomes the occasion for "celebration" as Paul's theology gives rise to prayer.

A final comment is in order. At the end of *Religious Experience in Earliest Christianity*, as Johnson reflects on the implications of his study, he concludes that "serious engagement with earliest Christianity demands recognition that its adherents . . . considered themselves caught up by, defined by, a power not in their control but rather controlling them, a power that derived from the crucified and raised Messiah Jesus." He goes on to insist that "any effort to interpret the writings of early Christianity . . . that does not proceed on this assumption is fated to fall short of a satisfying interpretation."[40] I agree entirely with Johnson's insistence that the study of early Christianity take seriously the way in which the biblical texts reflect this conviction about "a power not in their control but rather controlling them." Perhaps one reason this motif of thanksgiving and praise is given relatively short shrift in the scholarly literature on Romans is because it is assumed that the language is simply conventional, and therefore insignificant, alongside the weighty discourse of the letter. But Romans is not simply an act of thought but also of celebration. The letter itself is an invitation to praise and thanksgiving of God's powerful invasion of and liberation from the slavery of Sin and Death. In that sense, Romans confirms Johnson's conviction that we must attend to both the "front" and the "back" of the church, in this case the way in which conviction about God's powerful activity comes to expression in praise and thanksgiving.

ECSTASY AND *EXOUSIA*: RELIGIOUS EXPERIENCE AND THE NEGOTIATION OF SOCIAL POWER IN PAUL'S LETTER TO THE GALATIANS

SZE-KAR WAN

In his widely used introductory text, Professor Luke Johnson makes an insightful suggestion for understanding Paul's strategy in Galatians. To try to win his converts back from the seduction of itinerant teachers, unnamed save the derisive "agitators," Paul reminds the Galatians of their religious experience, "that they have been given life through the Holy Spirit, mediated through the preaching of the cross and received in faith."[1] In so doing Paul gives his readers/hearers no choice but to side with him: "If the Galatians agree, then his argument is cogent; if they disagree, they deny their own experience."[2] Given the unspoken tendency among modern scholars to rationalize or excise all hints of ecstasy or mysticism, Johnson's work has done a service in reminding us that Paul lived in a world in which ecstatic experiences, frenzied utterances, magic, witchcraft, and sorcery all exerted powerful influence on its inhabitants, and that interpretation of and reports about them carried dire personal and social consequences. We ignore them at our peril.[3]

Experience is inherently slippery, and *religious* experience is even more so. But Johnson is careful to place it in dialectic with interpretation, so that there can be no *factum brutum*, only "*interpreted reality*, that is, the experience itself is at least partially constituted by the interpretation of the experiencing subject.... Language is therefore part of experience's embodiedness, for every individual subject's perception is particular and conditioned not only by the symbols available but also by that individual's apprehension of those symbols."[4] At the same time, Johnson hastens to add,

> The term *experience* points to something real in the world that is not completely captured by our preset explanations and interpretations. The traffic, in short, moves both ways. Our language shapes our experience, but our experience also stretches, reshapes, and sometimes even shatters our language.[5]

Accordingly, religious experience is understood as "a response to that which is perceived as ultimate, involving the whole person, characterized by a peculiar intensity, and issuing in action."[6]

While the long-term impact of his contribution is still being assessed, I want to acknowledge my debt by applying his insights to a more thorough reading of Galatians—not only along the line he has suggested, but also to extend it into the social and communal realm in order to come to a firmer grasp of the power dynamics behind the Pauline congregations. Accordingly, this essay will focus not so much on the phenomenology of religious experience, as Prof. Johnson has so ably done already, as on Paul's use of such experience for the negotiation of social power. Specifically, I will explore how Paul uses religious experience not just as a rhetorical strategy but also as a means of triangulating the relationship among himself, his Galatian converts, and the emerging hierarchy within the burgeoning Jesus-movement.

EXPERIENCE AS RHETORICAL STRATEGY

Paul's appeal to experience plays a pivotal role in his rhetoric from the beginning. After his highly theological prescript (Gal 1:1-5), Paul famously begins his castigation of the Galatians, sans thanksgiving or conjunctive, with a blunt declaration, "I am shocked (*thaumazō*) that you have so quickly departed from the one who called you in grace" (1:6).[7] The use of *thaumazō* ("I am amazed or shocked") is common in ancient epistolography. An early second-century C.E. letter chastises the recipient's failure to write, with the words *thaumazō pōs . . . ouk antegrapsas moi* ("I am astonished that you have not written me," Pap. Mich. 479.4-5), and follows with a request for a letter in return.[8] *Thaumazō* is a common feature in Greek legal and political rhetoric as well and is frequently used in such context as "a device of indignant rebuttal and attack of things the opposition party has done and is about to do."[9] As a rhetorical formula, therefore, it is used in Gal 1:6 to convey to the Galatians that it is unthinkable for the Galatians to have departed from the God who called them in grace.

But the word is not merely rhetorical. It conveys a sense of wonderment as a result of having witnessed something extrahuman, extramundane—thus "I am astonished" in some translations. In the LXX, the verb is "a distinctive expression for the anthropocentrically determined piety of experience in the LXX, especially where it characterizes the object of experience as something which transcends all human possibilities. It thus embraces *miraculum* and *mirabile* and may express any degree of wonder or astonishment."[10] Sometimes it is used by a narrator as a stylistic device to underline "the greatness or significance of a fact or event by showing its effect on those who saw it."[11] In the New Testament, *thaumazein* is found mostly in the Synoptic Gospels, especially the Gospel of Luke, where it is a literary device to signify the greatness of the miracles by depicting their effects on the crowds. The accent there is placed not so much on the crowds' psychology as on the miracles (e.g., Matt 9:33; Luke 11:14).[12]

Similarly in Galatians 1:6, Paul is shocked to discover that the Galatians are "so quickly deserting" (NRSV) the God who called them. The present tense of *metatithesthe* indicates desertion is ongoing and is not yet completed, but by the same token it also adds a vivid sense of urgency as Paul tries to address a problem that is unfolding before his eyes.[13] The agitators are still in Galatia in Paul's absence, and the situation remains fluid and unpredictable. It has been suggested that "so quickly" echoes the Hebrews' apostasy in worshiping the golden calf (LXX Exod 32:8: *parebēsan tachy ek tēs hodou*, "they turned so quickly from the way") and their departure "quickly from the way" (*tachy ek tēs hodou*) at the times of the Judges (LXX Judg 21:17).[14] Such conscious use of Septuagintal language is certainly within the purview of Paul, especially since "the Way" was how the early Jesus-followers called their faith.[15]

But while *thaumazein* might obliquely point to extraordinary events, its primary referent is first and foremost the emotional state of a subject experiencing cognitive dissonance. This might be a sense of wonderment or dread in the face of a *mysterium tremendum*.[16] In LXX Isaiah 52:15, e.g., at the sight of the servant of God, the nations "will be in awe" (*thaumathesthai*) because of the wonderfulness as well as dread represented by him. The same dread is depicted graphically by the kings shutting up their mouths. Here *thaumazein* is paralleled by *existanai* (lit., "to be in ecstasy, to be out of one's mind") of 52:14. The word can also be used negatively to imply irritation. In LXX Sirach 11:21 the verb is used in a negative sense: *mē thaumaze en ergois hamartōlou* ("Do not be shocked by the works of a sinner"). Here *thaumazein* means not so much "to marvel" as "to be irritated, shocked, irate, indignant, even offended," as a result of the enormous injustice of the present state of affairs.[17]

So while Paul in 1:6 introduces the reason for his writing—to address the waywardness of the Galatians with the underlying hope of winning them back—he at the same time interjects himself into the appeal by telling them how shocked and astonished he is by their actions. Such a personal reading of *thaumazein* would correspond with the first-person tones throughout the letter. In 1:11-12, he explains the otherworldly nature of his gospel in starkly personal terms: "I did not receive it from a human being, nor was I taught it, but [I receive it] through a revelation (*apokalypsis*) of Jesus Christ" (1:12). His prophetic call to be an apostle to the Gentiles likewise came to him through divine revelation (1:15-16). Even the decision to go up to Jerusalem he claims to have been based on a revelation (2:2).

Why Paul insists on the divine origins of his gospel is not hard to fathom. He feels his apostleship is being denied him because doubters from the outside have begun to persuade his Galatian converts to the contrary. Not only is the would-be apostasy unbearable and unthinkable, it is also profoundly personal. That is why Paul throughout the letter does not hesitate to exhort (e.g., 5:13), cajole (6:1-10), reprimand (e.g., 5:2), even threaten the Galatians (6:11, 17), though he reserves his most ferocious barbs for his enemies (3:1; 5:12; 6:12). If Paul's emotions are on such ample display throughout the letter, it might make better sense to see in 1:6 a concerted effort to vest a standard formula with emotional as well as emotive freight, in the hopes of halting the Galatians' transfer of allegiance to the outsiders.

In his effort to vie for authority in the Galatian congregation, Paul also uses his own religious experience as an instrument of legitimation for his position, which is perhaps why he rarely speaks in the first person or recounts his ecstatic experiences without polemical overtones. This is a common tactic of Paul's, as we see in 1 Corinthians 9:1, where he insists that his vision of the resurrected Lord gives him a status equal to the apostles'. He is therefore as entitled as they in receiving remuneration for his work in the congregation, even as he is simultaneously refusing it. Likewise in 1 Corinthians 15:1-11, he again adduces his vision of the resurrected Lord as a form of self-legitimation and suggests that his own experience should be included as standard tradition in the preaching of the gospel. And when he thinks his opponents, the so-called "superapostles," are boasting of their ecstatic visions and extravagant prowess, he recounts his own experience of being caught up in third heaven, Paradise, where he witnessed things unutterable (2 Cor 12:1-10). In all these cases, Paul uses ecstatic experiences in the context of personal controversy. These attacks are, of course, not merely personal; they deeply affect his standing in the congregation. In adducing these ecstatic experiences, therefore, Paul seeks to legitimate his standing in the emerging hierarchy of the Jesus-movement and in the process distances himself from the other leaders.

If that is the case, Paul's use of his personal experience would seem to serve a double function. Rhetorically it accentuates the problem at hand, namely, the Galatian apostasy. But it also serves the political function of drawing a sharp distinction between Paul and his detractors. By exaggerating the Galatians' consideration to follow the agitators' leadership with an astonishment-rebuke formula, Paul aims at showing the enormity of changing sides. In other words, the emotional *thaumazō* is part of an effort to create a binarism between Paul and the outside teachers. It accomplishes the same rhetorical intent as the narrative of his tortuous history with the Jerusalem church (1:18-2:10; 4:21-5:1) and with the Antioch church, including his erstwhile colleague Barnabas (2:11-14). Through it all, Paul insists, he stands alone against the world, supported by no one except the revelation of God.

Paul's reaction and his chosen response are not unique in the history of religion. It has long been observed that men and women turn to ecstasy when they seek to strengthen and legitimate their authority. Whereas scholars of an older generation once attributed such a move to religious leaders and the elite,[18] more recent studies have discovered that established religious leaders are in fact forever suspicious of ecstatic authority. So the anthropologist I. M. Lewis based on his field work on African ecstatic religions:

> The more strongly-based and entrenched religious authority becomes, the more hostile it is towards haphazard inspiration. New faiths may announce their advent with a flourish of ecstatic revelations, but once they become securely established they have little time or tolerance for enthusiasm. For the religious enthusiast, with his direct claim to divine knowledge, is always a threat to the established order.[19]

Ecstasy, according to Lewis, is a "philosophy of power" favored by oppressed and marginalized groups, for whom the only avenue to escape from a tyranny buttressed by rational structures and fortified by rigid dogmas is through direct revelation or mystical power. Such social and environmental factors must be accounted for in the rise of ecstasy:

The circumstances which encourage the ecstatic response are precisely those where men feel themselves constantly threatened by exacting pressures which they do not know how to combat or control, except through those heroic flights of ecstasy by which they seek to demonstrate that they are the equals of the gods. Thus if enthusiasm is a retort to oppression and repression, what it seeks to proclaim is man's triumphant mastery of an intolerable environment.[20]

Seen in this light, Paul's appeal to religious experience is part and parcel of a negotiation, a struggle with what he perceives to be the power nexus of Jerusalem-Antioch.[21] By inserting his personal reaction into his evaluation of the Galatians' action and by singling out his extrahuman experience of conversion and call to be a prophet to the Gentiles, he succeeds not only in conveying to the Galatians the cause of his anger but, more importantly, in setting up an absolute, exclusive binarism between him and the established order. In this political binarism, there can be no fence-sitters.

SORCERY AND THE SOCIOLOGY OF BINARISM

This binarism Paul develops further in 3:1, where he cries, plaintively, "O, foolish Galatians, who has *bewitched* you?" *Baskainein* means literally "to cast an evil eye upon somebody."[22] In Sirach 14.8, the greedy man is evil for he will do anything, even deeds of injustice, just to increase his profit: *ponēros ho baskainōn ophthalmō* ("He who casts an evil eye [i.e., he who has an envious eye] is evil"). The word is a New Testament *hapax*, but it might stand behind the gospel references to the eye (Matt 6:23; Luke 11:34). By its frequent association with *phthonein* ("to envy; Mark 7:22; Matt 20:15; Sir 14:10), it has come to mean the use of magical means for unrighteous gains.[23]

In 3:1, the word is regularly interpreted as a mere metaphor or a rhetorical trope by the vast majority of scholars.[24] Ernest Burton's nearly century-old pronouncement on this matter is still representative: "It would be overpressing the facts to infer from Paul's use of this word that he necessarily believed in the reality of magical powers, and still more so to assume that he supposed the state of mind of the Galatians to be the result of such arts. It is more probably that the word, while carrying a reference to magical arts, was used by him tropically, as we use the word 'bewitch,' meaning 'to pervert,' 'to confuse the mind.'"[25] But even if we admit that Paul is using *baskainein* metaphorically, it does not answer the question why Paul would choose a term rich in connotations of sorcery and witchcraft to make his point. In non-philosophical writings, the term is often taken seriously in its literal sense of casting an evil spell or its transferred sense of invoking magic broadly conceived for malicious intents.[26] Plutarch describes it as primarily a psychic and bodily process whereby a sorcerer manipulates natural or demonic energies for harmful or injurious purposes; it also has profound connections to envy (*Quaest. conviviales* 681d-82a).[27] Basic to the belief, according to John Elliott, is "the conviction that certain individuals, animals, demons, or gods have the power of casting an evil spell or causing some malignant effect upon every object, animate or inanimate, upon which their eye or glance may fall."[28]

But what is crucial for our interpretation of Paul is not so much whether there is reality behind his accusation but rather *why* he would accuse the outside teachers of practicing magic and sorcery. If ecstasy and the practice of magic are born from social tension and are instruments of power in the negotiation of authority in community or society, accusations of sorcery or witchcraft, too, should function in the same manner. The answer is to be located in the turf war between Paul and the outside teachers.[29] Specifically, accusations of sorcery function in the social context to reinforce the boundaries between insiders and outsiders and, once the offending members are identified and recognized, to expel them from the in-group. According to Neyrey's reading of Mary Douglas, such accusations are especially prevalent in cultures that display and value a strong impulse towards high organization and systematization of people, things, rituals, body, cosmology, and so on (what she calls "strong group"), but where individuals in that culture have little agreement over how that systematization should take shape ("low grid").[30] According to Neyrey, these characteristics mark "a highly competitive society marked with strong rivalry and strong ambition. In this context, the accusation functions to denigrate rivals and pull them down in the competition for leadership. Such accusations, in short, are idioms of social control."[31]

Sorcery and witchcraft accusations also function in a context where there is an inequality of power. When comparing the phenomena of possession by a malicious spirit and sorcery accusations in African cultures—which despite appearance both function as protest in a competitive society in which all members believe in magic and spirits—I. M. Lewis notes a difference. Possession by an evil spirit "is regularly used by the members of subordinate social categories to press home claims on their superiors."[32] They accomplish this by turning their illness or misfortune, which are ascribed to evil spirits that plague the weak and the unsuspecting, into social power. Claims of possession in situations of conflict and tension with one's social superiors allow the so-called possessed to garner attention and respect, thereby gaining a measure of authority or social status, however short-lived, over one's superiors in that society.[33] "Witchcraft (or sorcery) accusations, on the other hand, run in different social grooves. Typically, they are launched between equals, or by a superior against a subordinate."[34] Thus, possession is an expression of subordination, and it merely serves to vent frustration and aggression more or less within the bounds of society but does not seek to overthrow or depart from that society. When inferior members bring up charges of sorcery or witchcraft, however, they do so against their social superiors. That is a highly risky move, for failure would mean termination of membership in that society. It is therefore a calculated move as well, one which signifies either a disillusionment of prevailing values of said society or a readiness to assert one's leadership in replacement of the old guard. In other words, it directly challenges the current power arrangement in which one is structurally disadvantaged. "For witchcraft accusations represent a distancing strategy which seeks to discredit, sever, and deny links; and ultimately to assert separate identity."[35]

Such anthropological study would cast much insight on what Paul intends to accomplish in Galatians. His laborious attempt to distinguish himself from the Jerusalem leaders is consistent with the assertion of independence intrinsic to the sorcery accusation of 3:1.[36] He insists that his gospel is not from any human source and that he was never taught it by any human teacher (1:11-12), in order to privilege his own form of divine possession (using Lewis's language). His reception of divine revelation and commission to Gentiles set him apart from his contemporaries (1:15-16). Even when he has to suffer the indignity of having to submit his version of the gospel to those "who appear to be somebody" for approval, he is quick to point out that he does so prompted by divine revelation (2:2), the same revelation that commissioned him to be apostle to the Gentiles (1:15-16). At the meeting with the "alleged pillars" (*hoi dokountes ti einai*, 2:2, 6 [twice], 9), Paul reports that the divine grace which he was granted placed him on equal footing with Peter (2:8, 9), and that this was so well recognized that the pillars had to agree to an egalitarian division of labor and turf (2:9). Paul's summary of the whole meeting is therefore an assertion of independence: While the meeting was conducted between representatives from the Jerusalem and Antioch church, and while Paul *and* Barnabas attended as delegates from Antioch, Paul's minutes leave his readers with the distinct impression that the decisions reached at the meeting have been based on *his* gifts. Note, for example, the tension between the plural ("me and Barnabas") and the first person singular in 2:9: "And upon recognizing the grace that had been given *me*, James, Cephas, and John, the alleged pillars, gave to *me and Barnabas* the right hand of fellowship, in order that *we* might go to the Gentiles and they to the circumcised."[37] This is because at the time of writing, Barnabas and he had already gone their separate ways (2:11-14). In so doing, he asserts his separation and independence from the parent church.

EXPERIENCE IN GROUP SOLIDARITY

Not only does Paul assert his independence from Jerusalem, he insists that the Galatians must choose sides. He accomplishes this by structuring a series of binaries in his opening salvo (1:6-9), all of which are designed to remind the Galatians of their own ecstatic experiences at the time of their conversion. The first binary opposes "the one who called" the Galatians to "a different gospel" (1:6). In calling what the agitators are advocating "gospel," Paul in no way concedes that point to his opponents. In all likelihood, this is a term used by the latecomers themselves, whose teaching might well be a form of Jesus-messianism centered on the Torah.[38] Whether they perceive their message to be antithetical to Paul's is open to question, but Paul, making explicit his reaction, clearly thinks so. He calls it sarcastically "a *different* gospel" but immediately distances himself from the possibility that there can be "another" gospel. It only appears so because "some are continual agitators (note the present participle)" who "wish to change (*metastrephein*)[39] the gospel of Christ" (1:7). In other words, the agitators' "gospel" is the binary opposite of "the gospel of Christ, and Paul represents the opposite of the agitators.

The next two verses (1:8-9) carry the binaries further by appealing to the Galatians' own experience of the gospel. At first glance, Paul's argument appears to be an exegetical sleight of hand. In the strongest condemnatory terms Paul says, "But even if *we ourselves* or an angel from heaven would proclaim a gospel contrary to what *we* proclaimed to you, let the person be damned!" (1:8). The repetition of the first person pronoun is what makes this statement circular. While placing himself under the same judgment as everyone else ("even if we ourselves were to preach . . ."), he ends up reaffirming his old message, "what we proclaimed to you," as the final court of appeal. What Paul puts forth in one hand he takes away in another. Is this a fair reading of Paul's strategy?

It should be noted that "we" might refer to different actors in the involvement with the Galatians. In his founding visit, Paul preached as a missionary under the auspices of the Antioch congregation; by the time of writing, however, he had already left Antioch (2:11-14). It is possible that Paul here stresses the authoritative nature of the Galatians' initial experience over all subsequent ones. This is, of course, a strategic move to relativize the importance and possible impact of the agitators, outsiders and, more importantly, latecomers. As such, their message must be judged by standards established earlier.

This, I submit, is the purpose of Paul's second anathema in 1:9.[40] It is formally similar to the first, "If someone is to preach to you a gospel contrary to what you received, let the person be damned!" Now the criterion of truth is not Paul's earlier preaching in presumably his founding visit (the first anathema) but what the Galatians *received*. The stress is shifted from Paul's preaching to the Galatians' experience.

The verb *paralambanein* is a semi-technical term used frequently by Paul in the context of the transmission and reception of traditions of the Lord. That is how the term is used in 1 Corinthians 11:23 (tradition regarding the Lord's supper); 15:1, 3 (the gospel in traditional form; note especially the coordinated verb *paradidonai* "to deliver"); 1 Thessalonians 2:13 ("receiving the word of God"). It might also carry this sense in Galatians 1:12, although what Paul means by receiving the gospel "through a revelation" has prompted endless speculation.[41] But the term has a broader referent than simply the repetition and reception of tradition in its technical sense. In Philippians 4:9, Paul exhorts the Philippians to practice all that they learned and received and heard and saw *in him*. While this may include the gospel in its narrative form, the parallels with "learning," "hearing," and "seeing" would seem to indicate a more general sense of following Paul's personal example. Similarly in 1 Thessalonians 4:1, Paul exhorts his readers to behave as they "received" (*parelabon*) from him how they ought to behave (*peripatein*) and to please God. What is being delivered in this case is not a technical tradition but a manner of living that proves pleasing to God.

If that is the case, then Paul's appeal in the second anathema is meant to remind the Galatians of not just the propositional aspect of the gospel but also their experience at the reception of the gospel. In other words, Galatians 1:9 is meant to anticipate 3:1-5, where Paul reminds the Galatians of their experience at the time of their conversion. The criterion for judging the "truth of the gospel" is ultimately experience.

From the time of Luther, commentators have largely accepted that the center of Paul's argument in 3:1-5 is experience, in particular the ecstatic experiences of the Galatians at the moment of their conversion.[42] The references to the reception of the Spirit (vv. 2, 3, 5) and mighty deeds of miracles (v. 5) would confirm the supernatural character of such experiences, while the compact phraseology of "hearing of faith" (vv. 2, 5) would point to the initial preaching of the gospel that led the Galatians to faith in Christ. The power of the Spirit also results in the Galatians' ability to speak in tongues, for once they have become heirs, according to Paul, "God sent the Spirit of his son into our hearts crying 'Abba!'" (4:6). It is possible that the reference to a public demonstration of Christ's crucifixion (v. 1) might allude to some form of ecstatic vision, but it is just as likely to be a re-enactment of the passion story.[43] In light of the context, the best translation of *paschein* (v. 4) would seem to be "to experience" rather than "to suffer."[44] If the Galatians have indeed experienced so much, Paul reminds them, "Have you experienced them all for nothing?" If the Galatians do not deny their own experience, they can only agree with Paul.[45]

Such an appeal to the Galatians' experience paves the way for Paul to build his argument. The exegesis of the faith of Abraham in 3:6-14 reaches its climax with the reception of the Spirit through faith (v. 14), which Paul equates to the fulfillment of the Abrahamic promise.[46] The ecstatic experience of the Galatians thus results into making them authentic children of promise, in contradistinction to those who are fleshly (3:3) and who boast in the mutilation of the flesh (6:13).

What is latent in Paul's appeal to the Galatians' experience is therefore discrimination and differentiation. The polemical implications of 3:1-5 are already anticipated by the series of binaries set up in 1:6-9. "Who" of 3:1 refers to the "agitators" of 1:7. To them belong the categories of "works of the Law" (3:2, 5) and "flesh" (3:3), whereas the Galatians' experiences include a public demonstration of Jesus' crucifixion (1:1), reception of the Spirit (3:2, 3, 5), "hearing of faith" (3:2, 5), and the witness of mighty deeds (3:5). The vivid reminder of the Galatians' ecstatic experiences, on the other hand, not only helps them to recall the early days of their faith but especially compels them to distance themselves from the outsiders:

> In this factional struggle for the faith and commitment of the Galatians, Paul and his rivals confront each other with equal claims to authority: apostolic credentials and the word of God. In this situation where a superior legal authority for adjudicating conflicts is absent, both contending parties are subject finally to the court of public opinion.... The experience of the Galatians ... and public opinion are Paul's court of final appeal. Their experience, he argues, makes it clear that it is not he but his opponents who are the malicious agents of evil and strife infecting the community.[47]

CONCLUSION

What makes religious experience in Galatians stand out is how Paul exploits its potentials for group solidarity and for negotiating status and power. Paul understands the social and communal power of religious experience and uses it to his own advantage. In his attempt to win back the allegiance of the Galatians to himself, he discloses to them his own personal experiences with God, Christ, and divine revelation. He does this for strategic reasons. First of all, he suggests that his experience with the risen Messiah is so unique and so decisive that it sets him apart from other missionaries. The distance between them is so great and so absolute that anyone who deviates from him can potentially become his mortal enemy. In this Paul transforms his personal experience into an us-versus-them binarism. Second, Paul uses religious experience to encourage the Galatians to identify their experience with his, thereby binding them to him and creating an identity based on group solidarity. In this Paul exploits the power of social cohesion engendered by religious experience. Contrary to modern belief, which insists on taking religious experience as an individualist activity, Paul regards religious experience as sharable, mutually recognizable, and articulable in public idioms. Finally, since such group identity is cultivated in the context of Pauline binaries, it results in a sharply drawn boundary marking insiders from outsiders. This demarcation requires the Galatians to take sides. They do so with a criterion of truth that turns out to be based also on experience. By placing his readers on the knife-edge of decision, Paul taps, unwittingly, into the divisive potentials of experience.

THE BEATITUDES: JESUS' RECIPE FOR HAPPINESS?

CARL R. HOLLADAY

Any discussion of ancient attitudes about happiness must include treatment of the Beatitudes, the stylized list of nine blessings that constitute the opening section of Jesus' Sermon on the Mount in Matthew's Gospel (5:1-13). In English translations, each item is formulated using the same basic structure: a pronouncement of blessing on those who exhibit a commendable character trait ("Blessed are those who...") followed by a clause introduced by "for" stating the basis of the pronouncement.

The term "blessed" renders the Greek word *makarios*, which signifies the state of being fortunate, happy, or especially favored.[1] Possible translations include "fortunate," "happy," "blessed," and "privileged."[2] In the Latin Vulgate, the equivalent term is *beatus*, which means "happy," "prosperous," "blessed," or "fortunate."[3] Its noun form, *beatitudo*, a word coined by Cicero, signifies "the condition of the *beatus*, happiness, a blessed condition."[4] Since the Greek term *eudaimonia*, which can be translated "prosperity," "good fortune," "opulence," and signify "true, full happiness,"[5] is typically rendered in Latin by one of two words, *beatitudo* or *felicitas*, any Greek or Latin text that employs terms within this semantic field is relevant to a discussion of ancient views of happiness.

In this paper, I explore several questions relating to the Beatitudes, primarily to acquaint those who are not biblical specialists or theologians with issues relating to their interpretation.[6]

TWO VERSIONS OF THE BEATITUDES IN THE NEW TESTAMENT

When people think of the Beatitudes in the Gospels, they usually have in mind the formulation in Matthew's Gospel (5:1-13). Less familiar but equally important is the version found in Luke's Gospel (6:20-26), in his Sermon on the Plain. Blessings are pronounced elsewhere in the New Testament, especially in prayers that introduce some New Testament letters (2 Cor 1:3-7; Eph 1:3-14; 1 Pet 1:3-12). But these represent a distinct literary form reminiscent of the *berakah*, which is well known from Jewish prayer books. The Beatitudes in Matthew's Sermon on the Mount and Luke's Sermon on the Plain, rather than being prayers of blessing, more closely resemble proverbial speech. Even so, they do not easily fit into the literary form of proverbs, which typically encapsulate wise sayings that illuminate some aspect of life.

LITERARY CONTEXT

The Matthean Beatitudes introduce the Sermon on the Mount, the first of five discourses in Matthew's Gospel.[7] Comprising chapters 5–7, this opening address inaugurates Jesus' teaching ministry and introduces Jesus as an authoritative teacher who gives bold, provocative interpretations of the "law and the prophets" (5:17-48). Especially critical of common religious practices that tend to become empty rituals rather than sincere expressions of inner devotion, most notably almsgiving, prayer, and fasting (6:1-18), Jesus continues by offering miscellaneous instructions on such topics as true riches (6:19-21), loyalty to a single master (6:24), freedom from anxiety (6:25-34), judging others (7:1-5), the golden rule (7:12), self-deception (7:21-23), hearing and doing (7:24-27).

Some see Matthew's Sermon on the Mount as the first of five discourses that correspond to the Five Books of Moses in the Pentateuch.[8] While Matthew's Jesus certainly offers authoritative interpretations of well known aspects of Moses' teaching (esp. 5:17-48), he does so as the Messianic

Teacher who uniquely combines several identities, including Messiah, Son of God, Son of Man, Son of David, and rabbi. Each of these titles has its own distinctive valence in Matthew's Gospel, but Jesus' didactic role receives special emphasis. Accordingly, the Beatitudes introducing the Sermon on the Mount must be read as pronouncements of the church's pre-eminent teacher. Like the other material in the sermon, as well as the other four discourses, the Beatitudes reflect Matthew's own literary artistry. They stem from his conviction that Jesus, during his Galilean ministry, articulated a vision that would guide the disciples after his death. In this sense, they are timeless teachings that transcend Jesus' own lifetime or even the earliest generations of disciples that succeeded him.

Luke's Sermon on the Plain occurs at a different point in his overall storyline. Rather than serving as Jesus' inaugural sermon (a role filled by Jesus' sermon at his hometown synagogue in Nazareth, Luke 4:16-30), the Sermon on the Plain is delivered after his ministry is well under way. Several healings have already occurred, along with some controversy stories. Perhaps most important, Luke reports Jesus' choosing the twelve apostles (Luke 6:12-16) and his ministry of teaching and healing (Luke 6:17-19) immediately prior to the Sermon on the Plain.

Luke's sermon, considerably shorter than Matthew's, may not be inaugural in the sense that Matthew's Sermon on the Mount is, but they both offer compact summaries of Jesus' teaching. Each can be read as a position paper in which Jesus outlines the major emphases of his ministry. One of the most remarkable differences between the Matthean and Lukan versions of the Beatitudes is the highly stylized antithetical literary form adopted by Luke: four blessings juxtaposed with four woes, with each woe expressing the antithesis of its counterpart in the same order. This doubtless reflects Luke's well known penchant for literary forms in which reversal is a central element.[9] If the "blessing-woe" formulation draws on prophetic traditions from the Jewish Bible, as some scholars argue,[10] this distinctive formulation may further enhance Luke's portrait of Jesus as the Messianic Prophet.[11]

Like Matthew's Sermon on the Mount, Luke's Sermon on the Plain introduces themes that are developed further in the remainder of the Gospel. The contrasting fates of the poor and rich anticipate Luke's numerous stories depicting tragic wealth and noble poverty. Luke's interest in the addictive power of possessions is a major theme in his Gospel and its sequel the Book of Acts.[12] A complementary motif is the distinctive Lukan emphasis on non-reciprocity. Jesus' disciples are instructed to love, do good, and lend "expecting nothing in return" (6:35). Called for here is spontaneous generosity that is devoid of calculation. Loving action should not be taken as a quid pro quo. Instead, love should be extended as a non-calculating act that stems from a generous spirit. Here, and elsewhere in Luke's Gospel, generosity of spirit emerges as one of the prime expectations of Jesus' followers.

LITERARY FORM AND STRUCTURE

That both evangelists open their sermons with beatitudes suggests that they may be following a well-established rhetorical pattern reminiscent of the Psalter that opens with the well known psalm in which righteous people are promised lives of blessing and delight (Ps 1:1-3) and the wicked receive dire warnings about their ultimate fate (Ps 1:4-6). The structural differences between Matthew's and Luke's beatitudes, however, are striking. Whereas Matthew's opening section comprises a cluster of nine beatitudes, Luke reports two neatly symmetrical sets of blessings and woes.

As noted, each Matthean beatitude reflects the same literary pattern: a pronouncement of blessing ("Blessed are . . . ") followed by a reassuring promise. The first seven beatitudes are uniformly succinct, whereas the last two are longer and are connected thematically with the persecution motif. The first seven are also uniform in presenting the recipients of blessing and their corresponding promise in the third person. In the last two, the first of the pair of beatitudes relating to persecution is framed in the third person, but the second one is formulated in the second person, which breaks the previous pattern. This may suggest that in an earlier form Matthew's beatitudes consisted of eight members, all of which were uniformly formulated literarily, and that the ninth beatitude, which amplifies the eighth by intensifying the description of persecution as well as the promised hope, represents a later editorial addition.

Rather than a single list of nine blessings, Luke presents a fourfold literary structure in which each blessing has its antithetical counterpart in the list of four woes. The first three blessings (and woes) are also found in Matthew, although in a different order. Luke's first item—poor and rich—also comes first in Matthew, although Matthew's formulation "poor in spirit" is attitudinal, whereas Luke's unembellished language constitutes straightforward social description. What we make of this difference depends on our view of literary and traditional sources being used by the evangelists. If Matthew and Luke are drawing on a common (oral) tradition (Q), the two versions show them taking the saying in different directions.[13] On this showing, Matthew reflects a spiritualizing tendency. If Luke is using Matthew directly (the Griesbach hypothesis), his language may reflect an anti-spiritualizing tendency which gives Jesus a more sharply profiled social ethic.[14]

Luke's second blessing and woe reflect a similar difference in perspective. Its counterpart is Matthew's fourth beatitude about hungering and thirsting *after righteousness*. Luke's formulation, however, accents *actual* rather than *spiritual* hunger. Those envisioned are neither abstract nor distant; they are hungry and full *now*.

Luke's third blessing and woe—weeping and laughing *now*—also connect with the world we experience every day, in the here and now. Again, the Matthean counterpart, with its promise that those who mourn "will be comforted," has a somewhat softer edge than Luke, who frames human experience between the extremes of weeping and laughing.

Like its Matthean counterpart, the Lukan blessing and woe relating to persecution is more fully amplified than the previous items. Much of Luke's phrasing echoes Matthew, although here Luke reverses his earlier trend toward compactness and becomes more expansive. Persecution that occurs "on account of the Son of Man" and mention of "false prophets" move beyond Matthew.

Also worth noting is how the evangelists envision the relationship between Jesus and his hearers (Luke's readers). By formulating the first eight beatitudes using the third person, Matthew portrays Jesus engaged in generalized teaching. Hearers are invited to imagine people "out there" who exhibit these qualities. Only in the final beatitude does he switch to the second person, thereby moving toward direct address. Persecution envisioned as a possibility for someone else in the eighth beatitude now becomes an expected reality for those listening to Jesus. Luke, by contrast, consistently uses the second person in all four blessings and woes, thereby creating a heightened sense of immediacy between Jesus and his hearers (and Luke's subsequent readers). Luke's Jesus speaks directly to his disciples, pronouncing blessings and woes that relate to life as they experience it every day.

THE MATTHEAN BEATITUDES

1. "The poor in spirit" (*hoi ptōchoi tō pneumati*). The phrase is unique in the New Testament, but its Hebrew equivalent occurs in the Qumran War Scroll, in which God strengthens the faint-hearted for war and apparently gives power to the "poor in spirit" (*'anwê rûax*).[15] Given the context, we should probably imagine one whose spirit is impoverished in the sense that it is weakened or deflated. In the Matthean formulation, the qualifying phrase "in spirit" clearly moves "poor" in a figurative direction. One suggested rendering is "lacking in spiritual worth."[16] Understood this way, the phrase would suggest someone who is dispirited and who operates with low self-esteem. If so, Matthew's first beatitude does not speak of humility in the classic sense—the opposite of pride— but psychological or spiritual depression.[17]

Those who experience spiritual ennui are promised "the kingdom of heaven" (*hē basileia tōn ouranōn*),[18] one of the most elusive phrases in the New Testament. Mentioning the kingdom first underscores the prominence of this theme in Matthew's Gospel. John the Baptist's ministry is inaugurated by his proclamation of the kingdom's imminence (Matt 3:2). Once Jesus begins his ministry in Galilee, he takes up the same theme (Matt 4:17).

The promise of the kingdom is repeated in Matthew's eighth beatitude, in which those who are persecuted are offered the same hope as the spiritually depressed of the first beatitude. If Matthew's ninth beatitude is a later editorial amplification of the eighth beatitude, and the original list consisted of eight items, the mention of the "kingdom of heaven" at the beginning and end would reflect the use of *inclusio*. By bracketing the initial list of beatitudes with this theme, Matthew anticipates its prominence not only in the remainder of the Sermon on the Mount (5:19-20; 7:21), but also in the rest of his Gospel (twenty-five times). His understanding of the "kingdom of heaven" is especially unfolded in Jesus' "parables of the kingdom," seven of which constitute his third major discourse (ch. 13).[19]

2. "Those who mourn." Although the Matthean formulation does not specify the cause of mourning, Matthew's language resonates with Isaiah's promise to those returning from Babylonian exile that God would "comfort all who mourn" (Isa 61:2). Those who "mourn in Zion" are promised "the oil of gladness instead of mourning" (Isa 61:3; also see Sir 48:24). If Isaiah forms the backdrop for Matthew, we can imagine sadness prompted by exile—the loss of land, home, and cherished religious institutions such as the temple. Consolation occurs through return and restitution. Neither does Matthew specify the source of comfort, but the Isaiah context suggests that it is God. This conviction was shared by Paul, who speaks of "the Father of mercies and the God of all consolation, who consoles us in our affliction" (2 Cor 1:3-4). We can confidently imagine that mourners will be comforted *by God*.

3. "The meek." The language of the third beatitude is drawn directly from Psalm 36, where enjoying the blessings of the land God has given the people is a recurrent theme (Ps 36:11 LXX). Those who trust in the

Lord and do good are promised secure life in the land (v. 3). The wicked are cut off (from the land), while "those who wait for the Lord shall inherit the land" (v. 9). The meek who will inherit the land are promised abundant prosperity (v. 11). Those whom the Lord blesses "shall inherit the land," whereas those whom God curses "shall be cut off" (v. 22). Not only will the righteous inherit the land, but they will also live there forever (v. 29). Abiding in the Lord's ways exalts people, enabling them to "inherit the land" (v. 34).

The cumulative effect of these repeated references underscores the connection between righteous living and sharing in the abundant blessings of the land that God had given Israel (Deut 4:38). When 1 Enoch 5:7 promises that the elect who experience "light, joy, and peace" will "inherit the earth," an enhanced version of the land of Israel is probably in view. Meekness is one of several characteristics that constitute the profile of righteousness. Rather than being contrasted with those who are proud or arrogant, the meek are rather set over against "the wicked."

Should we understand Matthew's promise that the meek will inherit the earth as being tied specifically to the land of Israel? Or should it be read in the broader sense that those who are not overly impressed with their own sense of self-importance but instead are "gentle, humble, [and] considerate" will participate in the earth's abundance? Probably the latter. By the time this beatitudinal formulation appears in the Sermon on the Mount, it appears to have become detached from the land of Israel, as was the case in the Psalter.

4. "Those who hunger and thirst for righteousness." When Psalm 107 (Ps 106 LXX) mentions wanderers in the desert experiencing hunger and thirst (v. 5) and promises that the Lord "satisfies the thirsty, and the hungry he fills with good things" (v. 9), physical starvation is in view. Making "righteousness" (*dikaiosynē*) the object of one's innermost desires, however, gives this beatitude a distinctive spiritual accent. In this form, the beatitude moves toward the Johannine formulation, in which Jesus as the bread of life promises that those who follow him will never be hungry or

thirsty (John 6:35). Just as John's Gospel insists that God is the ultimate provider of the manna from heaven (John 6:32-33), so should we imagine God as the subject of the promise in Matthew 5:6b: those who hunger and thirst for righteousness will be satisfied by God.

Accenting the quest for righteousness reflects Matthew's theological interest.[20] Just as Jesus' submission to John's baptism "fulfills all righteousness" (3:15), so are Jesus' disciples expected to pursue righteousness as the highest moral good. The eighth beatitude is starkly realistic when it insists that persecution is the inevitable price one pays for living righteously (Matt 5:10). Jesus' disciples must exhibit a form of righteousness that surpasses their religious counterparts, the scribes and Pharisees (Matt 5:20).

It is worth noting that the fourth beatitude sees righteousness as a fully attainable goal. It is neither elusive nor mysterious. Nor does Matthew share the view of the Johannine apocalypse that only in heaven will hunger and thirst be completely eliminated (Rev 7:16). Matthew, by contrast, suggests that longing after righteousness, far from being an eschatological vision, is an everyday pursuit that is fully achievable in this life. The future tense—"they will be filled"—should be understood as future attainment in this life rather than eventual attainment in the future life.

5. "The merciful." The parable of the unforgiving servant, which is unique to Matthew, captures the essence of mercy (Matt 18:23-35). A king forgives the huge debt of one of his slaves, who in turn imposes harsh demands on a fellow slave who owes him a pittance. The king severely rebukes the first slave by asking, "Should you not have had mercy on your fellow slave, as I had mercy on you?" While mercy is not defined in the parable, its meaning is clear: empathetic concern for someone in need and the extension of kindness and consideration to that person. The parable occurs within Matthew's fourth discourse, which addresses issues relating to community life. Recognizing the inevitable tensions that occur when people try to live together in communities of faith, this discourse on "community rule" identifies the difficulty of forgiveness as a special concern.

In the parable, the king clearly symbolizes God, who embodies and extends mercy. In a wide range of religious traditions, mercy is preeminently a characteristic of God. Exodus 34:6-7 typifies the biblical tradition: "The LORD, the LORD, a God merciful and gracious, slow to anger . . . forgiving iniquity and transgression and sin." Deities in other traditions, such as Amenophis and Isis, also extend mercy.[21]

In Matthew's Gospel, those afflicted with disease repeatedly approach Jesus, imploring him for mercy (Matt 9:27; 15:22; 17:15; 20:30-31). While some of these healing stories are also found in Mark's Gospel, Matthew especially emphasizes the role of Jesus, Son of David, as a messianic figure who establishes his identity by extending physical and psychological healing. These stories give a therapeutic dimension to Matthew's understanding of mercy.

The parable of the unforgiving servant is useful in deciding from whom the merciful will obtain mercy. It underscores both the divine and human dimensions of mercy. God treats humans mercifully, and since humans should reflect God's nature, they are expected to treat each other mercifully. Accordingly, those who act mercifully will be treated mercifully in the first instance by those to whom they extend mercy and, in the second instance, by God, the "Father of mercies."

The parable of the unforgiving servant also portrays dramatically what James 2:13 states aphoristically: "judgment will be without mercy to anyone who has shown no mercy; mercy triumphs over judgment." Just as harsh, unsympathetic action toward someone in need engenders hard-edged responses, so does mercy prompt mercy.

6. "The pure in heart." Psalm 24 establishes the conceptual framework of the sixth beatitude. Prescribing a liturgy for entering the sanctuary, the psalmist calls for worshipers approaching the temple to have "clean hands and pure hearts" (v. 4). Bodily purity metaphorically expresses moral purity: refraining from what is false and from swearing deceitfully (v. 4). People who display such integrity "will receive blessing from the LORD" (v. 5). This places them in the company of those who "seek the face of

the God of Jacob" (v. 6). Being pure in heart—morally unblemished—directs the devout worshiper toward the presence of God. It is in this sense that they "see God." Elsewhere the psalmist promises that "God is good to the . . . pure in heart" (Ps 73:1).

7. "Peacemakers." Essentially a relational term, peace *eirēnē* signifies a state of concord or harmony that exists between groups or individuals. The former may range from kinship units (tribes, clans, or families) to more formally organized political units (governments or nations), while the latter may be related to each other in a variety of ways, ranging from casual or deep friendships to highly formalized contractual agreements between business associates. Depending on the nature of the relationship, the absence of peace may be war between nations or a personal dispute between friends. In one case, differences may be resolved through military action and agreements formulated in treaties, in the other through argument and discussion that concludes with a handshake or a warm embrace.

Linking peace with general well-being and health is fully understandable, given the physical and psychological toll that disharmony, strife, and enmity can take. When early Christian greetings acquired the formulaic two-part structure, "Grace and peace," this literary development recognized the therapeutic dimension of peace.[22] Drawing on the rich connotations of *shalom* in the biblical tradition, Christians extended greetings to each other that created the possibility for forming communities characterized by gracious dealings and a healthy sense of well-being.

Given the rich, multi-layered dimensions of peace, it is not surprising that it would figure as a central element in visions of the future, whether seen as messianic, utopian, or eschatological visions. One interpretive question, however, is whether the term peace always has this robust meaning in which it calls to mind everything associated with personal and corporate well-being. Rather than regularly interpreting peace in this fully expanded theological sense, some prefer to see it in more modest terms as a description of normalcy.[23]

How we understand "peacemaking" in the seventh beatitude depends on how we construe the term peace. When President Carter quoted this beatitude at the ceremony honoring the peace agreement between President Anwar Sadat and Prime Minister Menahem Begin, he was trading on its generality and open-endedness. Given the religious outlook of each participant, the inclusive tone of "children of God" became fully appropriate in a public setting.

While the beatitude does not explicitly connect the activity of peacemaking with achieving the status of God's children, we can easily deduce the unstated premise: the deity is a God of peace. According to the logic of this beatitude, those who make peace share in God's nature.

The biblical tradition provides some glimpses of the "God of peace." After an encounter with an angel of the Lord, Gideon, one of Israel's judges, receives a reassuring promise from the Lord: "Peace be to you; do not fear, you shall not die." In response, he built an altar to the Lord and called it, "The LORD is peace." (Judg 6:23-24). In Solomon's response to Joab, God is portrayed as the giver of everlasting peace (1 Kgs 2:33). By helping Israel's kings win their wars, God gives peace (1 Chr 22:9, 18; 2 Chr 14:6-7). One of Job's friends, Bildad, begins his third speech by asserting, "Dominion and fear are with God; he makes peace in his high heaven" (Job 25:2). In the Psalter, God is entreated as one who can "bless his people with peace" (Ps 29:11; see Pss 83:1; 85:8; 147:14). These biblical references may be scattered and somewhat sporadic, but they are frequent enough to establish the framework for early Christian writers, such as Paul, who regularly mentions the God (Lord) of peace (Rom 15:33; 16:20; 1 Cor 14:33; 2 Cor 13:11; Phil 4:7; 1 Thess 5:23; 2 Thess 3:16; see Heb 13:20). By extension, Christ is an agent of peace (Eph 2:14-15; Col 1:20; 3:15).

As for the act of peacemaking itself, Proverbs 10:10 offers straightforward advice: "the one who rebukes boldly makes peace." James 3:18 does not offer blessing to peacemakers but comes close in promising that "a harvest of righteousness is sown in peace for those who make peace."

8. "Those who are persecuted." Explicit language relating to persecution occurs infrequently in the Jewish Bible.[24] By contrast, it occurs three times as frequently in the New Testament.[25] Regardless of its frequency, language of persecution is loaded. Implicit, especially to heirs of the Enlightenment, is an inherent sense of injustice, especially if "persecute" *diōkō* means "to harass someone, especially because of their beliefs."[26] We can imagine only bad forms of persecution. Good persecution is an oxymoron.

To be persecuted "for righteousness' sake" is clarified by the NRSV rendering of 1 Pet 3:14, which probably echoes Matthew's eighth beatitude: "But even if you do suffer for doing what is right, you are blessed." These reassuring words from 1 Peter probably reflect localized resistance to the early Christian movement. Whether the readers are mainly experiencing psychological harassment or are encountering physical abuse, their critics apparently regard them as "evildoers" (1 Pet 2:12). This description captures the paradox of religious persecution: the persecuted see themselves as good but are seen by their persecutors as evil. A single set of convictions creates resolved devotion in one group and violent resistance in the opposing group. Those persecuted claim "righteousness" as the basis for their steadfast devotion, but so do their detractors. Persecutors also operate with a sense of "doing what is right."

The eighth beatitude, however, is partisan toward those being persecuted. Since "righteousness" has special valence in Matthew, serving as shorthand for all that is noblest and best as one seeks to live before God, it is rightly seen as the target of opponents. Righteousness defines Jesus' mission (Matt 3:15) and sets expectations for his followers (Matt 6:33). Those who live to "do what is right" are assured that the "kingdom of heaven" is theirs. The Matthean formulation leaves unstated whether this heavenly reign is present or future. The ambiguous language used elsewhere about the coming kingdom leaves open both possibilities. Taken at face value, the language reassures those who suffer for righteousness' sake that they can experience God's heavenly reign in this life.

In the language of 1 Peter 2:20: "if you endure when you do right and suffer for it, you have God's approval." Although the present tense is used, the promise can be read just as easily as a future promise.

9. "Being reviled and persecuted." With the shift of language to the second person plural, the ninth beatitude becomes more direct. It amplifies the essential message of the previous beatitude through triple formulaic language, some of which echoes Isaiah 51, which employs direct speech as it addresses "you who know righteousness, you people who have my teaching in your hearts." Hearers are advised not to fear the reproach of others or be dismayed when they are reviled (Isa 51:7). Anticipating the more extended warning in Jesus' second major discourse relating to mission (Matt 10:16-23), this beatitude targets false accusations directed against the disciples. So closely are the disciples identified with Jesus that attacks against them occur "on my account."

In the face of unrelenting abuse and persecution, Jesus' disciples are expected to "rejoice and be glad." The basis for such resilience is explicitly eschatological: they will be rewarded greatly in heaven. In the previous beatitudes, references to hope or bliss in a future life have been muted. Coming in the final beatitude, this assurance of future blessedness acquires a climactic quality. So positioned, it has probably had a retroactive effect, prompting readers to interpret the previous beatitudes as promises of blessedness after death. Appealing to the fate of earlier prophets who experienced outright resistance and rejection creates experiential continuity intended to strengthen the hearers' resilience (see Neh 9:26). This rhetorical strategy anticipates the more fully elaborated appeal that later occurs in the fifth formal discourse (23:29-36).

THE LUKAN BLESSINGS AND WOES

1. "You who are poor." Although the scribal tradition tried to align Luke's first beatitude with its Matthean counterpart by adding "in spirit," textual critics rightly see this as secondary harmonization. Luke's

unembellished language is straightforward social description: those in poverty. Mentioning "the poor" (*hoi ptōchoi*) first reflects the priorities of the biblical tradition in which various Hebrew terms are employed in giving extensive attention to those living at subsistence levels.[27] Prophetic critiques of those who oppress the poor typify the way in which biblical writers align themselves with those who are deprived of the world's goods, especially through unjust practices of their oppressors. New Testament writers across the board reflect a similar stance.[28] Luke's first beatitude succinctly expresses the early Christian view: poverty may be widespread, even inescapable, but it is not determinative in shaping human worth. The poor may not be blessed physically but they can experience God's blessings: "yours is the kingdom of God." The same outlook is echoed in James 2:5: "Has not God chosen the poor in the world to be rich in faith and to be heirs of the kingdom that he has promised to those who love him?"

This proverbial benediction comes to life in the parade of poor characters who populate Luke's Gospel, beginning with Jesus' own parents. That they were people of modest means is shown when they offer a pair of turtledoves or two young pigeons instead of a sheep in presenting Jesus in the temple (Luke 2:22-24). And yet, Mary is blessed by Elizabeth as "the mother of my Lord" (Luke 1:42-43). Quoting Isaiah 61:1-2 in his inaugural address, Jesus claims the anointing of God's Spirit in announcing "good news to the poor" (Luke 4:18). Along with those who are imprisoned, blind, and oppressed, the poor are given the hope of participating in "the year of the Lord's favor" (Luke 4:18). Blessing becomes concrete for numerous people in Luke's Gospel who are healed by Jesus (Luke 4:40-41). The leper (Luke 4:12-16), the paralytic (Luke 4:17-26), the man with the withered hand (Luke 6:6-11), to mention only those who are healed prior to the Sermon on the Plain, are different manifestations of the poor. While their economic status is not in the forefront, they clearly typify those without access to traditional sources of healing or who are otherwise desperate for care.

Luke's first beatitude privileges the poor not only by mentioning them first but also by presenting them as rightful heirs to God's kingdom. His unfolding narrative chronicles the reality of this promise. The poor whom Jesus encounters in their many different forms are embraced rather than excluded. They may be socially marginalized, but they occupy the center of Luke's narrative, his way of signaling that they stand squarely in the center of God's vision of the world.

2. "You who are hungry now." Luke's emphasis on "those who hunger now" (*hoi peinōntes nun*) stands in sharp contrast to Matthew's spiritual hunger. Earlier in Luke's narrative, Jesus has already experienced extended hunger: a forty-day fast left him famished (Luke 4:2). The story of Jesus' temptation echoes biblical traditions relating to the hunger Israel experienced in the forty years of wilderness wandering. Reflecting on the wilderness crisis, Psalm 107 graphically depicts the desert wandering in which the Israelites hunger and thirst, experience fainting souls within themselves, cry out in distress, and finally thank God for satisfying their thirst and hunger with "good things" (Ps 106:4-9 LXX). Luke's language of "hungering now" and "being filled" (*chortasthēsesthe*) echoes this psalm.

Distinguishing the hungry as a separate group from the poor sets the stage for later Lukan episodes that feature beggars, most notably the prodigal son who experienced hunger at the most humiliating level (Luke 15:17), Lazarus who begged for crumbs at the rich man's table even as stray dogs licked his sores (Luke 16:20-21), and the blind man at Jericho (Luke 18:35-43).[29] Stories of miraculous feeding and banqueting give visual realization to how the hungry are fed. The father's lavish feast for his returning son amply illustrates how those who are "hungry now" get fed (Luke 15:23-24). The story of feeding the five thousand (Luke 9:10-17) shows the hungry being filled *en masse*. Other stories, such as the great banquet (Luke 14:15-24), make the same point indirectly.

As the Lukan narrative unfolds, filling the hungry is depicted at the physical level, but there are plenty of signals that more is in view than dispensing food. In some instances, beggars are healed. In others, they experience heavenly bliss that sharply contrasts with their life of earthly poverty. Stories of hospitality, meals, and banqueting convey more than well-spread tables; they are occasions when people who are hungry gather to experience Jesus' presence as he teaches, heals, and entertains questions. In the tradition of the Greek symposium, these meals cannot occur without food and drink, but they are about far more than satisfying physical hunger and thirst. If the wilderness traditions are the immediate background for understanding this second Lukan beatitude, we can most certainly assume that the one who will satisfy urgent hunger is God.

3. "You who weep now." Lament figures so prominently in the biblical tradition that it constitutes one distinct type of psalm. In psalms of lament, however, those who weep do not always receive immediate assurance that they will eventually laugh. They may vent their anger against God and rehearse their many troubles and afflictions. They may even be reminded of God's faithfulness or the prospect of divine deliverance. Reflecting on God's deliverance, they may express trust in God's steadfast love and experience heartfelt joy that breaks out in song (Ps 13:5-6). But the promise of laughter as an antidote for sorrow is not the main thrust of lament psalms. Even so, the psalmist can exclaim to the Lord, "You have put gladness in my heart" (Ps 4:7).

Reflecting a broad spectrum of human experience, Luke includes episodes in which people grieve. Encountering the funeral procession of the son of the widow of Nain, Jesus comforts her, saying, "Do not weep." After Jesus restores the man's life, Luke marks the moment by noting that "God has looked favorably on his people!" (Luke 7:16). While Luke does not report the mother's grief turning to laughter, her experience certainly illustrates the promise of the third beatitude. The sinful woman who anointed Jesus with precious ointment expressed her contrition through her tears (Luke 7:36). By extending unconditional forgiveness to her, Jesus enacts the bestowal of blessedness. At the funeral of the synagogue leader's daughter, bystanders were "weeping and wailing" (Luke 8:52), but Luke's third beatitude is enacted a third time when the young man was restored to life.

Not all weeping turns to joy in Luke. Those excluded from the kingdom of God will experience "weeping and gnashing of teeth" (Luke 13:28). To the company of mourners following Jesus to the scene of his crucifixion, he retorts, "Daughters of Jerusalem, do not weep for me, but weep for yourselves and for your children" (Luke 23:28).

4. "You who are hated, excluded, reviled, and defamed." As in Matthew, the final beatitude deals with the prospect that Jesus' disciples will experience stiff resistance, mainly in the form of verbal harassment and defamation. The specific mention of the elusive christological title "Son of Man" as the object of abuse (Luke 6:22) connects with Luke's four passion predictions in which Jesus anticipates suffering and death in his role as Son of Man (Luke 9:21-22; 9:43-45; 17:24-25; 18:31-34). As Jesus emphasizes later, his disciples will share his fate (Luke 9:23-27).

Joy as the appropriate response to persecution is exemplified especially in the sequel to Luke's Gospel, the Book of Acts. Upon their release by the Sanhedrin, the apostles display this behavior (Acts 5:41). Paul and Silas are portrayed praying and singing while imprisoned in Philippi (Acts 16:25). Like Matthew, Luke mentions the eschatological motivation: "your reward is great in heaven" (Luke 6:23). He also links the disciples' experience with that of Israel's persecuted prophets (Luke 6:23b; cf. 2 Chron 36:16).

5. "You who are rich." Those who are rich (*plousios*) receive repeated warnings in the Gospel narratives. Especially memorable is the "rich young man," whose sad fate is reported in all three Synoptic Gospels (Matt 19:16-30; Mark 10:17-31; Luke 18:18-30). While Luke knows Jesus' teachings about the dangers of wealth from his earlier sources, the Gospel of Mark and the Q tradition, he amplifies this strand of the Jesus tradition. This is especially evident in the narrative episodes and teachings that are unique to Luke's Gospel, the so-called "L" material. Much of this material is included in Luke's Travel Narrative (Luke 9:51–19:27). Prominent in these materials are memorably depicted characters who display the addictive power of riches: the rich fool (Luke 12:13-21); the prodigal son (Luke 15:11-32); the rich man who neglected Lazarus (Luke 16:19-31). Each of

these illustrates the truth of Luke's first "woe." Similarly tragic fates are experienced by Ananias and Sapphira in the Book of Acts (Acts 5:1-11).

Juxtaposed with these examples of tragic wealth are other cases that offer hope to the rich: the Good Samaritan (Luke 10:29-37); Zacchaeus (19:1-10); the early Christian community (Acts 2:43-47); Barnabas (4:32-37); the church at Antioch (Acts 11:27-30). Each of these illustrates that through the proper disposition of wealth, the sharp warning of the first Lukan beatitude can be avoided.

6. "You who are full now." "Being full *now*" echoes its counterpart "being hungry now." Each reinforces the other: physical hunger and satiety here and now. Prophetic indictments of self-indulgent behavior typically target excessive eating and drinking (Joel 1:5; Amos 6:4-7). Isaiah 5:22 offers warning to those who "are heroes in drinking wine and valiant at mixing drink." Reflecting this sharp-edged prophetic critique of satiety, Luke provides some glimpses of those who eat to excess: the prodigal son who "squandered his property in dissolute living" (Luke 15:13) and the rich man "who feasted sumptuously every day" (Luke 16:19). By depicting the rich man's fate after death as one of irreversible deprivation, Luke underscores what it means to be empty.

7. "You who are laughing now." Once again, the addition of "now" recalls its counterpart: "weeping *now*." It is a reminder that both states are temporary and short-lived. A reversal of these conditions is imminent.

Luke's third woe reflects the doleful tone of James 4:9: "Lament and mourn and weep. Let your laughter be turned into mourning and your joy into dejection." Luke's outlook may be shaped by prophetic oracles in which Israel is urged to lament in the face of impending disaster (Joel 1:2-12).

8. "When all speak well of you." One of the standard definitions of a false prophet is someone who receives popular adulation by delivering crowd-pleasing messages (Isa 30:9-11; Jer 5:30-31; 6:13-14; 23:16-17). A recurrent feature of Luke's portrait of Jesus is his strident prophetic preaching. This is already evident in Jesus' inaugural sermon at Nazareth,

in which he manages to infuriate his own hometown (Luke 4:16-31). The four Lukan woes continue the theme of unsettling prophetic preaching, and they are reinforced by two sets of fourfold woes addressed to Pharisees (Luke 11:42-44) and lawyers (Luke 11:45-52). Similarly harsh preaching also occurs on Jesus' lips elsewhere in Luke's Gospel (Luke 10:13; 17:1; 21:23; 22:22).

CONCLUSIONS

Although the Matthean and Lukan versions of the Beatitudes share many common elements, they reflect distinctive differences. Both sets of sayings are attributed to Jesus, but in Matthew we hear the Messianic Teacher pronouncing blessings on people who experience a wide range of character traits, emotional dispositions, and behaviors. In Luke, by contrast, Jesus' pronouncement of blessings and woes has a more distinctly prophetic tone. Biblical echoes are heard throughout the Matthean and Lukan formulation, suggesting that the immediate frame of reference is a liturgical or catechetical setting in which biblical interpretation figured centrally. While the language of both versions resonates with literary formulations from non-Jewish traditions, differences should be respected. We may hear some echoes of Greek moral discourse about the virtues in the beatitudes, but neither Matthew nor Luke presents a virtue (or vice) list. Some may read Matthew's "poor in spirit" as a synonym for humility, but such an easy equation is problematic. Nor is it clear that "blessed" (*makarios*) in this context signifies "well-being" (*eudaimōn*) in the Aristotelian sense.

For all the differences between Matthew and Luke, they share a common frame of reference. They may formulate God's heavenly reign differently, but both stand within the tradition of Second Temple Judaism in which biblical perspectives inform their understanding of the past and present and shape their visions of the future.

PART TWO

THEOLOGICAL APPROPRIATION OF THE NEW TESTAMENT

KERYGMA AND MIDRASH:
A CONVERSATION WITH
LUKE TIMOTHY JOHNSON AND C. H. DODD

RICHARD B. HAYS

STARTING A CONVERSATION

Because Luke Johnson has contributed to New Testament studies in many and various ways, it is all too easy for some of his important insights to get lost in the thicket of his abundant writings. He is perhaps insufficiently credited for the important work he has done on the ways in which the New Testament writers interpreted Israel's Scripture. This is a topic of considerable significance as we seek to reflect on our own interpretative engagements with scriptural traditions. The present essay, therefore, will focus particularly on some of the hermeneutical implications of Johnson's treatment of the New Testament's interpretation of the Old.[1]

For the most part, Johnson's insights on this topic are imbedded in his commentaries or scattered about in his journal articles or other writings. But he has published at least one short monograph, *Septuagintal Midrash in the Speeches of Acts*, that offers a substantial, highly condensed analysis of scriptural interpretation by one of the NT's major witnesses, the author of Luke-Acts.[2] This little book will provide the focal point for the present essay. To be sure, we should be cautious about drawing general conclusions from a single study of a few passages in one NT writing. In what follows, I do not presume to describe fully Johnson's understanding of the intertextual hermeneutics of the NT. Johnson himself has repeatedly warned against efforts to construct comprehensive synthetic accounts of the theology of the NT, preferring instead to pursue close readings of individual texts.[3] It is perhaps appropriate, then, that we treat Johnson's own writings with similar circumspection by focusing closely on a single monograph, and asking how its findings might inform our reflections about hermeneutics.

This inquiry will be enhanced if we set Johnson's work alongside another significant treatment of similar questions; the comparison will bring some of the distinctive features of Johnson's contribution into sharp relief. I propose, therefore, to compare and contrast Johnson's study of midrash in Acts to C. H. Dodd's classic study, *According to the Scriptures*.[4]

The juxtaposition of these two works might at first seem surprising. Dodd's book, published in 1952, represents the perspective of an earlier generation of British NT scholarship, whereas Johnson's book, published exactly fifty years later, reflects the state of the art in NT criticism in America at the beginning of the twenty-first century. Yet these two works share a number of common characteristics that will make the comparison fruitful. Both books originated as public lectures: Dodd's as the Stone Lectures at Princeton Theological Seminary, Johnson's as the Père Marquette Lecture at Marquette University.

The demands of the public lecture format forced each of these two formidably erudite scholars to present their ideas in a concise, lucid form. Each of them packs much information into a few pages of artful prose. Each of these two rather different scholars foregrounds the role played by OT citations in the Acts of the Apostles,[5] and each is convinced that the patterns of scriptural interpretation in Acts can provide important insights and models for the church's ongoing practice of biblical interpretation and preaching. The half-century gap between these books serves to highlight some of the ways that the discipline has progressed over time; nonetheless, some of Dodd's concerns still stand in significant counterpoint to Johnson's views. In the following pages, we shall attempt to open a conversation between these two important readers of the NT.

STRUCTURE AND CONTENT OF THE TWO STUDIES: AN OVERVIEW

DODD: ACCORDING TO THE SCRIPTURES

Dodd's book was widely influential in its day, but it has long been out of print, and his arguments are less well known today than formerly; consequently, it will perhaps be useful to summarize the main lines of his analysis. *According to the Scriptures* builds upon his earlier work, *The Apostolic Preaching and Its Developments* (1936). That study had sought to isolate from the diverse NT writings a common primitive tradition, the *kerygma*, which provided the fundamental content of early Christian proclamation, summarized in an outline of historical events. Here is Dodd's account of that kerygmatic tradition:

> The events in question are those of the appearance of Jesus in history—His ministry, sufferings and death and His subsequent manifestation of Himself to His followers as risen from the dead and invested with the glory of another world—and the power and activity of the Church as a society distinguished by the power and activity of the Holy Spirit, and looking forward to the return of its Lord as Judge and Saviour of the world.[6]

In *According to the Scriptures*, Dodd proposes to advance this analysis by distinguishing between the apostolic *kerygma* itself (i.e., the narration of these events) and the OT texts that are cited to explain the significance of the events. Using the metaphor of church architecture, Dodd likens the *kerygma* to the ground plan of a cathedral, and suggests that the early interpretations of OT texts constitute the "substructure" of the edifice.[7] On this common ground plan and foundation, then, the various NT writings such as the letters of Paul, the Gospel of John, and the Letter to the Hebrews construct their diverse theologies. "As church architecture, based upon a universal general plan, may show the various characteristics of Romanesque, Gothic, or Baroque, so each of these theologians builds after his own style."[8] The salient point is this: Dodd sets out to demonstrate the hypothesis that the NT's scriptural quotations—or at least a great many of them—belong to a common early tradition that antedates the individual writings in the canon. The aim of *According to the Scriptures* is to trace the evidence for this common tradition that constitutes the OT substructure on which the NT authors build.

In order to test this hypothesis, Dodd surveys all the "passages from the Old Testament which, being cited by two or more writers of the New Testament in *prima facie* independence of one another, may fairly be presumed to have been current as *testimonia* before they wrote."[9] For example, Psalm 2:7 ("You are my son; today I have begotten you") is quoted both in Acts 13:33 and in Hebrews 1:5, 5:5. Furthermore, it shows up in the Gospels both in the baptism and transfiguration narratives. Consequently, Dodd infers that the passage must have been used as a pre-canonical "*testimonium* to the messiahship of Jesus."[10] The second chapter of Dodd's work identifies fifteen instances in the NT of such multiple citations.

This is precisely the sort of evidence that had led J. Rendel Harris, earlier in the twentieth century, to hypothesize that the NT authors were drawing not directly on a reading of the OT books but rather on compilations of messianic prooftexts collected in anthologies of *testimonia*.[11] Dodd, however, rejects Harris's theory, because he notices numerous cases in which different NT authors drew on different bits of material from the same OT context, suggesting that they were in fact reading larger textual units, not merely isolated prooftexts. An example of this phenomenon is the citation or echoing of different excerpts from Psalm 69 by several different NT writers: John 2:17; Romans 15:3; John 15:24; Matthew 22:34; Mark 15:36; John 19:28; Acts 1:20.[12]

Dodd therefore, in his third chapter, sets himself the task of identifying and categorizing the major extended "portions of Scripture" from which the NT authors drew their testimonies and interpreted the meaning of the *kerygma*. He groups these OT texts into four categories: "Apocalyptic-eschatological Scriptures" (chiefly Joel, Zechariah, Daniel); "Scriptures of the New Israel" (Hosea, parts of Isaiah, Jer 31:10-34); "Scriptures of the Servant of the Lord and the Righteous Sufferer" (the servant songs in Isaiah along with numerous psalms); and finally the less than helpful category of "unclassified Scriptures" (Psalms 2, 8, and 110; Genesis 12 and 22; and Deuteronomy 18).[13] Having surveyed the evidence, Dodd argues strongly that the earliest Christian interpreters, even before Paul, were engaged in "an original, coherent and flexible method of biblical exegesis" that read extended passages of Scripture in a contextually sensitive fashion and found in these large units of Scripture a prefiguration of precisely the events narrated by the *kerygma*.[14]

In a much briefer fourth chapter, Dodd explores the ways in which these portions of Scripture organically gave rise to the early community's doctrines of the church, of Jesus' messiahship, and of the atoning significance of his death. A famously provocative ending to this chapter proposes the theory that Jesus himself was the source of the early church's christological exegesis of the OT: "To account for the beginning of this most original and fruitful process of rethinking the Old Testament we found need to postulate a creative mind. The Gospels offer us one. Are we compelled to reject the offer?"[15]

Finally, the book's concluding chapter discusses "whether the principles and methods followed by the early oral tradition of Old Testament interpretation lying behind the New Testament have continuing validity as a means to the theological understanding of the gospel facts."[16] Not surprisingly, Dodd gives a positive answer to this question, though with sophisticated qualifications. He contends that the NT's reading of the Old often represents "an organic outgrowth or ripening of the original thought," based on "a genuinely historical understanding" of the history of Israel as a whole.[17]

JOHNSON: SEPTUAGINTAL MIDRASH IN THE SPEECHES OF ACTS

Johnson's work, as we have noted, is more modest in its scope. Rather than investigating the NT as a whole, he focuses chiefly on the practices of biblical interpretation found in the apostolic speeches in the Acts of the Apostles. He begins by noting the many unresolved problems about the date and genre of Luke-Acts and its puzzling "mingling of Hellenistic and Jewish elements." As a way of getting a handle on this challenging work, he proposes to study "the way Luke shows the first Christians interpreting the texts of Scripture that form the common symbolic world of messianist and non-messianist Jews of the first century, as well as their most obvious field of contention."[18]

Johnson begins by surveying recent critical perspectives on the speeches in Acts. He takes note immediately of Dodd's work, describing it as "the last credible effort to salvage the so-called missionary speeches as historical evidence."[19] Despite the conciliatory adjective "credible," Johnson is thoroughly unpersuaded by Dodd's argumentation. Noting that the diction and theology of the apostolic speeches is consistent with Luke's own language elsewhere in the narrative, Johnson opts firmly for reading the speeches as Lukan compositions that express Luke's own viewpoint and style of biblical interpretation. Thus, the speeches are "a form of authorial commentary, placed in the mouths of the characters."[20] Johnson finds, consequently, that the most fruitful approach is to analyze the speeches in terms of their narrative functions within Luke's unfolding story. For example, in Stephen's narration of the story of Moses (Acts 7:17-50) Luke structures the tale to create a typological correspondence between the Exodus story and "the double visitation of Jesus to Israel"—once leading to rejection, the second time with the Spirit-given power of signs and wonders. Thus, the pattern of this speech provides readers "with an interpretive key for [Luke's] entire two-volume composition."[21]

Next, Johnson gives a more general overview of Luke's use of Scripture throughout his two-volume work. Luke skillfully weaves his Scripture citations into the spoken discourse of his characters. Most significantly, these citations repeatedly depend upon specific nuances and textual peculiarities of the Septuagint (LXX), rather than the Hebrew textual tradition. (This is an important point to which Johnson will return in his concluding observations.) Johnson emphasizes the vexing complexities of textual criticism of Acts, but on the whole finds that Luke prefers the LXX, while also exercising the prerogative to alter its readings freely where necessary to underscore a theological point.

Finally, with these prolegomena out of the way, Johnson turns to a detailed substantive analysis of the actual patterns of scriptural interpretation in Acts. He concentrates attention on three speeches that illustrate different "modes of Scriptural interpretation."

First, Stephen's speech in Acts 7:2-53, a retelling of Israel's history, is shown to be comparable to the targumic style of renarration found in *Jubilees* and in the *Biblical Antiquities* of Pseudo-Philo.[22] Luke stays close to the verbal formulations of the LXX, but he fills narrative gaps in a haggadic fashion. Thus, this speech exemplifies what Johnson provocatively calls "septuagintal targum."[23]

Second, Johnson proposes that the prayer of the apostles in Acts 4:24-30—which, despite being a prayer, bears all the earmarks of a speech—illustrates an interpretative strategy virtually identical to the *pesher* exegesis found in the biblical commentaries at Qumran.[24] The prayer cites LXX Psalm 2:1-2 verbatim and then explicates it line by line, showing that the text's prophetic meaning is fulfilled in the present experience of the community.

Third, Johnson shows that Paul's sermon at Pisidian Antioch (Acts 13:16-41) weaves together a tapestry of numerous texts, partly through word association, to argue for the resurrection of Jesus. Johnson draws particular attention to verses 32-37, in which Psalm 2:7, Isaiah 55:3, and Psalm 15:10 LXX are linked together in a way that presupposes the reader's recollection of earlier speeches in Acts and also requires the hearer to remember the specific OT contexts from which the fragmentary citations are taken. So, for example, Paul's citation of Psalm 2:7 (Acts 13:33) reminds us of the earlier *pesher*-style reading of the same psalm in Acts 4:25-26 and at the same time asks us to construe the entire psalm as foreshadowing Jesus the Messiah: "It is as though we are invited, through the medium of Luke's speeches, to read with Peter and Paul all of Psalm 2 with a messianic perspective shaped by the death and resurrection of Jesus, so that the Anointed One rejected by the rulers in Psalm 2:1 is also the 'begotten son of God' of Psalm 2:7."[25] Johnson characterizes this mode of scriptural interpretation as "a kind of haggadic midrash" on the LXX.[26]

We should pause here to observe that Johnson's analysis provides a detailed demonstration of one of the points Dodd was seeking to establish. Luke was reading Psalm 2 *as a whole* messianically, and encouraging his readers to do the same. Whether such a reading was part of pre-Lukan tradition is a question that Johnson does not entertain, but at least at the level of Luke's composition, we see him doing precisely what Dodd suggested early Christians did in their interpretation of Israel's Scripture.[27] On the other hand, Johnson's treatment takes more fully into account than Dodd's the complex intertextuality of Luke's midrash, which makes its argument through the collocation of several texts at once.

In the concluding section of Johnson's essay, he sums up his findings, partly reiterating points already made, but also advancing the argument by teasing out the implications of his detailed analysis. He emphasizes six points: (1) The interpretation of Scripture in the apostolic speeches is Luke's own. (2) Luke expects his readers to have "a reading competence sufficient to catch [his] allusions and echoes," and "the full force of Luke's exposition is rarely obvious within a single speech."[28] One has to read the full narrative of Acts to see the scope of the messianic midrashic argument. (3) Luke contends that Scripture must be "read prophetically in order to be properly understood."[29] (4) Unlike other Hellenistic Jewish interpreters, Luke avoids allegory. "Instead, his methods resemble those found among Palestinian Jews whose text was Hebrew rather than Greek: targum, *pesher*, haggadah."[30] (5) The closest parallels to Luke's interpretative practice are therefore to be found in the Qumran scrolls and in Paul. (6) If we take seriously Luke's own creative work as a biblical interpreter, this will lead us to regard him as a member of "the Pauline school," applying proto-rabbinic and sectarian interpretative methods to the LXX rather than to Hebrew textual traditions.[31] The last three of these points, taken together, articulate the central thesis that Johnson is advocating in this book.

Johnson then closes by propounding three further open questions raised by his findings. Should Luke be seen as closer to Paul, both historically and theologically, than mainstream NT criticism has thought? Should we recognize that "the LXX is really the Christian Old Testament"?[32] And "to what extent does Luke's way of interpreting Scripture serve as example and legitimation for our own?"[33] The second of these questions is a particularly explosive one for our understanding of the canon of Christian Scripture. And Johnson's highly significant answer to the third will concern us in more detail as we undertake a comparison of his book to Dodd's.

In any case, both Dodd and Johnson offer densely reasoned and informative accounts of the practices of scriptural interpretation that stand at the heart of the NT's witness, especially in the Lukan writings. We turn now to some comparative reflections about their findings.

CONTRASTING METHODS

Despite treating similar material, Dodd and Johnson are actually looking for quite different things. Dodd's book concerns itself not at all with explicating Lukan theology and hermeneutics; rather, he is searching for an antecedent layer of traditional material *behind* the NT texts. He is seeking to trace a diachronic line of historical development from Jesus to the apostles to the oral tradition of the early communities—or, more accurately, he is seeking to trace this line backwards from the NT to its underlying sources and finally to its origins. "This would give us," according to Dodd, "a genuinely chronological starting point for the history of Christian thought."[34]

Furthermore, Dodd is confident that the pre-canonical traditions that he reconstructs will disclose a structure or pattern that is common to all of them. At the surface level, the different NT writings may seem to manifest theological diversity, but at the level of "sub-structure"—hence his book's subtitle—they share a unitary foundation. By working backwards from the canonical texts, we can discover the basis of the NT's unity, in the primitive *kerygma* and in the earliest traditions of interpreting that *kerygma* through appeal to specific OT texts. This is a matter of great theological significance, for Dodd suggests that "the fundamental and regulative ideas of Christian theology as it meets us in the New Testament arise directly out of the understanding of these scriptures in relation to the evangelical facts."[35] The two adjectives here, "fundamental" and "regulative," are illuminating pointers to the goals of Dodd's exegetical work: he is seeking to show that the church's Rule of Faith has a strong historical claim to be based on foundational teachings from "the earliest period of Church history to which we can gain access."[36] That is to say, the church's subsequent christological doctrines and ideas about the fulfillment of Old Testament scriptures are not late superimpositions on the earliest traditions about Jesus, nor are they diffuse and inconsistent. Rather, they are deeply historically grounded and fundamentally coherent as a reading of Israel's history.

It is not always clear whether Dodd's belief in the unitary substructure of NT theology is the result or the presupposition of his inquiry. Most probably, it is both: his intuition about the unity of the underlying structure prompts his analysis of the evidence, and at the same time his analysis of the evidence reinforces the original intuition. In any case, Dodd's method is simultaneously *excavative* and *synthetic*.

When we turn to Johnson, the picture is very different. Though he is certainly interested in historical questions, he is skeptical about the possibility of reconstructing pre-canonical traditions—at least in the case of Luke–Acts.[37] In particular, if the apostolic speeches in Acts are Luke's own creative compositions, their interpretations of the OT simply cannot with any confidence be attributed to an alleged substructure of thought in the early church—and still less to the Jesus of history. (Of course, the quest for "the historical Jesus" is another topic that arouses an acute allergic reaction in Johnson.)[38] Johnson therefore turns his attention to narrative analysis of the Lukan material. He seeks to understand how the speeches function in the narrative of which they are a part, and how they both create and participate in a particular symbolic world.

Johnson's "turn to narrative," if we may so describe it, has several noteworthy consequences. First, he tends to give deeper and more detailed readings of particular Lukan passages than anything found in *According to the Scriptures*. He is reading the text to hear its own voice and its own theological witness, not merely to extract evidence from it for a developmental history of Christian thought. Second, in comparison to Dodd, he gives the reader a much fuller appreciation for the overall shape and emplotment of Luke's story. His recognition that the midrashic argument throughout Acts depends on the cumulative effect of all the speeches taken together is one good example of the gains achieved by his methodology. Third, Johnson's approach allows us to appreciate Luke as a significant theologian and hermeneutician. The fact that his works take the form of narrative does not disqualify him as a "creative mind"; on the contrary, his intricately patterned narrative gives evidence of a profound and subtle theological understanding of Israel's Scripture in its septuagintal form. And fourth, Johnson's attention to the distinctive contribution of Luke's narrative theology complicates the question about the unity of the NT. In *Septuagintal Midrash*, Johnson does not address this issue directly.[39] But he leaves us in no doubt that any attempt to reflect on the unity of the canon must, at the very least, reckon with the distinctive narrative form of Luke's testimony.

The differing aims of Dodd's and Johnson's projects naturally give rise to differing methods of inquiry. As we have noted, Dodd identifies the passages that he will discuss by pinpointing OT texts that turn up independently in two or more NT writings. And, having identified the OT sites of interest, he widens the focus to see how the broader context of the explicitly cited material might shed additional light on the way that the NT authors employ the cited material. Thus, his working method anticipates more recent studies of intertextuality and echo effects in the NT.

Let us consider a single example. In his discussion of citations of Isa 40:3-5 in the NT, Dodd notes that John's Gospel, in the self-identification of John the Baptist, explicitly quotes Isa 40:3: "I am the voice of one crying in the wilderness, 'Make straight the way of the Lord,' as the prophet Isaiah said" (John 1:23). This much is clear. But Dodd then goes on to suggest that it is "not entirely improbable that the same passage is echoed in two other places of the Fourth Gospel." Noting that the LXX of Isaiah 40:5 reads *ophthēsetai hē doxa kyriou kai opsetai pasa sarx to sōtērion tou theou* ("the glory of the Lord will be seen, and all flesh will see the salvation of God"), Dodd proposes that there are "reminiscences" of this text in John 11:40 (*opsē tēn doxan tou theou*, "you will see the glory of God") and perhaps 1:14 (*etheasametha tēn doxan autou*, "we saw his glory").[40] This is a lovely example of an intertextual reading that identifies a subtle echo of a text not cited explicitly by John. Unfortunately, having made the observation, Dodd fails to trace out its implications. He does not discuss what it would mean for the reader to hear Jesus, standing before Lazarus' tomb, echoing Isaiah's prophecy of the end of exile, or what significance we might attach to the Johannine prologue's subliminal evocation of the same passage. Dodd is only concerned to accumulate evidence that Isaiah 40:3-5, taken as a whole, must have been understood as a *testimonium* "in the pre-canonical tradition."[41]

Thus, while Dodd's book is full of numerous fascinating examples of intertexual echoes, he repeatedly fails to cash out their literary potential in his discussion of the texts. To be fair to Dodd, he sometimes may be assuming that his readers will connect the dots. But more often, it seems to me that he is simply operating with a certain historically oriented methodology that occludes the potential literary effects of the intertextual connections he discovers. It would be anachronistic to blame Dodd for failing to employ literary-critical methods that were nowhere on the horizon in the biblical studies guild in the early 1950s. But I would suggest that Dodd's book actually contains numerous nuggets of insight that still lie buried in his historical discourse, waiting to be discovered by someone who can polish them up and display their true literary and theological value.

Johnson's method, by contrast, focuses on a particular type of narrative unit (apostolic speeches) and studies the different interpretative techniques employed in these passages. Though Johnson does occasionally note echoes of the wider original context of the OT texts cited, this is only a minor point of interest in his study. He is more interested in delineating the strategies that Luke actually employs in interpreting the material he explicitly cites.

This is the point where Johnson's historical interests come strongly to the fore. His methodology is much more *comparative* than Dodd's, placing Luke's interpretative techniques within a broad field of hermeneutical practices in Mediterranean antiquity. In particular, Johnson is concerned to situate Luke on the map of Jewish biblical interpretation in his time. He announces his intention clearly at the beginning of his analysis:

> My goal is to take both aspects [e.g., Luke's creative authorial contributions and Jewish hermeneutical methods] with full seriousness first by treating his scriptural interpretation within speeches as fully his own work, reflecting his literary and religious preoccupations, and second by comparing his interpretation as such with Jewish practice.[42]

Thus, Johnson places the speeches in Acts in comparison to similar material in Josephus, Philo, *Jubilees*, the *Biblical Antiquities*, and other Jewish writings. Most importantly, he turns again and again to the Dead

Sea Scrolls to find important parallels to Luke's hermeneutical techniques. For example, noting that 4Q Florilegium cites Nathan's oracle to David (2 Sam 7:12-14) as a messianic prophecy, he shows how the same scriptural text, along with Psalm 131:11 LXX, underlies Peter's statement that "God had sworn with an oath to [David] that he would put one of his descendants on his throne" (Acts 2:30).[43] And, as we have seen, he likens the interpretation of Psalm 2 in the apostolic prayer of Acts 4:24-30 to the *pesher* exegesis of the Qumran biblical commentaries, citing both 1Qp Hab and 4Q Psalms Pesher.[44]

Of course, Dodd wrote *According to the Scriptures* very shortly after the initial discovery of the Dead Sea Scrolls and well before they had been edited, published, and translated. He can hardly be reproached, therefore, for giving these texts little or no role in his analysis. Nonetheless, when one sets Johnson and Dodd side by side, the contrast is striking. For the most part, Dodd seems to think of early Christian biblical interpretation as an intra-ecclesial enterprise, developing its own distinctive readings and traditions through direct encounter with the Old Testament texts; Johnson, on the other hand, sees early Christian interpretation emerging within a conversational field shaped by Jewish tradition and methods. To borrow Umberto Eco's term, Luke's "encyclopedia of production" was the cultural-linguistic frame of reference common to early first-century Jewish interpreters, now reshaped by the early community's experience of Jesus and the Holy Spirit. We need not belabor the point that Johnson's method represents a significant advance in historical understanding for the field of NT studies.

COMPARING FINDINGS: SELECTED TOPICS

A thoroughgoing comparison between the particular exegetical findings of these two stimulating studies would expand the present essay far beyond its permitted length. Instead, foregoing any pretense of completeness, I want to draw attention to just four substantive points where the juxtaposition of the two books is of particular interest.

A. DAVIDIC AND MOSAIC TYPOLOGY

Perhaps nowhere is the limitation of Dodd's methodology more glaringly apparent than in his cursory dismissal of the importance of Davidic and Mosaic typology in the NT.

Dodd takes note of precisely the same passages on Jesus as the Son of David that Johnson emphasizes (Acts 2:30 and 13:33-37) and observes the connection, as does Johnson, of these passages to 2 Samuel 7:12-14, Psalm 132:11 (Ps 131:11 LXX), Psalm 16:10 (Ps 15:10 LXX), and Isaiah 55:3. For good measure, he notes that Psalm 2 is also connected to 2 Samuel 7:14 in Hebrews 1:5, and that other passages such as Acts 15:16-17 and Romans 1:3-4 also presume or assert the Davidic lineage and messiahship of Jesus. Yet in spite of this evidence, he inexplicably writes that "the idea of the Messiah as the son of David is not conspicuous in the primary body of *testimonia*." He then concludes that "so far as our evidence goes, it does not appear that [the Davidic descent of Jesus] played any great part in the shaping of Christian theology."[45]

By contrast, anyone who reads Luke–Acts as a continuous narrative, as Johnson does, will have been alerted as early as Luke's story of the annunciation that Davidic messiahship is at the very heart of Jesus' identity and mission. The angel Gabriel declares to Mary, "And now you will conceive in your womb and bear a son, and you will name him Jesus. He will be great, and will be called the Son of the Most High, and the Lord God will give to him the throne of his father David. He will reign over the house of Jacob forever, and of his kingdom there will be no end" (Luke 1:31-33). This prophetic announcement is precisely what is reaffirmed in the apostolic speeches of Peter and Paul in Acts 2 and 13. Johnson's detailed discussion of these passages (*Septuagintal Midrash*, 35-46) amply confirms the centrality of this Davidic motif. Dodd's method of screening *testimonia*, in this case, results in swallowing several gnats but missing a camel.

Similarly, Dodd's method identifies the passage in Deuteronomy 18:15-20 about a future "prophet like Moses" as a primitive *testimonium*. But because he does not find it explicitly quoted elsewhere than Acts 3:22-23 to elucidate the *kerygma*, he reaches the conclusion that "The prediction of the 'prophet like Moses' had little significance for the development of New Testament theology."[46] Once again, this is a finding that is 180 degrees opposite from Johnson's reading. Johnson takes precisely this motif as the interpretive key to the whole of Luke-Acts, in which the motif of "the prophet and the people" is at the heart of the narrative logic of the two-volume work.[47]

These differences between our two authors starkly highlight what is at stake in their differing methodologies. Johnson's focus on the bigger narrative picture allows him to see major patterns of allusion that elude Dodd's quest for pre-canonical *testimonia*.

B. THE PROBLEM OF SUPERSESSIONISM

The second point to be considered in this comparison is not so obvious as the first, but it nonetheless bears careful reflection. Dodd's manner of interpreting the evidence leads him into some unfortunate statements about the relation between the church and Israel. For example, "If then the whole episode of the beginnings of Christianity is to be understood, as the first Christians understood it, in the light of prophecy, what happened was that the existing Jewish community ceased to represent the true Israel of God, as the embodiment of His purposes for mankind, and its place was taken by the Christian *ecclesia*." Dodd is careful to say that this transposition occurred not because the Christians were "wiser, more virtuous, or more capable than their Jewish contemporaries, but because they had been the objects of an act of God."[48] Nonetheless, the theology affirmed here is classic replacement theology in a fairly strong form. And once again, it seems to represent an inference from prooftexts divorced from their narrative context.[49]

Johnson's approach is more promising in two ways. First, as we have noted, he situates early Christian (or at least Lukan) hermeneutics within a matrix of emphatically Jewish interpretation and debate. From this point of view, the NT's readings of the Old appear not as alternatives to "the existing Jewish community" but as sectarian mutations within it—or, if one prefers a less pejorative characterization, as offshoots from the roots and trunk of Jewish tradition. This perspective is both more historically nuanced and more theologically fruitful for thinking through the admittedly difficult problems surrounding the sibling rivalry and eventual parting of the ways between early rabbinic Judaism and emergent Christianity.[50] Second, Johnson's embrace of narrative interpretation requires us to locate the apostolic scriptural citations within a more complex and comprehensive picture of relations between Jewish and Gentile believers in the story that Luke tells. The place of the Jewish people within Luke's unfolding story has remained a debated question among interpreters of the NT.[51] But Johnson's hermeneutical method at least gives the church resources to gain theological leverage against radical supersessionism.

C. THE SEPTUAGINT AS CHRISTIAN SCRIPTURE

Johnson's detailed text-critical observations lead him to the conclusion that Luke tends to presuppose the LXX, rather than the Hebrew text, as the scriptural text on which his characters base their interpretations. And this in turn moves Johnson to ask whether it is really the LXX that should be regarded as the Christian OT.[52] Dodd, on the other hand, presents a more mixed picture. His comments on particular texts reflect an awareness of text-critical issues, but he offers no generalizations about the textual tradition followed by the interpreters who developed the pre-canonical substructure that is the focal point of his study. At several points, he takes pains to point out examples where the NT's scriptural citations take a non-septuagintal form.[53] Indeed, the further back one can trace these pre-canonical traditions, the more improbable it is that the LXX would have been the basic scriptural text for the early Palestinian community. Thus, though Dodd does not address the question directly, his overall approach would tend to minimizing the centrality of the LXX for early Christian biblical interpretation.

Johnson forthrightly notes that Western Christianity since Jerome's Vulgate translation has (de facto) treated the Hebrew text as the authoritative Old Testament, and he speaks of the West's "long estrangement from the LXX."[54] Should that estrangement be overcome in light of modern critical study? This is one point where Johnson's exclusive concentration on Luke-Acts may skew the evidence slightly. If one looks at NT citations across the range of the NT canon, as does Dodd, the picture is more complicated, though it remains true that in cases where the LXX and MT diverge, the majority of NT citations follow the LXX textual tradition. It does seem to me that Johnson raises a valid point here, and that—at the very least—the theological burden of proof lies upon those who would advocate "the Hebrew Bible" as the exclusively authoritative text for teaching and preaching in the church.

D. THE POSSIBILITY OF THEOLOGICAL SYNTHESIS

Finally, Dodd and Johnson represent very different critical convictions about our ability to identify theological common ground that can unify our reading of the NT documents. Dodd regards this project as both possible and necessary, while Johnson regards it as reductive and dangerous. How are we to respond to these starkly opposed alternatives? I would like to offer a suggestion that might move at least some way towards rapprochement between these positions.

In many respects, as my comments in this essay have suggested, Johnson's working methodology is exegetically preferable to Dodd's. The first responsibility of the NT interpreter is to trace sensitively the literary shape and message of the actual texts before us in the canon. But surely that first responsibility is not the only legitimate critical operation for interpreters in the church. Once we have carefully described the literary and theological contours of the individual NT witnesses—Luke, Paul, Matthew, John, and all the rest—is it not a fair question to ask whether their messages hang together and how they might collectively inform Christian doctrine?

The problem with Dodd's approach is twofold: it seeks unity behind rather than through the witness of the texts, and it is therefore prematurely synthetic. I would propose, then, that the same sort of careful synchronic reading that Johnson performs on the Lukan apostolic speeches needs to be carried out for each major unit of material in the NT, asking precisely Johnson's questions about how the individual text carries out the practice of reading Israel's Scripture. But once that descriptive task has been patiently done, surely we might go on to pose the question of coherence among the messages of the various texts. Granted that their strategies for reading the OT are not identical, what can be said about what they have in common? Any points of convergence that we might identify are not (*pace* Dodd) necessarily evidence of primitive tradition behind the texts. But such points may nonetheless be *theologically* significant and informative for the church's faith and teaching.

It is also very interesting that one result of Johnson's inquiry is to interrogate the conventional view that the theologies of Luke and Paul are incommensurable. If Johnson is right that the theological perspectives of these two writers "are not so disparate as sometimes supposed," and indeed that Luke may best be understood as belonging to a "Pauline School,"[55] might that not push us back slightly in the direction of Dodd's predisposition to look for unity within the NT canon?

TRADITION VS. EXPERIENCE?

Finally, we turn to address the question of what it might mean to take the NT's interpretative practices as normative for our own hermeneutical endeavors. Perhaps not surprisingly, we once again find our two formidable conversation partners seriously at odds. Both of them conclude their studies with explicit reflections on exactly this question, and they draw dramatically different conclusions.

The last page of Johnson's book revisits a recurrent theme that runs through his whole body of scholarly work: the NT writings are fundamentally to be understood as efforts to interpret *religious experience*.[56] His concluding sentences deserve to be quoted in full:

> It is daunting to realize how deeply and thoroughly both [Luke] and his readers were involved in the imaginative world of Scripture. Luke suggests that it is impossible to speak the good news, impossible to tell the story of Jesus, without using the words of Scripture. But even more challenging is Luke's assumption that God's Holy Spirit continues to work in the lives of believers. Luke thinks that the Spirit continues to lead them into new and surprising experiences of God, continues to open their eyes to meanings of Scripture that study alone could never have yielded. Luke believes further that God's Spirit continues to guide the church in its process of discernment and decision making, if Christians trust this same Holy Spirit. Letting the Spirit work in us this way requires not scholarship but the obedience of faith.[57]

Standing alone, this paragraph is tantalizingly open-ended, but when we read it in conjunction with Johnson's other works, such as *Scripture and Discernment* and *Faith's Freedom*, we see that it articulates clear and deeply-held convictions about the way in which the NT informs Christian faith.[58] Rather than giving us a set of authoritative teachings, the NT offers us models of receptivity to the work of God's Spirit. Our task as interpreters is not just to repeat the NT's message but to learn to "imagine the world that Scripture imagines" and to respond freshly and authentically to the work of God in our own living experience.[59]

With Johnson's experientially oriented program in mind, it is fascinating to return to the closing pages of Dodd's study, in which he seeks to rebut the emphasis on "religious experience" that characterized the thought of many NT interpreters earlier in the twentieth century, a movement that has now, Dodd opines, "spent itself." For the advocates of this viewpoint, the Apostle Paul was the parade example of a witness whose theology was based on experience, both in his dramatic conversion on the Damascus Road, and in his mystical heavenly visions (2 Cor 12:1-4).

Dodd witheringly observes that even Paul did not make such exalted experiences the basis for his teaching:

> It is of course true that any theology speedily becomes abstract and barren which does not verify itself in experience; Paul's did so verify itself. But this is a different matter from making such experience its ground, and this Paul never did. He expressly bases his theology upon the *kerygma* as illuminated by the prophecies of the Old Testament; or, in other words, upon the historical facts which he had "received" (*ho kai parelabon*) from competent witnesses, set in the larger historical framework witnessed, both as fact and as meaning, by the prophetic writers. ... [S]till more is this true of other New Testament writers, whose experience in any case has to be conjectured, since they say nothing about it. This was not what early Christian preachers talked about. On the day of Pentecost, we are informed, their theme was not the amazing experience of being possessed by the Holy Spirit: it was "the mighty works of God."[60]

In his account of Paul's theology, Dodd of course leans heavily on 1 Corinthians 15:3-5. But we might ask whether his comments entirely do justice to 1 Corinthians 15:8, or to Galatians 1:11-12. Likewise, while we may readily concede that the author of Luke-Acts tells us nothing about his own religious experience, he certainly does give vivid accounts of the experiences of his characters and, as Johnson has delineated more clearly than anyone, shows how those experiences come to shape the early community's understanding of God's will.

How then shall we evaluate this debate? Must we choose between—on the one hand—Dodd's emphasis on Christian proclamation based in the historical events of Jesus' death and resurrection, authoritatively conveyed to us through tradition interpreted by Israel's Scripture, and—on the other—Johnson's emphasis on the living, ongoing work of the Holy Spirit in the lives of believers? Readers acquainted with my work will not be surprised to learn that on this point—in contrast to some other issues treated in this essay—my sympathies stand more closely in agreement with Dodd than with Johnson. With regard to doctrine and practice, the kerygmatic story in its scriptural matrix remains the source and touchstone for our lives. But it is not coincidental that in the two lengthy quotations above, each of our disputants acknowledges some validity to the other position: Johnson declares that "it is impossible to speak the good news, impossible to tell the story of Jesus, without using the words of Scripture," while Dodd, even while writing in a somewhat more polemical tone, concedes that "any theology speedily becomes abstract and barren which does not verify itself in experience."

The heremeneutical challenge that we face is somehow to do justice to the truth of both positions. The message of the gospel is authoritatively given in the traditions that we have received from the earliest church, *and* the Holy Spirit is truly and powerfully at work today, sometimes in surprising ways. On this much, Dodd and Johnson, standing fifty years apart in different ecclesial and cultural settings, might agree. The hard work of theological hermeneutics is always to bring these twin truths together in patient and faithful discernment concerning disputed questions about what God requires of us in our time.[61]

JESUS MADE REAL IN MUSIC: *LA PASIÓN SEGÚN SAN MARCOS* AND LUKE TIMOTHY JOHNSON'S EXPERIENCE/INTERPRETATION MODEL

GAIL R. O'DAY

Luke Timothy Johnson's career has been marked by an unquenchable energy and an intense passion to draw his students and his colleagues into a conversation about the New Testament as an expression of the religious life of Christians throughout the ages. Johnson is fully versed in the details of the first-century Mediterranean world in which Christianity took root, but for him, the essential questions are not those that can be answered by solving some puzzle of the past but are those that begin with religious experience.

This set of concerns shapes Johnson's book, *The Real Jesus: The Misguided Quest for the Historical Jesus and the Truth of the Traditional Gospels*.[1] This book is in many ways a tour de force: a succinct and searing assessment of fifteen years of historical Jesus research ("the misguided quest") followed by an eloquent and passionate articulation of the religious truth of the "real" Jesus of the Gospels. His passion to move to the essential questions of religious experience—and his impatience with those who do not share this need—is very much in evidence.[2]

Johnson does not eschew history in this book; *The Real Jesus* contains a chapter in which Johnson identifies a judicious list of "what's historical about Jesus."[3] But the heart and soul of this book is its plea to reassess the very function of historical reconstruction as a tool for determining religious meaning. To quote Johnson himself, "Christian faith has never—either at the start or now—been *based on historical reconstructions of Jesus*, even though Christian faith has always involved some historical claims concerning Jesus. Rather, Christian faith (then and now) is based on religious claims concerning the present power of Jesus."[4]

The Real Jesus presents in condensed form one of the overarching questions of Johnson's work: the limits of history as a conduit into present religious experience. Investigations of the historical Jesus highlight the limits of history because, for Johnson, such research entails a confusion of the mutually exclusive categories of history and faith. Faith is not grounded in the past; faith is grounded in the present.[5] As Johnson writes in what is essentially the theme sentence of the book, "the *real Jesus* for Christian faith is not simply a figure of the past but very much and above all a figure of the present, indeed, who defines believers' present by his presence."[6]

In many ways, the heart of Johnson's work in this book is not his searing critique of Jesus quests (although that has received the most attention).[7] The heart of his work is the constructive proposals for how to study the New Testament with which he concludes. In the "Epilogue" to *The Real Jesus*,[8] Johnson calls for a more comprehensive model of critical biblical scholarship that attends to the anthropological, the literary, and the religious alongside the historical. Johnson calls this model the "experience/interpretation" model.[9] This model employs a hermeneutic that "begins with the premise that God's Spirit is working in the world to transform people into the image of the 'real Jesus.'" Through this ecclesial hermeneutics, "the complex texts of human experience are brought into conversation with the complex and often conflicting normative texts of tradition."[10] This model names the complexity of both sets of "texts"—those of human experience and the normative written texts of Christian tradition—and suggests that in the creative intermingling of these complexities, the real Jesus emerges.

Attention to religious experience opens the doors to the lived experience of people of faith that may reconfigure ecclesial categories. For Johnson, the "experience/interpretation" model is inherently and explicitly ecclesial. His explicit hope for this model, as the epilogue title, "Critical Scholarship and the Church," makes clear, is that it will enable "a community of faith that also experiences the powerful presence of the risen Lord to engage these texts (along with those of Torah) in a continuing conversation," by providing "a framework for interpreting these compositions within the life of the church."[11]

Yet this model, with its emphasis on present human experience, also provides a hermeneutical lens for looking at explorations of the meaning and present experience of Jesus for contemporary life that are not conventionally ecclesial. Johnson's emphasis on attention to the anthropological dimensions of New Testament texts, with anthropology's attendant focus on cultural symbols, invites a new range of partners into the conversation. Attention to the literary dimensions of the NT comes not only in careful literary analysis, but in the recreation of those literary elements and aesthetics in other media, for example, painting or music. Attention to Christian religious experience invites conversation with forms of religious experience that move beyond what is normally held to be "church." In this essay, I will follow the threads of Johnson's "experience/interpretation" model outside the conventional ecclesial setting to look at how a non-ecclesial contemporary artistic retelling of the Jesus story employs the multi-textual hermeneutic that Johnson recommends to make Jesus "real."

LA PASIÓN SEGÚN SAN MARCOS: OVERVIEW

The year 2000 marked the 250th anniversary of the death of Johann Sebastian Bach. To commemorate this anniversary (and to mark the new millennium), Helmut Rilling of the Internationale Bachakademie Stuttgart commissioned four contemporary composers to write modern passions. Each of the works, known collectively as "Passion 2000," was presented in repertory in the Bach anniversary celebrations in Stuttgart in August and September of 2000. The four composers were Ozvaldo Golijov (Mark), Tan Dun (Matthew), Wolfgang Rihm (Luke), and Sofia Gubaidulina (John). Rihm and Gubaidulina wrote passions that adhered to the European musical styles, while Golijov and Dun drew on musical traditions from outside of Europe—Golijov on Latin American music and Tan Dun on Asian music. Each of the works was well received, but the works by Tan Dun (*Water Passion after St. Matthew*) and by Golijov (*La Pasión según San Marcos*) have received repeated international performances since their premieres.[12]

While the *Water Passion* could also be investigated for the ways in which it uses music to make the Jesus story real for the contemporary listener, I will focus on Golijov and *La Pasión según San Marcos* for several reasons. First, in each of its repeat performances, *La Pasión* has been universally acclaimed as a masterwork of contemporary classical music.[13] Second, the Golijov passion is more textual than the Tan Dun passion, and so provides more access to its portrayal of the Jesus story for a New Testament scholar. Third, I have heard *La Pasión* performed live and can therefore speak more to the immediacy of the work than I can to *Water Passion*, which I have heard only on a recording.

Golijov's passion seems to adhere completely to Kähler's famous footnote in which he describes Mark as a "passion narrative with a long introduction."[14] In the Gospels, the passion narrative is on one level the story of the death of Jesus, but on another level, it is about much more than that. If the entire Gospel serves in some way as an introduction to the passion narrative, then when the reader finally arrives at the passion narrative, themes of the nature of humanity, the identity of God, and God's hopes for the world resonate out of this narrative. *La Pasión* claims the centrality of the death of Jesus in Gospel stories and makes the grand sweep of the Markan passion narrative vividly present to the listener. This piece creates musical, theological, and spiritual resonances that are larger than the particular story of the death of Jesus.

Like the passions of J. S. Bach, in whose honor the work was commissioned, Golijov's passion follows the text of Mark quite closely. Its structure follows the outline of Mark 13:35 (the call to watchfulness) to Mark 15:38 (Jesus' death), and while some narrative details are omitted (e.g., the preparation of the upper room), none of the narrative plot is overlooked. *La Pasión según San Marcos* is exactly that: the passion narrative of Mark set to music.[15]

Golijov followed Bach's model in other ways as well. One of the voices in his passion is Mark himself, corresponding to the Evangelist in Bach's Matthew passion. Golijov, like Bach, used contemporary poetry and music to comment on the biblical text, and these contemporary texts enhance, rather than replace or supplant, the words of the NT. As in Bach's passions, the arias, recitatives, and choruses of *La Pasión* provide commentary on the biblical story. Golijov, like Bach, honored the words of the Gospel text, giving pride of place to the words of the NT itself, and also like Bach, did not confuse his commentary on the biblical text with the biblical text itself.[16]

Yet for all the similarities, there is one significant difference between Bach's passions and the passion of Golijov. Bach was a German Protestant Christian and wrote his passions to be performed as part of a Good Friday liturgy. Bach wrote his passions as a churchman for ecclesial life. Golijov is an Argentine Jew and wrote his passion, not for a worship service, but as noted, in response to a commission. The ecclesial context that completely informed Bach's work is largely absent from Golijov's, and the act of composition as an explicit expression of Christian faith is also not part of the story of *La Pasión*. Yet this difference may not be as dispositive as it first appears, because the overwhelming majority of the performances of Bach's passions are now in concert halls, not worship services (and have been ever since Felix Mendelssohn, himself a Jew, rediscovered the Bach St. Matthew passion in 1829).

Golijov's Jewish upbringing in a predominantly Catholic Latin American country brings new partners into the gospel conversation, and attention to this dimension of the work accords with Johnson's emphasis on common cultural symbols and religious experience. While Bach drew on familiar hymn tunes to draw the audience into the work, Golijov drew on popular Latin American melodies, rhythms, and instruments to make a connection between the world of the first century and *La Pasión's* contemporary world.

The language of *La Pasión* is predominantly Spanish, with a few short passages of Latin and Aramaic. And the Spanish is quite intentionally the Spanish of the people; Golijov worked with a wide assortment of Spanish translations of the Gospel of Mark, many of them pamphlet-style versions that were given out free in churches and sold by street-corner evangelists.[17] Golijov's reading of Mark was influenced by the interpretation of Reynolds Price, who notes how the story of Mark "reels out at full-tilt speed and with what seem the first words at hand," words marked by "energy and efficiency."[18] Golijov's language choice is a pivotal interpretive act: it mirrors his experience of the language of the Gospel of Mark and infuses the passion with the voice of the people, suggesting that the Jesus story belongs to everyone.

Even though Jesus was not the object of his own religious faith, Golijov worked intentionally in this piece to capture what it means to have faith in Jesus:

> I want to record—like Rembrandt recorded the Jews. I want to record the Christians, simply that. For example, my great grandmother had a picture of "Jeremiah Lamenting the Fall of Jerusalem" by Rembrandt. It's the greatest Jewish picture ever and he was not a Jew. I cannot aspire to be Rembrandt, but if at least one section of the Passion has the truth about Christianity that Rembrandt's paintings have about Judaism, I'll be all right—that's enough.[19]

The relationship between an explicit ecclesial context and the power of the music to make Jesus "real" is a theme to which we will return.

The largely Latin American origins of *La Pasión* determine many of its distinctive characteristics. Within what is essentially a very traditional adherence to the passion oratorio form as practiced by Bach, Golijov uses unconventional rhythms and orchestrations to bring the Jesus story to life. To quote Golijov again,

> I feel that I have to present a Jesus that is as true as Bach's but has so far remained for the most part unheard. Jesus can be very pale and very European—but in Guatemala he is black. . . . The main thing in this Passion is to present a dark Jesus, and not a pale European Jesus. It's going to be about Jesus' last days on earth seen through the Latin American experience and what it implies.[20]

The Latin American rhythms and the unusual instruments, including a range of percussion instruments like the agogó bell, atabaque drum, berimbau, claves, guaguanco, and maracas, give the music its distinctive character, as the lively music draws the listener into the story that is being sung and eliminates any distance between the story of the past and the listener's present experience of the passion.

The musical choices Golijov made are also pivotal interpretive acts that bring the distinctiveness of the Markan passion into focus. One of the distinguishing traits of the Gospel of Mark is the intensity and speed with which events take place. There is no lag time in the Gospel of Mark, no time for leisurely reflection; the narrative moves and snaps. The adverb "immediately" occurs forty-two times in Mark, compared to seven times in Matthew, once in Luke, and three times in John, all of those much longer Gospels. Interestingly, thirty-eight of the forty-two uses occur outside of the Markan passion narrative.[21] It is as if Mark, in his storytelling, is racing to get to the story of the death. Once Mark arrives at the story of the death, it is no longer necessary for him explicitly to say "immediately" or "at once" as often, because the story itself has arrived at the point of relentless immediacy.

Golijov's music captures and conveys Mark's pace and intensity. The whole piece is under ninety minutes in length, but in those ninety minutes one's senses are constantly stimulated; the breakneck speed of the Gospel of Mark is captured by the various rhythms and orchestrations of Golijov. One imagines that the first listeners who heard the stories of Mark spoken or read out loud were always on the edge of their seats, knowing that if they relaxed for just a moment, something would unfold and they would miss it. It is the same with this music—one daydreams at one's listening peril, because even what seem to be interludes carry the momentum forward.

La Pasión also includes dance as one of the media through which the gospel story is brought to life. Golijov was quite self-aware about this enacted dimension of his passion; "unlike a Protestant Passion which is about meditating and commenting, this Passion is about enslavement and ritual. It's a synthesis of Latin American traditions: Catholicism and the Yoruba religion brought by African slaves."[22] *La Pasión* is a musical enactment of the passion story, not simply its proclamation. This embodiment of parts of the passion narrative on stage contributes to the sense of immediacy experienced by the audience of *La Pasión*.

LA PASIÓN SEGÚN SAN MARCOS: TEXTUAL NOTES

I turn now to specific sections of *La Pasión*, focusing on two complementary aspects of Golijov's interpretation of Mark through music—the ways in which Golijov's composition gives voice to the silences in the Gospel, and relatedly, the ways in which he gives musical voice to the speaking voices of the Gospel's characters.

FILLING IN THE GAPS WITH MUSIC

One characteristic of all biblical storytelling is the economy of narration. Biblical stories are lean, and there are many narrative gaps compared to contemporary storytelling. There is little description of what people looked like or what they are thinking, for example, and transitions from one scene to another are not always smooth. These gaps leave much to the imagination of the hearer, and the music and texts that Golijov has put in the gaps in the Markan passion narrative are some of the most powerful parts of *La Pasión*. Musical interpretations of a biblical text, whether the classic oratorios like those by Bach, Mendelssohn, and Handel, requiems like those of Brahms and Britten, or more contemporary compositions like those commissioned for Passion 2000, exploit the balance between what is spoken and what is left unsaid in biblical texts in ways that the written word, even when read aloud in worship, does not. The musician can create worlds through the interplay of sound and silence that are quite distinct from a solely text-based world.

For example, *La Pasión* begins with two wordless numbers that introduce all that follows. The two opening numbers, an instrumental piece entitled "Vision: Baptism on the Cross," and an instrumental and dance segment entitled "Dance of the Ensnared Fisherman," are outside the narrative flow of Mark 13–16 proper and function as an overture to what follows. These two very brief units (their combined length is two minutes) introduce what will be key for *La Pasión*—reflective and embodied engagement with the death of Jesus. Interestingly, in the libretto for *La Pasión*, Golijov assigns words to the first section, even though no words are sung at this juncture. The words of the opening section are identical to the words with which *La Pasión* reflects on Jesus' crucifixion at the end of the piece.[23] They are a composite of verses from Mark 1:11 ("And a voice came from heaven, 'You are my Son, the beloved; with whom I am well pleased.'"), Jesus' words on the cross at Mark 15:34 ("My God, my God, why have you forsaken me?"), and Lamentations 1:12 ("Is it nothing to you, all you who pass by? Look and see if there is any sorrow like my sorrow").

Interestingly, the words from Lamentations which are attributed to the people in this opening section are spoken by Jesus in the work's conclusion. This is one way in which this passion makes the people's story of suffering coextensive with Jesus' story.

These two introductory units highlight the evocative play between sound and silence. This play allows Golijov to give his listeners an option: to experience the beginning of the piece with musical sound but textual silence, letting the listeners' own interpretation of the music and the dance set the tone, or to listen while reading the words that he sets to music in the opening section and thus have a narrated guide through the music. The textual silence creates a space for something like meditation or prayer; the listener is not led to one meaning, but is allowed his or her own mode of engagement.

This transformation of narrative gap into a powerful moment of listener engagement can be observed in many sections of La Pasión.

THE ANOINTING AT BETHANY[24]

La Pasión begins to follow Mark's narrative in sequence starting at Mark 13:35. Two brief musical numbers precede the anointing at Bethany—Jesus' call to watchfulness and an announcement, sung by "Mark," of the plan to kill Jesus (Mark 14:1-2). The anointing follows as the first major unit of the work, and is a good example of Golijov's musical and textual technique.

For a reader of the Gospel, the narrator's voice guides the interpretation of everything that happens in the Gospel. In the anointing, for example, not only does the narrator present the scene of the anointing (Mark 14:3), the voice of the narrator also describes the disciples' reaction to the anointing and reports their words ("But some were there who said to one another in anger," "And they scolded her," 14:4-5). Jesus' words are introduced by the narrator ("But Jesus said," 14:6). The anointing in La Pasión begins with the voice of Mark singing the setting and action of the anointing (vv. 3-4), but after that, the other voices of the story speak without the guiding voice of the narrator. In Mark, while the narrator reports, "they said to one another in anger," Golijov has a chorus sing: "Por que? Por que?" over and over again, this repeated refrain punctuating the chorus's singing of the disciples' words of verse 5 and the solo voice of Jesus with words of response (vv. 6-9). The music moves quickly, with intense Latin rhythms, so that the setting of the anointing, a table in a house in Bethany, comes alive with conversation for the audience. The anointing lasts almost four minutes in *La Pasión*, far longer than it takes to read this story. The difference of opinion between the disciples and Jesus about the anointing jumps off the page, into the music, and into the listeners' experience.

The Markan account of the anointing ends with Jesus' affirmation of the woman: "Truly I tell you, wherever the good news is proclaimed in the whole world, what she has done shall be spoken of in memory of her" (v. 9). These words are not singled out in Golijov's music, but sung by Jesus as part of the give and take between Jesus and the disciples that characterizes this scene. Yet even though the libretto does not linger over these words, the music does. The anointing is followed immediately by an instrumental number called "Aria with Crickets (the silent woman in Bethany, instrumental)."[25] This number fills an important gap in the Markan text, for nowhere in the narrative has the woman's voice been heard. She is silent in the story, and the instrumental music gives voice and place to the silent woman. The number lasts for over two minutes, half the length of the anointing scene itself, and through its music, the audience has to linger with the woman and her act. Golijov fills in Mark's silence and makes audible the continuing remembrance of the woman's act, which exists in Mark only as a future promise.

THE LAST SUPPER

The anointing at Bethany is followed immediately in Mark by the narrator's announcement of Judas's agreement to betray Jesus (14:10-11), the preparation for the Passover meal (14:12-21), and the institution of the eucharist (14:22-24). Golijov follows the outline of Mark completely in this section, although his musical arrangement of the text places the emphasis on the theme of betrayal and on the character of Judas as the lead-up to the eucharist. In a relatively lengthy segment (over four minutes), Golijov's Mark sings of Judas's betrayal, as the disciples (through the chorus) wonder about the betrayal, "Will it be I?" The narrator and choral parts are then joined by Jesus' own announcement of the betrayal (Mark 14:20).[26]

In Mark, Jesus' announcement of the betrayal is followed immediately by the institution of the eucharist. Golijov, however, creates a musical interlude between the announcement of the betrayal by Jesus and the narration of the eucharist. Just as Bach used arias to give his interpretation of the biblical story, here Golijov inserts his first interpretive aria, the Aria of Judas.[27] For Judas's aria, Golijov uses an anonymous poem, "I wish to forswear," set to a flamenco melody.

In this aria, Golijov fills in a very powerful silence in the Markan narrative that has intrigued centuries of Christians: what is Judas thinking; what is the motivation for his actions? This aria, which gives voice to the aftermath of Judas's decision to betray Jesus, gives voice to Judas's despair and his sense of his dislocation in the world ("I wish to forswear this world completely . . . to see whether in a new world I could find more truth"). The betrayal results in only loss for Judas, not triumph, for he still is not in possession of any truth. The aria, and the despair to which it gives voice, makes Judas's betrayal an act that any human being could have committed. This possibility is underscored by the setting of the aria, because Judas begins to sing it immediately after the chorus asks one another for one last time, "Is it I? It can't be me! Could it be me? I am not the betrayer." By filling in a narrative gap, the aria creates a dramatic moment that lends poignancy to all that surrounds it.

The musical number that follows Judas's aria, the eucharistic meal, could not be more different musically from what has preceded it. The institution of the eucharist is set to music that evokes a Gregorian chant—there is almost no instrumentation, the rhythms are simple and chant-like, so that the words of institution, sung by Jesus and the chorus, are the center of attention. It is a moment of transcendent peace, made even more powerful by the fact that it follows the musical frenzy of the betrayal segments.[28]

In Mark, the eucharistic meal is actually a Passover meal (14:12); the meal that Jesus celebrates with his disciples is the first seder of the Passover. Jesus transforms that meal during the course of it, but when he and his disciples sat down at the table, they sat down together to celebrate the seder. Golijov conveys this dimension of the meal by filling in another silence in the text—the hymns of celebration with which the Passover meal ends. That hymns are sung is noted in Mark (14:26, "When they had sung the hymn, they went out to the Mount of Olives"), but in the Gospel, the hymn singing is reported to the reader, not experienced. In Golijov's imaginative recreation of the moment after the eucharistic meal, music does what no written text can ever do—it enables the listener to hear the hymns. Golijov sets fragments of Psalms 113–118 to choral variations on a song, "Todavía Cantamos," by the popular Argentine singer Víctor Heredia to create a hymn of praise for this meal. It is an appropriately celebratory moment, in which the praise of God takes center stage.

Golijov's use of a Heredia melody here is similar to Bach's use of familiar tunes in his passions and functions very much like one of Bach's chorales. The chorale was "designed to express appropriate responses on the part of the worshipping congregation to the story of salvation. . . . The use of familiar words and tunes to interpret the Gospel text enhanced corporate participation in the praise and the prayers which the text elicited."[29] The singing of psalms of praise, to a tune of the people, provides the context against which the whole passion is to be understood—God is faithful, and regardless of what happens in life or death, God should be celebrated in song.

PETER'S ARIA

In passions, there is a tradition of Peter singing an aria at the moment of his betrayal of Jesus. This is probably because the moment after Peter's denial is one of the heaviest moments of silence in the entire NT. Mark's account of the aftermath of Peter's betrayal is, as in all the Gospels, tersely matter-of-fact ("And he [Peter] broke down and wept," 14:72). Peter is given no words in any of the gospels at this moment—only tears. Golijov translates a Galician poem by Rosalia de Castro to give voice—not to Peter—but to translate his tears. The title of the poem is "Colorless Moon," and Golijov subtitles it, "Aria of Peter's tears." The aria is a three-stanza poem; in each stanza the singer addresses the colorless moon ("star of orphan souls"), who looks down to observe the singer's despair. Peter's tears quite literally sing.

By using a contemporary poem at this point, Golijov breaks through the distance of time, makes Peter real, and draws the listener into Peter's sadness.

GIVING VOICE

Just as music can fill in the narrative gaps in the Gospel text, music can also make immediate and direct that which is only reported in the Gospel. For example, at the last supper, Mark 14:19 reads, "They [the disciples] began to be distressed and to say to him one after another, 'Surely not I?'" As noted above, Golijov is able to turn single sentences like this into rich choral moments, giving musical voice and depth to what is left to the imagination in the Gospel accounts. The intensity of feeling—whether that be anger (e.g., the disciples' response to the anointing at 14:5), distress (as at the prospect of being the betrayer), worshipful awe (the eucharistic psalms), mockery (15:25-32), or sorrow (Peter's response to the denial)—becomes part of the listeners' experience of the Gospel, rather than simply a narrator's observation. The chorus plays a significant role in giving immediate voice to the events of the Gospel story, as do the shifting rhythms and dramatic instrumentation of the work.

For example, through Golijov's use of contemporary Latin rhythms and instrumentation, he creates a vivid sense of life on the street, of constant movement and activity. This captures a dimension of Mark that is hard to convey with the written word, that Jesus' passion takes place in the middle of a festival, when hundreds of thousands of pilgrims would be in Jerusalem to commemorate and celebrate their deliverance from slavery in Egypt. It is a lively, sacred time in Jerusalem. Jesus' death takes place in the midst of it, but appropriately, does not stop the festival completely. Life goes on, and the vividness and vitality of festival street life adds to the power of the passion story.

One of Golijov's more interesting musical decisions in *La Pasión*, and one that is quite different from the pattern of Bach with whom Golijov is so clearly in conversation, is that there are no set voices for singing roles. Whereas Bach has one voice for the Evangelist (a tenor) and one for Jesus (a bass), Golijov allows for a variety of voices to sing a character's part, so that there is no identification between any one voice and a particular character. Judas's and Peter's arias, for example, are both sung by women. The deconstruction of conventional character roles is particularly striking in the way it informs the musical presentation of Jesus. Jesus' words are sung by a male voice, an alto, a soprano, the chorus, a quartet of tenors; Jesus' actions are embodied by the dancers on the stage. Golijov describes the effect he is looking for this way:

> In this Passion, I thought that most of the time the voice of Jesus would be the choir because for me Jesus represents the voice of the people, transformed into a collective spirit. At other times, his voice will be the male soloist and sometimes the female soloist. I have sections where there are three choirs—they divide themselves into three—because a lot of my piece has to do with processionals. I imagine choirs from three villages proceeding down from the tops of the mountains—this is based on South American Easter tradition. There are some sections that are divided into two choirs, especially when one represents Jesus and the other the people, or the mob, and then there will be sections where they are just one.[30]

Through this multiple and dynamic voicing, Golijov frees his passion from any pretense of historical reconstruction and so moves the passion narrative completely into the present of the listeners' experience. For listeners who want historical verisimilitude in even their musical interpretations of the Gospel story, this deconstruction of conventional dramaturgy can be disconcerting.[31] But if one listens to Golijov through Johnson's categories, in which the presence of Jesus is not based on historical reconstruction, Golijov's deconstruction of conventional character lines can be experienced differently. Johnson says that the fourfold canonical gospel

> symbolizes the infinite replicability of the story of Jesus in the lives of human beings. . . . But in what sense can the story of Jesus be replicated? Surely not in the specifics of his ministry, which are irretrievably past: his maleness, Jewishness, celibateness, beardedness, itinerancy. Such historical elements are not repeatable. But neither are they important to repeat.[32]

By using multiple voices to give voice to Jesus in *La Pasión*, Golijov moves the Jesus story dramatically into the present experience of the listener, where historical "facts" (Johnson's list of maleness, beardedness, etc.) cannot be relied upon as markers into the Jesus story. Instead, the listener must attend carefully to the voice of Jesus and follow the pattern of his life and death without easily recognizable markers. By decentering the representation of Jesus, Golijov's emphasis falls on the voice of Jesus that reverberates into the present.

Golijov has commented that he could not end the work with Jesus' cry of agony in death (Mark 15:37), and so he does not.[33] But he does not end the crucifixion scene the way Mark ends it either, with the centurion's announcement, "Truly this man was the Son of God" (Mark 15:39). The soprano soloist sings the cry of dereliction of Mark 14:34 (*Eloi, Eloi, lema sabachthani*), but the rest of the death scene is conveyed by instruments, not words.[34] After Jesus has died, Golijov takes the listener back to the very beginning of the work. The voice from heaven that was the basis of the vision of the opening number is now heard ("Thou art my beloved son, in whom I am well pleased"), so that God, not the centurion, announces Jesus' sonship. This is followed immediately by the words of Jeremiah's laments in Latin (sung by Jesus), the only Latin of the work. These two musical numbers hold together the tension of the passion—the joy of heavenly blessing and the pain and sorrow of lament.

In a moment of genuine pathos, *La Pasión* ends with the Kaddish, the traditional Jewish prayer for the dead:

> May His Great Name grow exalted and sanctified! Amen!
> May His Great Name be blessed forever and ever.
> Blessed, praised, glorified, exalted, extolled, mighty, upraised and lauded be the Name of the Holy One,
> Blessed is He beyond any blessing and song,
> Praise and consolation that are uttered in the world
> And say: Amen[35]

One of *La Pasión*'s first reviewers wrote, "At the very end, Kaddish is sung for the man on the cross, and the music undergoes an even more mysterious metamorphosis: the language is now Aramaic, the cantillation is Jewish, and the centuries have slipped away like sand."[36] It is an ending that honors the sacredness of human life and of human death and places the whole story of the passion where it belongs: in the hands of God.

A NON-ECCLESIAL "REAL" JESUS

The response to *La Pasión según San Marcos*, as noted, has been overwhelmingly positive. At its world premiere in Stuttgart, the audience gave the piece a thirty-minute standing ovation; it was given the same reception at its U.S. premiere in Boston six months later. Certainly, much of the positive response comes from the dynamism and drama of the music itself, as the Latin American rhythms, singing styles, dance, and instruments draw the listener into an almost irresistible musical world. Yet it is wrong to assume that these musical elements, in the service of a different story, would generate the same response. Rather, the genius of this work is the way in which Golijov has recreated the dynamics that make Bach's passions such classics: by finding a musical vocabulary that seamlessly speaks the Gospel story for a new day.

La Pasión según San Marcos was composed by an Argentine Jew for a concert, not ecclesial, setting. It is neither primarily a theological nor an ecclesial creation, yet one is hard pressed to say that the Jesus it creates is not a real presence for many of those who experience this piece. This can be seen most acutely by looking at the choir that sings the choruses in all of the performances of this piece. The choir, the Schola Cantorum of Carácas, is a group of non-professional singers who bring tangible energy and passion to each performance of La Pasión. As Golijov notes, "They all tend to have full-time jobs, so when they travel [to perform] they have to take vacation time. This had to be a Passion to engage their emotions."[37] The choir members embrace an "evangelical-style Catholicism," and so when they sing the religious and musical popular idioms of this work, they are singing in their own language. The story that they sing is their story, and the singers' connection with the story accounts for much of each performance's power. Jesus is real for this choir as they sing, and they create an occasion for Jesus to become real in the experience of the audience. In the lives of the performers and quite frequently the audience, there is an experience of the living Jesus.

Golijov's interactions with this choir had an impact on La Pasión at the composition stage as well. He was working with this choir when, at Christmas 1999, mudslides destroyed many of Carácas's poorest neighborhoods, including homes of some of the choir members. The pain of the city and of affected choir members helped to focus his work:

> All these disconnected thoughts and ideas that had been floating in my head sort of found a focus in all the misery. I think a situation like that unleashes passions and forces that can be tremendously creative. St. Mark wrote the first of the Gospels and he wrote fast, a bit like a journalist, so I took my inspiration from that, too. So we had this incredibly concentrated burst of creativity in Carácas after that.[38]

Golijov also names the faith of his great grandfather as one of his own life experiences that gave him an insight into what is at stake in the passion narrative:

> A crucial thing in my life was when my great grandfather shared my bedroom when I was seven or eight years old. He was in his nineties. He slept in the other bed in my room for many nights after two of his sons died. I would wake up and he would be next to the window praying the phylactery. He would finish the prayer, then put on his overalls and begin to fix things in the house. I remember being amazed that somebody who has lost children could keep praying and fixing things.[39]

Neither Golijov's engagement with the religious life of the choir or his memory of his great grandfather's prayer constitutes an ecclesial setting for the composition and performance of this work. *La Pasión* remains by origin and definition a secular piece, yet it moves deep into the religious experience of composer and performer. And because of, not in spite of its secular origins, *La Pasión* creates an occasion for fresh access to Jesus as a living presence. Osvaldo Golijov has attended to the four dimensions of the NT that Johnson hopes will occupy NT scholars—the anthropological, the historical, the literary, and the religious—not as a confessing Christian, but as an artist moved to tell the story of the intersection of the Jesus story with contemporary life.

"WATCH HOW YOU HEAR": THE HEALING OF *kōphoi* ["DEAF-MUTE"] PERSONS IN LUKE

DENNIS HAMM, S.J.

Luke Timothy Johnson has been a significant contributor to the collaborative enterprise of reading Luke-Acts whole.[1] This paper, inspired in part by Johnson's work, attempts to contribute to that ongoing project by teasing out the narrative and theological implications of Luke's healing of persons described with the ambiguous term *kōphos*—a word that can mean deaf or mute, or both deaf *and* mute—within the broader theme in Luke-Acts of hearing the word of God as a source and defining element of Christian discipleship.

Johnson's commentary on the Gospel of Luke provides a perceptive narrative analysis of that Evangelist's version of the Beelzebul controversy.[2] One minor point of disagreement with him has led me to explore new connections between that passage and the rich Lukan theme of hearing God's word. At the beginning of his interpretation of this pericope, Johnson says, "The exorcism of the mute demon is brief (11:14) and serves mainly to set up the charge against Jesus that he performed exorcisms under the aegis of the devil himself."[3] He is right to say that the narrative of the exorcism is brief (indeed, the deliverance and its result occupy a single verse!) and that it serves to set up the charge against Jesus. But that its *main* service is to set up the charge of demonic collaboration on Jesus' part—this, I will, argue, catches only part of what is going on here. That the man is healed from the condition of being *kōphos* contributes to Luke's highly developed theme of the disciple's hearing and responding to the word of God mediated by Jesus, a theme that the rest of Johnson's commentaries on Luke and Acts bears out.

This paper will move through eight steps: (1) to take a fresh look at the word *kōphos*; (2) to review the meaning of *kōphos* and the broader theme of hearing (and *not* hearing) in Luke's favorite source, the Greek version of Isaiah (hereafter LXX Isaiah); (3) to review, for the purpose of comparison, the healing of *kōphos* persons in Mark and Matthew; (4) to explore the relationships between the three *kōphos* passages in the Third Gospel; (5) to survey the theme of hearing (and its opposite) in the first ten chapters of Luke; (6) to bring all of this to bear on Luke's redaction of the Beelzebul controversy as introduced by the healing of the man with a *kōphos* demon; (7) to briefly sketch the theme ("heart-listening") as it continues through the remainder of Luke-Acts; and (8) to indicate some implications of this passage and the larger theme of deep listening for contemporary pastoral theology.

THE WORD *kōphos*

The Greek word *kōphos* is an adjective whose primary meaning is "blunt, dull."[4] The "dullness" can pertain to a lack of speech capability, meaning *mute*, as in Philo, Josephus, and certain biblical passages. Or it can pertain to hearing disability, meaning *deaf*, as frequently in the Bible and in other ancient sources. Or it can mean both mute and deaf, as when used figuratively of idols, which neither hear nor answer.[5] The verbal form, *kōphoō* to "make blunt" or "dull," has been used in the passive to become deaf or to be rendered speechless.

A little reflection on human experience makes it clear why a word whose primary meaning is "blunt" or "dull" should be applied to both muteness and deafness. Hearing, of course, is the normal way of learning to speak. A child imitates the speech of the persons around him or her. And a profoundly deaf child, without special intensive training, will be unresponsive to speech, and will learn to speak only with great difficulty. Consequently, a deaf person may give the appearance of dullness (the root sense of *kōphos*), although the disability may mask acute intelligence. I suspect a contemporary speaker of Greek would avoid using *kōphos* for a deaf and mute person, much as we today generally avoid the word "dumb"—whose informal meaning is "stupid," though its traditional meaning is "speechless." Nevertheless, this brief linguistic reflection helps one realize why the same word, *kōphos*, came to be applied (albeit negatively) to persons with disabilities both of hearing and of speech.[6]

kōphos IN THE SEPTUAGINT—ESPECIALLY ISAIAH

The adjective occurs a dozen times in the Septuagint—six in Isaiah and six elsewhere.[7] The six instances in LXX Isaiah, in each case meaning inability to hear, are particularly pertinent for understanding Luke. The four instances in Second Isaiah, chapters 40–55, all refer to the deafness of recalcitrant Israel (LXX Isa 42:18-19 [2x]; 43:8; 44:11), whereas the two instances from First Isaiah prophesy the healing of the deaf— Isaiah 29:18 (the deaf will hear the words of the book); and 35:5 (the end-time vision of healing, "Then the eyes of the blind shall be opened and the ears of the deaf shall hear").

These references to *kōphoi* persons in the LXX Isaiah are part of a massive theme running through the entire scroll—the theme of Israel's hearing, or failing to hear, the word of God. This theme appears at the beginning, when the prophet we call First Isaiah addresses the leadership and the people with the words, "Hear the word of the Lord [*akousate logon kyriou*], you rulers of Sodom; attend to the law of God, you people of Gomorrah" (LXX Isa 1:10) and in the final chapter, where Third Isaiah conveys a final scolding, "for I called them, and they did not hearken to me: I spoke, and they heard not [*elalēsa kai ouk ēkousan*]. . . . Hear the word of the Lord [*Akousate rhēmata kyriou*], you that tremble at his word [*ton logon autou*]" (LXX Isa 66:4-5).

Especially significant for our study of Luke is the passage about the call and commission of Isaiah of Jerusalem—Isaiah 6:1-10. Because this passage is quoted and echoed frequently in New Testament writings—most conspicuously in John 12:40-41; Revelation 4–5; Matthew 13:14-15; Mark 4:12; Luke 8:10; and Acts 28:26-27—it warrants special attention.

The first thing to notice is that a reference to a *dead* king (Uzziah) is followed by the description of a vision of God as a *living king enthroned and reigning* from his temple—in other words, an image of the kingdom of God (verse 1). The prophet hears a voice telling him to say something in the name of the Lord. He receives a necessary purging of his lips by burning coal. The message he is sent to speak to the people is, "You shall hear indeed, but you shall not understand [*akoē akousatê kai ou mē synēte*] and you shall see indeed, but you shall not perceive" (LXX Isa 6:9).

Then follows a prediction regarding Israel's response:

For the <u>heart</u> of this people has become gross[8] [*epachynthē gar hē kardia tou laou toutou*]
 . . . and their <u>ears</u> are full of hearing [*kai tois ōsin autōn bareōs ēkousan*]
 . . . and their <u>eyes</u> they have closed,
 . . . lest they should see with their <u>eyes</u>
 . . . and hear with their <u>ears</u> [*tois ōtousin akousōsi*]
and understand with their <u>hearts</u> [*kai tē kardia synōsi*]
and be converted and I heal them. [*kai epistrepōsi kai iasomai autous*]
(LXX Isa 6:10)

Especially notable here is the way the chiasm—

    heart
        ears
            eyes
            eyes
        ears
    heart—

binds together the association of *hearing, seeing,* and *heart-understanding,* a connection that Luke will allude to more than once in his story of Jesus and the church in Luke-Acts.

In Isaiah, the heart is the ultimate seat of reception or rejection of God's initiative. It is the seat of righteous living (32:4; 38:3; 51:7), deep listening, understanding (6:10; 40:2), and place of conversion (46:8, 12). It is also the seat of pride (9:9; 14:13; 47:7-8), error, hardness, rejection/sin (6:10; 21:3-4; 29:13; 32:6; 44:18, 20; 51:7; 57:11; 59:13; 63:17), inner weakness (57:15), and the site of wonder (49:21). The heart is both the seat of sorrow (1:5; 15:5; 19:1; 61:1; 65:14, 16) and the site of joy (60:5; 66:14); indeed, the entire scroll of Isaiah begins with rebellious Israel described as a sick person with a sad heart (1:5) and it ends with the hopeful vision of Israel with a rejoicing heart (66:14).

THE HEALING OF *kōphos* PERSONS IN MARK AND MATTHEW

To appreciate what Luke does with the *kōphos* tradition, it helps to review the healing of *kōphos* persons in Mark and Matthew. Mark uses the word *kōphos* in two passages—first, regarding the deafness of the deaf-mute of Decapolis (twice, 7:32, 37), and second, describing the deafness of the demonized deaf-mute boy that the disciples were unable to cure after the Transfiguration (9:25). In both cases the person is said to be *kōphos* and *alalos* (speechless). The distinction (between deafness and muteness) is reinforced in the crowd's response to the healing of the deaf-mute of Decapolis: "He [Jesus] has done all things well; he makes the deaf [*kōphous*] hear and the mute [*alalous*] speak" (Mark 7:37), indicating that for Mark, as for Isaiah, *kōphos* refers specifically to deafness. Mark's debt to Isaiah becomes obvious when one notes Mark's first reference to the man as *kōphon* and *mogilalon* (v. 32). *Mogilalos*, occurring only here in the NT, is also a hapax in the Septuagint, at LXX Isaiah 35:6, where the prophet speaks of a future time when "the ears of the deaf *ōta kōphōn* shall hear" and ". . . the tongue of the stammerers [*glossa mogilalōn*] shall speak clearly."[9]

Matthew understands the word differently. Except for his use of the Q allusion to Isaiah in "the deaf hear"—*kōphoi akouousin*—(Matt 11:5//Luke 7:21; LXX Isa 35:5-6), where *kōphos* means "deaf," Matthew's six other instances of the word clearly intend *kōphos* to mean "mute." In the complex of ten miracles in Matthew 8–9, the climactic healing is that of a "dumb demoniac [*kōphon diamonizomenon*]" (9:32), whose cure is described with the words, *elalēsen ho kōphos* ["the dumb man *spoke*," 9:33]. This episode has usually been taken to be a doublet of the cure of the demoniac introducing the Q account of the Beelzebul controversy. Indeed, when Matthew transmits that tradition, he describes it as the healing of a "blind and dumb demoniac" [*daimonizomenos typhlos kai kōphos*, 12:22], who then "*spoke* and saw," indicating, again, that for Matthew the word denotes muteness. Note that Isaiah 35 is the passage echoed in Mark 7:32, in his unique (in the NT) combination of *kōphos* and *mogilalos*.

In the place where Mark's story line presents the healing of the deaf-mute of Decapolis, Matthew omits that specific account and, instead, provides a summary of Jesus healing many "on the mountain"—"the lame, the blind, the deformed and the *kōphous*" (15:30). How Matthew understands that word becomes clear when he refers to the throng's wonder "when they saw the *kōphous lalountas* ("speaking") in the next verse.

Thus, whereas Mark uses *kōphos* only to refer to deafness (echoing LXX Isa 35:6 at 7:32), Matthew mainly uses the word to indicate *muteness*, the sole exception being his reference to Isaiah 35:6 at 11:5.

THE (DELIBERATE?) AMBIGUITY OF *kōphos* IN LUKE

If Isaiah's powerful theme of hearing (and being deaf to) the word of God is mediated by *kōphos* one way in Mark (meaning "deaf") and another way in Matthew (mainly meaning "mute"), Luke uses the word with what

"Watch How You Hear": The Healing of kōphoi ["Deaf-mute"] Persons in Luke

appears to be deliberate ambiguity. This should come as no surprise. Luke employs deliberate ambiguity elsewhere in his work. Sometimes he uses the same word two ways in the same passage, as in the use of "father" in the Finding in the Temple, when Mary complains to Jesus, "Your *father* [*ho patēr sou*] and I have been searching for you with great anxiety," and Jesus responds, "Did you not know that I must be in my *Father's* house [*en tois tou patros mou dei enai me*]?" (2:48-49). The same passage exemplifies another kind of deliberate ambiguity; that last phrase—*en tois tou patros mou*—can also be rendered "about my Father's business." The ambiguity can be taken as deliberate because Luke's work presents Jesus' mission as entailing a nuanced relationship with the temple: in this Gospel, Jesus' temple action is not so much a purging as taking over what is rightly his property. His Father's house is also indeed his Father's business, and Jesus' business as well. So the ambiguous Greek phrase works both ways. Another example of this kind of ambiguity: When the healed Samaritan leper returns, praising God, to thank Jesus, Jesus asks, "Has no one but this foreigner been found to give glory to God?"(17:16-17). Here thanking Jesus and giving glory to God are so conflated that the language seems to suggest the high Christology of equating thanking Jesus and glorifying God.[10] This readiness to exploit ambiguity to draw the reader into further meaning surfaces in a special way in Luke's use of *kōphos*.

Luke's first use of the adjective *kōphos* describes the condition of Zechariah, the father of the future John the Baptizer, who receives an apparition of the angel Gabriel while he is serving as the incense tender as part of the evening Tamid service in the temple sanctuary. Gabriel tells him that because he has not believed in the good news of Elizabeth's pregnancy, he will become silent [*esē siōpōn*] and "unable to speak" [*mē dynamenos lalēsai*] until the day when Gabriel's words to him come true (Luke 1:20). Meanwhile, the people were outside in the temple precincts waiting for Zechariah; this no doubt refers to the custom of receiving the public blessing spoken by the priest at the culmination of the incense ritual.[11] He is unable to speak the blessing and gesticulates to the crowd. Luke says *diemenen kōphos* (v. 22)—which must be translated, "He remained *speechless*," given that the problem is an inability to speak.

That his condition also seems to entail deafness becomes apparent on the day of his son's circumcision (1:57-66). When Elizabeth says that the child shall be named John, the neighbors and relatives object that no relative has that name. So they "made motions" [*eneneuon*] to Zechariah to learn what name he wanted the boy to have, indicating that he is not only speechless but *deaf*, or at least that they thought so (v. 62). When, in obedience to the command of the divine messenger, the priest asks for a tablet and writes, "His name shall be John," "immediately his mouth was opened, his tongue freed, and he spoke [*elalei*] blessing God" (v. 64). So, while his condition of being *kōphos* seems to have entailed being deaf, the main punishment and release had mainly to do with the inability to speak. And speak he does—the Benedictus(!). But the ambiguity of the priest's condition is sufficient to call attention to itself and to get the reader to think about his condition and how hearing and speaking are related. He could not speak because he did not hear with faith.

The next instance of *kōphos* in Luke occurs at 7:22. This is a Q saying also found in Matthew 11:4, Jesus' answer to John the Baptist's embassy echoing Isaiah:

> Go tell John what you have seen and heard: the blind receive their sight, the lame walk, lepers are cleansed, and the *deaf hear* [*kōphoi akouousin*], the dead are raised up, and the poor have the good news preached to them.

Here, as we have learned to expect from Greek Isaiah, *kōphoi* refers to those who do not hear.

Luke's third use of the adjective *kōphos* (here, twice in the same verse) occurs in the passage of our special interest, his description of the demoniac healed before the Beelzebul controversy: "Now he was casting out a demon that was mute [*kōphon*]; when the demon had gone out, the *kōphos* man spoke [*elalēsen ho kōphos*]" (Luke 11:14). Whatever it

"Watch How You Hear": The Healing of kōphoi *["Deaf-mute"] Persons in Luke*

means for a demon to be *kōphos*, the second clause in the verse is clear that it caused the disability in the demonized person.

The effect of the cure—that the man *spoke*—naturally suggests that the translation of *kōphos* here should reflect an inability to speak—being mute. But given that Luke's prior uses of *kōphos* (1:22; 7:22) imply both muteness *and* deafness in Zechariah's case and *specifically* deafness in the allusion to Isaiah 35:5 in Jesus' response to John's disciples, *kōphos* might be best rendered here "deaf-mute."

This is no small point in the interpretation of the Third Gospel, for this Evangelist develops a powerful theme of a *heart-felt hearing of the word of God that leads to speaking and acting upon it*. Indeed, the immediate context of Luke's setting of the Beelzebul controversy includes a major expression of that theme. For shortly after Jesus' response to the Beelzebul charge, Luke narrates the exchange of beatitudes between the woman in the crowd and Jesus regarding Mary:

> While he was speaking these things, a woman from the crowd called out and said to him, "Blessed is the womb that carried you and the breasts at which you nursed." He replied, "Rather, blessed are those who hear the word of God and observe it'" (11:27-28).[12]

Surveying the sweep of that theme in Luke-Acts will help us interpret more fully in the Lukan context the healing of the man with the *kōphos* demon and the Beelzebul controversy it introduces.

HEARING (OR NOT HEARING) THE WORD OF GOD IN LUKE 1–10

The Visitation. It is significant that the first time Luke refers to human beings *hearing* anything is during Mary's visit with Elizabeth (1:41-45). That Elizabeth's response to Mary's greeting should contain the confession of faith—that is, calling the unborn Jesus "my Lord"—indicates obviously that this is a special kind of hearing, hearing with faith.

Elizabeth's next statement to Mary—"Blessed are you who believed that what was spoken to you by the Lord would be fulfilled"—is significant in the way it contrasts with the unbelief of Zechariah fifteen verses prior to this moment, when he was rendered *kōphos* precisely because he did *not* believe in Gabriel's words "which would be fulfilled in their proper time" (1:20).

John's Circumcision. At 1:58 the neighbors and relatives are said to hear not simply that the post-menopausal Elizabeth had given birth to a son but "that the Lord had shown great mercy toward her," an interpretation indicating that this, too, was a hearing with faith. Further, the news of Zechariah's healing from being *kōphos*—apparently muteness and deafness in his case—evokes a special kind of hearing in the neighbors: "All who heard these things *took them to heart*, saying, 'What, then, will this child be?' For surely the hand of the Lord was with him" (1:66).

What the Shepherds Hear. Luke highlights that the experience of the shepherds is not only a matter of *seeing* the angel of the Lord and the heavenly army and the child in the manger. They report what they have *heard*, and the people respond to the message they hear from the shepherds, namely that this child is "savior, Messiah, and Lord"—a faith understanding of what is seen—and the people "marveled" [*ethaumasan*] (Luke 2:8-20).

The Finding in the Temple. Some important reciprocal hearing is going on here. Jesus is described as listening (*akouunta*) to the temple teachers, and they in turn are listening (*akouuntes*) to him, "amazed [*existanto*] at his understanding and his answers" (2:46-47).

Nazareth. At Jesus' homecoming and messianic debut in the Nazareth synagogue, applying the Greek text of Isaiah 58:6 and 61:1-2 to himself, the people are portrayed initially as listening with amazement [*ethauma zon*] to his gracious words, but later with hostility and rejection when they hear themselves compared with rebellious Israel during the ministries of Elijah and Elisha (4:22-29).

Summaries. The next three summaries in Lukan redaction show the crowds listening with general openness. In the setting of the miraculous catch of fish, the crowd is said to press upon Jesus "to hear [*akouein*] the word of God" (5:1). When the report went abroad after the healing of the leper (5:12-14), great multitudes gathered "to hear him and to be healed from their infirmities" (5:15). And the gathering of the audience for the Sermon on the Plain describes a great crowd of people who "came to hear him [*akousai autou*] and be healed of their diseases" (6:18).

Sermon on the Plain. Exactly what hearing Jesus entails and what blocks right hearing becomes clear in the Sermon on the Plain. After the four Beatitudes and the four Woes, Jesus says, "But to you *who hear* I say [*alla hymin legō tois akouousin*] . . ." That contrast signal, *alla*, makes a clear distinction between those to whom the four "woes" were just now addressed—the rich, full, laughing, and the well spoken of—and those who actually "hear"—presumably the poor, hungry, weeping, and excluded of the four Beatitudes. Evidently, only those so curiously blessed will truly *hear* the subsequent command to love enemies, do good to those who hate them, bless those who curse them, and pray for those who abuse them (v 27b). Eighteen verses later, just before the similes of the two foundations, Luke wraps up the teaching of Jesus' sermon with verse 45: "A good person out of the store of goodness in his *heart* produces good, but an evil person out of the store of evil produces evil; for from the fullness of the *heart* the mouth speaks." This connection between what is in the heart and speech that the heart produces is unique to Luke's version of the sermon and will affect our understanding of the Lukan meaning of what it means to truly *hear*. Hearing with the heart is exactly the opposite of the "gross/dull heart" that leads to the closed eyes and stopped ears of Isaiah's prophecy regarding the recalcitrant people of God (Isa 6:10).

As in Matthew's version of the sermon, the Lukan sermon ends with those two similes about the one who builds a house by digging deeply and making a foundation on rock and the one who simply builds on the ground without a foundation; the first representing the person who hears Jesus' word and acts upon it, and the second the person who hears Jesus' word but does not act upon it. The point is clear enough in Matthew's Sermon on the Mount, but by framing his brief version of the Q sermon with the references to hearing (vv. 27 and 46-49), Luke's version of Jesus' teaching is all the clearer regarding true hearing. What those who hear are asked to do is contained in verses 27-42: love enemies, respond to hostility nonviolently, share what they have to meet the needs of others, forgive, and not to judge. True hearing is the work of a responsive heart that gets up and does such things, using words when necessary.

The Centurion of Capernaum. Luke's segue to the next episode continues the theme: "After he had ended all these sayings *in the hearing of the people [eis tas akoas tou laou]*" (7:1), which seems to present the contents to the reader neutrally, waiting for commitment or rejection. And that is immediately followed by the good example of the faithful hearing of the centurion with the sick slave. "When he heard of Jesus [*akousas de peri tou Iēsou*], he sent him elders of the Jews . . ." (7:3). At the end of the episode, Jesus equates the centurion's understanding of and trust in the efficacy of his word as faith: "Not even in Israel have I found such faith" (7:9).

Jesus' Response to John's Question. With Jesus' response to the question of John's disciples ("Are you the one who is to come, or are we to look for another?"), we hear an answer echoing several passages in LXX Isaiah— 35:5-6 (regarding the blind seeing, the lame walking, and the *kōphoi* hearing); 29:18-19 (regarding blind seeing, *kōphoi* hearing, and the poor rejoicing); and 61:1-2 (regarding the blind seeing, and the poor having good news proclaimed to them). Given that the narrative of Luke-Acts provides specific examples of each of the four other kinds of healing referred to here, Luke probably understands that his two references to *kōphos* persons (Zechariah and the *kōphos* person whose deliverance introduces the Beelzebul controversy) suffer deafness as well as speechlessness.[13]

If we have any doubt that Luke's interpretation of these healings goes beyond the physical, we need only read a few lines further in this same context. Luke 7:29-30 makes a clear distinction between those who truly *listened* and those who "rejected the plan [*boulēn*] of God for themselves." "All the people who listened [*pas ha laos akousas*], even the tax collectors, who were baptized with the baptism of John, justified God [*edikaiōsan ton theon*]. But the Pharisees and scholars of the Law, who were not baptized by him, rejected the plan of God for themselves." The formal disjunction between *hearing* and *rejecting God's plan* in this statement invests the verb *akouein* with heavy thematic weight. In this case it is those who accepted John the baptizer as God's messenger and submitted to his baptism who are said to truly listen or hear. To hear fully is to listen responsively in faith. It was to receive John as a transmitter of the "word of God" (see Luke 3:2, *rhēma theou*; and see LXX Isa 40:8; 55:11; 66:5; Jer 1:1). Indeed, the vocabulary used in this bit of Lukan redaction echoes yet another part of LXX Second Isaiah, specifically LXX Isaiah 47:8-13:

> Remember these things and groan; repent, you that have gone astray, return in your heart and remember the former things of old . . . and I said, 'All my counsel [*pasa hē boulē mou*] shall stand. . . . Hearken [*akousate*] to me, ones who lost their heart, that are far from righteousness. I have brought *near my righteousness* [*ēggisa tēn dikaiosynēn mou*] and will not be slow with the salvation that is from me.

The Parable of the Sower. This parable, of course, focuses on hearing the word of God in all three synoptic versions ("Whoever has ears to hear, let him hear" 8:8). The paraphrastic citation of LXX Isaiah 6:9, with its reference to seeing that does not really see and hearing that fails to understand, drives the point home. The allegorical explanation of the Sower parable that follows in all three synoptic accounts explicates what inhibits responsive and faithful hearing (in Luke: the intervention of the devil, lack of perseverance, temptation, and the cares, riches, and pleasures of life). Luke nuances his explanation of what can go wrong or right in the process of hearing the word of God, and only Luke calls it "the word of God" [*ho logos tou theou*]. He does this with references to the heart. "Those on the path are the ones who have heard, but the devil comes and takes away the word *from their hearts that they may not believe and be saved*" (8:12).

The wording of this redaction implies that the word of God can be somehow planted in the heart and yet be snatched away before the person believes and experiences salvation. Without solving the philosophical question of how a person can be the passive victim of diabolic snatching, one can at least see that this is a matter of the core of the person, the heart, and that believing and salvation *follow from* possession of the word of God in the *heart*. Luke's version next speaks uniquely of the possibility of *believing for a while* and then *in time of temptation, falling away*. This heart-language resumes in the explanation of the "good soil," which represents "those who, when they have heard the word, *embrace it with a generous and good heart* and bear fruit *through perseverance*" (8:15). This would seem to be Luke's exposition of what Isaiah 6 means by the kind of hearing that leads to understanding.

The lamp imagery that follows in the sayings of verses 16-17 touches on the communication or sharing of the product of growth in the receptive heart. Indeed, it is an implicit mandate to share what grows from the seed of the word of God nurtured in the heart. Like a lamp in a darkened home, it is not to be hidden but placed where it can welcome those who enter. It is no accident that, where Mark has, "Take heed what you hear [*blepete ti akouete*]" (Mark 4:24), Luke has, "Take heed how you hear" [*blepete pōs akouete*] (8:18).

The True Family of Jesus, Formed by Hearing (Luke 8:19-21). That Luke is subtly pursuing a theme in this passage becomes clear in his placement and expression of the tradition about Jesus' true family. Whereas Mark had placed this episode (Mark 3:33-35) *after* the Beelzebul controversy and just *before* the section on the parables of growth, Luke places the episode here—with the connecting particle *de*—right *after* the explanation of the Sower parable and its attendant sayings about sharing the light and minding how one hears. Luke's revision of the words of Jesus, responding to the report that his family is outside wanting to *see* him, brings the theme home. Where the Markan Jesus said, "Whoever *does the will of God* is my mother, sister, and brother," the Lukan Jesus says, "My mother and my brothers are those *who hear the word of God and do it*" (8:21)—very much in the spirit of Luke's redaction of the Sermon on the Plain. And Luke *omits* Mark's reference to Jesus' looking around the room and those sitting around him and the statement, "Here are my mother and my brothers." This omission makes it easier to associate Jesus' words with the entourage mentioned just *before* the parable of the Sower, the Twelve and the healed women who supported them out of their own resources (Luke 8:1-3). They are the ones who have truly heard the word of God, the proclamation of "the good news of the kingdom of God" (v. 3). The women's readiness to support the ministry of the Twelve out of their resources (8:3) demonstrates that their hearing of the word has not been choked by "riches and the pleasures of life" (v. 14).

The Transfiguration. Luke's "great omission" (of Mark 6:45–8:26) allows for a quick segue to Peter's Confession, the first prediction of the Passion, and the Transfiguration, which culminates with the voice from heaven saying "This is my Son, my chosen one; *listen to him [autou akouete]*" (9:35). Though Jesus is *not* one of the prophets of old, he speaks with the divinely delegated authority ascribed to them. Indeed, as Son he speaks with even greater authority. This theme already inheres in Mark's version of the Transfiguration, of course. Luke may be enhancing the *content* of what is to be heard by asserting that the topic of Moses' and Elijah's exchange with Jesus was "the exodus he was about to accomplish in Jerusalem" (9:31).

The Second Passion Prediction. Luke's redaction of the second passion prediction and its aftermath is a surprisingly rich vehicle of his theme of hearing Jesus (9:43b-45).

> While they were still marveling at everything that Jesus was doing, he said to his disciples, "Put these words in your ears, for the Son of man is about to be handed over to the hands of men." But they did not understand this saying; its meaning was hidden from them [*parakekalymmenon ap'autōn*] so that they should not understand it [*hinamē aisthōntai auto*], and they were afraid to ask him about this saying.

In this Lukan abbreviation of a synoptic tradition, it is precisely the handing over of the Son of man which is not properly heard with understanding. The Lukan diction here is significant. The Greek word translated by this second reference to the disciples' failure to understand is *mē aisthōntai*. This NT hapax is rare in the LXX, where *aisthanomai* occurs only six times (Job 23:5; 40:18; Prov 17:10; 24:14; and Isa 33:11 and 49:26).

The Isaian uses are especially illuminating. The context in LXX Isaiah 33:10-11 is the rising, exaltation, and glorification of the Lord—"Now will I arise, says the LORD, now will I be glorified, now will I be exalted. Now you shall see, now you shall perceive [*aisthēthēsesthe*]." Even more pertinently, LXX Isaiah 49:26 occurs in the very passage to which Luke's version of the Beelzebul controversy and the healing of the *kōphos* man has given other evidence of consciously alluding to the image of the captured and despoiled strong one—Isaiah 49:24-26. The final clause of that passage reads, "And all flesh shall perceive [*aisthanthēsetai*] that I am the LORD that delivers you." This is precisely what the disciples are *not* able to do at this point in the Gospel account.

Luke's description of the disciples' response is also pertinent to the theme, with its linking of hearing, understanding, and the condition of the "heart."

> An argument [*dialogismos*] arose among the disciples about which of them was the greatest. Jesus realized the intention of their hearts [*dialogismon tēs kardias autōn*], took a child and placed it by his side and said to them, "Whoever receives this child in my name receives me,

and whoever receives me receives him who sent me. For the one who is least among you is the greatest (Luke 9:46-48).[14]

Whoever hears you hears me. (Luke 10:16). This is a Q saying occurring in the mission discourse, for which Matthew's version is, "He who *receives* you receives me, and he who *receives* me receives him who sent me" (Matt 10:40; see the Johannine parallel at John 13:20: "Truly, truly, I say to you, he who receives any one whom I send receives me; and he who receives me receives him who sent me.")[15] Two things about the Lukan version command our attention: (1) Where Matthew has *ho dexomenos hymas* ["whoever *receives* you"], Luke has, "*ho akouōn hymōn* ["whoever *hears* you"]; and (2) where Matthew's version continues with the clause about the one who receives Jesus receiving the one who sent him, Luke's version proceeds to describe the opposite of hearing/receiving as *rejection*: "and he who *rejects* [*athetōn*] you rejects me, and he who rejects me rejects him who sent me." This matches Luke 7:29-30, where *hearing/listening* people are said to "justify" God, and are contrasted with those who "reject" [*ethetēsan*] God's purpose for themselves. So Luke 7:29-30 and 10:16 both claim that failure to listen to God's sent ones is to reject God! These versions seem to be Lukan composition in chapter 7 and Lukan redaction in chapter 10.

When the seventy-two return from their first mission exulting at how the demons are subject to them in Jesus' name, Jesus says to them in private, "Blessed are the eyes which see what you see, for I tell you that many prophets and kings desired to see what you see, and did not see it, and *to hear what you hear, and did not hear it*" (Luke 10:24). It is obvious why Luke saw no need to edit this saying, which is a Q saying, parallel to Matthew 13:17. While the saying itself has not been edited, redaction shows up in the *placement* of this saying about seeing and hearing. The context in Matthew 13 was the parable of the Sower; in Luke's context the saying addresses the seventy-two and refers to the wonders they experience on mission, specifically how the demons were subject to them because of

Jesus' name. It follows immediately upon the prayer of 10:21-22, which includes, "All things have been handed over to me by the Father," suggesting a post-Easter moment. So what they see and hear are the wonders of mission as manifesting a revelation of the Father ("No one knows who the Son is except the Father and who the Father is except the Son and anyone to whom the Son wishes to reveal him—10:22).

The last expression of the healing theme before the Beelzebul controversy introduced by the deliverance of the man with the *kōphos* demon is the reference to Mary of Bethany sitting at the feet of the Lord, listening to his word [*ēkouen ton logon autou,* 10:39].[16]

The Beelzebul Controversy (Luke 11:14-23). There is much more to Luke's theme of hearing, or not hearing, the word of God, but having traced it from the beginning of the Gospel to chapter eleven, we are well prepared to appreciate Luke's redaction of the Beelzebul pericope with its inciting incident, the deliverance of the man with the *kōphos* demon, as it participates in that theme and further draws upon Luke's favorite part of Scripture, Isaiah.

> Now he was casting out a demon that was *kōphos* ["deaf-mute"?]; when the demon had gone out, the *kōphos* ["deaf-mute"?] spoke, and the people marveled [*ethaumasan*]. (v. 14)

The suggested translation of *kōphos* as "deaf-mute" reflects Luke's use of the word in the previous chapters, where the *kōphos* Zechariah (1:22b) is treated as both mute *and* deaf (1:62-64), and the allusion to LXX Isaiah 35:5b at Luke 7:22 ("the *kōphoi* hear") refers unambiguously to deaf persons. Since a similar incident occurs in Matthew's introduction to the Beelzebul controversy, we can take this as Q tradition. Matthew describes a *blind* and dumb demoniac who, when healed, speaks and sees. Does Matthew add the blindness, or does Luke omit the blindness? In either case, it is sufficient for Luke that the man is *kōphos*.

> But some of them said, "He casts out demons by Beelzebul, the prince of demons." Others, to test him, asked him for a sign from heaven. (vv. 15-16)

For Mark the adversaries were "scribes," whom Matthew changes to his favorite foils to Jesus, the Pharisees. Luke, by contrast, generalizes the challengers by simply referring to "some" and "others"—presumably of "the crowd" [*hoi ochloi*] mentioned in the previous verse. And to those "others" he ascribes a new challenge to Jesus, the request for a "sign from heaven." I take this as an ironic set-up for the punch-line of this proclamation story—Jesus' statement of verse 20, "But if it is by the finger of God that I cast out demons, then the kingdom of God has come upon you." By irony I mean the gap between the request for a sign from heaven and the reality that Jesus' deliverances from demonic oppression are themselves such a sign. Indeed the exorcisms are evidence of "the finger of God," a clear echo of Exodus 8:19, which reinforces Luke's portrayal of Jesus' ministry as a new exodus in the Isaianic sense of restoration after exile. Leveling and broadening the adversaries to some of the *ochloi* supports the theme of Jesus' resisters as replicating stiff-necked Israel of the wilderness period. And yet not all Israel resists, given that the "some" and "others" seem to form a subgroup of the crowd that is said to "marvel" at the healing in verse 14.

> But he, knowing their thoughts [*dianoēmata*], said to them, "Every kingdom divided against itself is laid waste, and house falls upon house." (v. 17)

Luke's use of the rare word *dianoēma* is a further hint that he still has Isaiah in mind. This NT hapax echoes meaningfully the single instance of this noun in LXX Isaiah: "But as heaven is distant from the earth, so is my way [*hē hodos mou*] distant from your ways, and your thoughts [*ta dianoēmata hymōn*] from my mind [*dianoias mou*]" (LXX Isa 55:9). The likelihood that this passage was in Luke's mind increases when we notice that the very next verse in LXX Isaiah 55 is the classic passage on the assured effectiveness of the word of God:

> For as the rains shall come down, or snow, from heaven, and shall not return until it have saturated the earth and it bring forth, and bud, and give seed to the sower, and bread for food; so shall my word be whatever shall proceed out of my mouth, it shall by no means turn back, until all the things which I willed shall have been accomplished (LXX Isa 55:10-11).

This Isaian context makes *ta dianoēmata* the apt word to describe the inappropriate responses to Jesus' ministry—the ascription of Jesus' healing power to Beelzebul and the (needless) search for a "sign from heaven." These ways of thinking exemplify the human ways that are not the ways of God. Such *dianoēmata* block a proper hearing of the word of God delivered by Jesus. Such auditors are *kōphoi* in Isaiah's sense.

Mark's version of the Beelzebul controversy does not carry the powerful Q statement interpreting the deliverance ministry of Jesus as evidence of the "finger/spirit of God" and the kingdom of God come upon them (Matt 12:17//Luke11:20). But the same idea of divine intervention is carried by the implied analogy of Mark 3:27 "But no one can enter a strong man's house and plunder his goods, unless he first binds the strong man; then indeed he may plunder his house." Many commentators, including the marginal note in Aland's *Synopsis*, recognize this image as derived from Isaiah 49:24-25, where it refers to YHWH's transcendent power to defend the people of Israel against imperial power and to restore them from exile in a new exodus. The liberation of demonized persons is, therefore, a sign that Satan has been bound and a sign that the Isaian new exodus is unfolding in the new reign of Jesus' healing action.

Intensifying the tradition in Mark, the Q tradition asserts divine victory as happening in Jesus' healings more directly with the Reign-of-God-come-upon-you saying (Matt 12:28, "by the Spirit of God"//Luke 11:20, "by the finger of God"), for which the binding-the-strong-man image becomes a kind of redundant reinforcement. However, Luke's redaction of that image takes yet another step. He introduces language that further echoes LXX Isaiah:

> but when one stronger than he assails him, he takes away his armor in which he trusted, and divides his spoil [*ta skyla diadidōsin*].(v. 22)

That is the only instance of *skylon* ["booty," "spoils"] in the NT; it occurs *twice* in LXX Isaiah's passage about taking the spoils of the strong man (Isa 49:24-25). Even more important to Luke may have been the link the word forges with LXX Isaiah 53:12, where it is said of the (exalted) Servant that *"he will divide the spoils of the strong"* [*kai tōn ischyrōn meriei skyla*]. Indeed, when one re-reads the Greek Isaiah's fourth Servant Song one is struck by the fact that this same passage begins with a prediction of the exaltation of the Servant and of the fact that "many nations shall be amazed at him" [*thaumasontai*] . . . and *those who have not heard will understand* [*kai hoi ouk akēkoasi synēsousi*]" (LXX Isa 52:15a, d). Thus the Lukan version of the Beelzebul controversy triggered by healing of the *kōphos* man mirrors the fourth Servant Song of Greek Isaiah 52:13-53:12 by framing the unit with a reference to an *amazed crowd* [*ethaumasan hoi ochloi*, 11:14; see LXX Isa 52:15] at the beginning and a reference to *dividing the spoils of the strong* at the end (11:22; see LXX Isa 53:12), and including *a movement from not hearing to understanding* (see LXX Isa 52:15). The prevalence of echoes from Greek Isaiah in Luke 11, together with his exploitation of the Isaian theme of hearing the word of God, suggests that this resonance is no accident.

THE THEME IN THE REMAINDER OF LUKE-ACTS: A "FAST-FORWARD" GLANCE

If we need confirmation that the author of the Third Gospel still has the challenge of properly hearing on his mind, we find it almost immediately after the Beelzebul pericope. To the woman in the crowd who blesses the womb that bore Jesus and the breasts that fed him, Jesus asserts that his mother is to be blessed for something more than her biological relationship to him: "Blessed rather are those who hear the word of God and keep it" (11:28).

And the theme continues: (1) in the responsive listening of the queen of the South to the wisdom of Solomon and of the Ninevites to the preaching of Jonah (11:29-32); (2) the repetition of the saying "Whoever has ears to hear should hear" culminating the sayings about the cost of discipleship at 14:35, and see 8:8; (3) the contrast between the tax collectors and sinners "listening" to Jesus as opposed to the stiff-necked "murmuring" of the Pharisees and scribes at 15:1; and (4) the statements of Abraham at the end of the parable of Lazarus and Dives: "They have Moses and the prophets. Let them listen to them" [*akousatōsan autōn*]. . . . "If they will not listen [*ouk akouousin*] to Moses and the prophets neither will they be persuaded if someone should rise from the dead" (16:29, 31).

The theme is heightened during the final week, when the rather nondescript "crowds" become a listening *laos* ("people," using the LXX word for the covenant people of God)—the people who are said to "hang upon him listening" [*ho laos gar hapas exekremato autou akouōn*] when Jesus takes over the temple precincts for daily teaching (19:48 and again at 21:37-38); and the *laos*, who at 23:13, 14, 27, and 35 are portrayed as refraining from joining the mockery, are simply present and witnessing the events during the crucifixion (especially at vv 27 and 35, framing the *via crucis* narrative). Although they are not explicitly described as listening, they are in fact "given an earful" in the three powerful sayings of Jesus from the cross about forgiveness (23:34), welcome into Paradise (v. 43), and entrusting of his spirit to the Father (v. 46). "When all the people [*pas ho laos*] who were gathered for this spectacle saw what had happened, they returned home beating their breasts" (23:48)—the final reference in the Third Gospel to responsive listening.

The theme continues in Acts. Suffice it here to note these highlights. The book is framed, at the beginning and at the end, with this theme. First, it shows up in the Pentecost narrative (Acts 2). Just as the gospel begins with a (punitive) miracle of (temporary) muteness and apparently deafness in the case of Zechariah, the Book of Acts begins with precisely the opposite, a miracle of hearing (vv. 5-8). Each of the visitors hears what the disciples prophesy in their own particular dialect. People are "confused," [*synechythē*] but the confusion is a reversal of the confusion of tongues that occurred at Babel (Acts 2:6; see LXX Gen 11:7) [*syncheōmen*]. It is a miracle enabling hearing with understanding. The ending of Acts is also thematized by the issue of hearing (or not), along with seeing (or not), in Paul's quotation of Isaiah 6:9-10 at Acts 28:26-27, followed by the crisp *pesher* interpretation: "Let it be known to you that this salvation of God has been sent to the Gentiles; they will listen [*akousontai*]" (v. 28).

The speech that Peter makes on Pentecost (Acts 2:22-41) evokes the theme of hearing with a response of the *heart* that leads to conversion. After claiming that the prophesying of the Twelve is a sign of the fulfillment of Joel's endtime vision, Peter prefaces his proclamation of healing and prophesying as signs of the resurrection of Jesus with the words, "You who are Israelites, *hear these words*" (2:22). The people's response to the speech is told in language reminiscent of Luke's redaction of the parable of the Sower and its explanation: "Now when they heard this, they were cut to the heart [*katenygēsan*], and they asked Peter and the other apostles, 'What are we to do, my brothers?'" (v. 37). That word, *katanyssomai* ["to be pierced to the heart," "to be deeply pained"], occurs only here in the NT. Rare in the LXX (19x), it occurs significantly in LXX Isaiah 6:5 (again, the call of the prophet), where it describes the prophet's sense of unworthiness when he hears the hymn of the seraphs (the Trisagion) in the temple. This is the passage Luke alludes to at Luke 8:10 (Isa 6:9) and the one he has Paul cite more fully at Acts 28:26-27 (Isa 6:9-10). As the call account of Isaiah 6 shows the prophet to be the exception to a deaf Israel, responding to what he hears with a vulnerable heart, so those hearing Peter in a way that can be described with the same word for the community described in 2:42-47—"those who were being saved" (v. 47).

It would take a monograph to spell out this theme fully, but these examples should be enough to show (1) that Luke-Acts has a carefully developed theme of Christian discipleship as heart-hearing of the word of God, (2) that he draws upon Isaiah's theme of Israel's failure to hear the word of God combined with end-time hope of its healing from the condition of being *kōphos*, and (3) that the healing of the man with the *kōphos* demon exemplifies the restoration of Israel in the Jesus people—the "dull" are enabled to hear and speak the word of God.

SOME IMPLICATIONS FOR PASTORAL THEOLOGY

Luke's theme of heart-hearing of the word of God has powerful implications (1) for understanding the giving and receiving of the word of God as initiated and sustained by God, (2) for the importance of knowledge of the Old Testament for reading the New Testament, and (3) for liturgical practice.

(1) The kind of hearing that creates disciples of Jesus is ultimately an act of God; the "word of God" is what the Father communicates, especially through Jesus, and those Jesus sends, and the human response to that word is facilitated by the Sender of the message. The conversion of Lydia in Acts 16 is described in a way that brings this out explicitly. In this first "we" section of Acts, Luke describes this moment of evangelization at a synagogue outside of Philippi in this way:

> We sat and spoke with the women who had gathered there. One of them, a woman named Lydia, a dealer in purple cloth, from the city of Thyatira, a worshiper of God, listened [*ēkouen*], and *the Lord opened her heart to pay attention to what Paul was saying* [*hēs hokyrios diēnoixen tēn kardian prosechein tois laloumenois hypo tou Paulou*]. After she and her household had been baptized, she offered us an invitation (Acts 16:13-15).

A narrative of healing from the condition of being deaf and mute, such as we find in Luke 11:14, symbolizes this reality powerfully. The narratives in Acts—such as the Pentecost experience and its attendant preaching with the conversion of those who hear it with the heart and the little vignette about Lydia—exemplify how this act of God's grace is typically mediated in very human acts of communication. This can encourage Christian evangelization today. One shares what one knows and trusts that the grace of God will facilitate the response of those ready to cooperate. Note that Luke mentioned that the woman already was a worshiper of God.

(2) Luke's frequent echoing of LXX Isaiah reinforces his theme that in Jesus God the Father is implementing his endtime project of restoring his people so that they can be a light and a blessing to many nations (see Paul's application of Isa 49:6—the Servant as "a light to the Gentiles"—to the Christian mission). This encourages contemporary Christians to understand their discipleship as collaborating with the God of exodus and restoration from exile in furthering our own liberation and restoration from exile. The Third Evangelist's frequent allusion to the First Testament, especially Isaiah, reminds us of the catechetical importance of promoting basic biblical literacy among fellow Christians. In the arena of scholarship, this ongoing discovery of biblical allusions in New Testament writings suggests that there remains much more to unpack in the New Testament writers' use of the Old Testament, especially in the Greek version.

(3) Luke's theme of deep listening has implications for liturgical celebration. The Third Evangelist's emphasis on heart-hearing, or hearing with faith, can encourage contemporary Christians to "watch how they hear" the word in communal worship. First, preachers need to hear the word deeply in the study and meditation on the text that is part of their preparation for preaching the homiletic interpretation of the readings of the day. The intimate connection between hearing the word of God with faith (being healed from deafness) and speaking (being healed from

muteness), suggests that having "something to say" to the assembled faith community requires having listened deeply to the word of God, especially as mediated by Scripture. This mysterious reality points to the need for those charged with preaching to integrate into their sense of identity and lifestyle a rhythm of biblical study and meditation.

Second, the theme can remind the entire congregation to devote some time to study and pray over the word even apart from the communal celebration. Like Lydia, people hear what they are prepared to hear. A gradual personal appropriation of the biblical traditions enables individuals to join the communal liturgy with an awareness of their continuity with the worship of the people of God down through the centuries, and to appreciate the homilist's applications to living the faith today.

Third, in the liturgical celebration itself, the way the lectors prepare and then perform their oral interpretation of the biblical text is very much a part of "watching how we hear." A thoughtful, heart-felt, and clearly articulated reading is a sign of the community's ultimately being gathered and constituted by responding to the word of the good news, as illustrated especially in Luke 8—the Sower parable framed by the community snap-shots of the Twelve and the healed and beneficent women (vv. 1-3) and the new family of those who "hear and do" the word of God (vv. 19-21). This focus on the importance of speaking and hearing the word of God suggests that it may be best to discourage congregants from eyeballing printed versions of the text that is being rendered orally. Reading silently a written copy of the text is essentially a private act, whereas listening together to a text rendered orally is a communal act. The hearing-impaired are an obvious exception, and will be helped by a written copy to join in the community response to the word. Those who are deaf and know deaf-sign will best experience the communal dimension of responding to the word through the ministry of a signer who interprets the word as it is being rendered orally.

This study's effort to interpret Luke's account of the healing of *kōphos* persons within his theme of hearing the word of God is another attempt to "read Luke-Acts whole." And that kind of study is yet another way to try to hear the word of God, for Luke's own prologue (Luke 1:1-4) tells us that his aim was nothing less than an effort to transmit that word to his readers (auditors). The work of Luke Timothy Johnson the exegete has helped us all take seriously the intent of Luke the Evangelist.

FROM THE SERVANT IN ISAIAH TO JESUS AND THE APOSTLES IN LUKE-ACTS TO CHRISTIANS TODAY: SPIRIT-FILLED WITNESS TO THE ENDS OF THE EARTH

WILLIAM S. KURZ, S.J.

It is a special honor and pleasure to contribute to this *Festschrift* for Professor Luke Timothy Johnson. We have shared scholarly beginnings and a recent new beginning. We were Ph.D. student classmates in New Testament at Yale University from 1971 to 1975. In 2002 we shared a quasi new scholarly beginning when we co-authored a conversation requesting a more explicitly theological future focus for Catholic (and implicitly Christian) exegesis.[1] As a friend I have admired Luke's teaching and scholarly career and his dedicated pastoral concerns and incorporation of religious experience in both his scholarly and popular writings. I write this in tribute to an extraordinary *Mensch* as well as scholar, teacher, and writer. May Luke have many more productive and happy years.

INTRODUCTION

Acts 1:8 is almost universally considered a thematic introduction to the Acts of the Apostles as sequel to the Lukan Gospel. However, it has received little explicitly theological consideration. Reflecting on this biblical verse theologically provides an occasion to combine, apply, and illustrate several of Luke Johnson's principal scholarly interests and contributions. Drawing on narrative and intertextual observations involving the servant motif in LXX Isaiah, this essay will consider implications of Acts 1:8 for the church's contemporary mission and witness.

My hope is that theological reflection on Acts 1:8 and on the biblical theme of Spirit-filled servant witness "to the ends of the earth" that it introduces will help correlate accounts in Acts that do not at first reading seem to have much theological relevance. The main goal of this theological reading of this scriptural passage and theme within the horizon of the overall biblical story of salvation is to articulate a unified biblical message about witness that is grounded in texts and themes from the Greek Jewish Scriptures on which Luke probably relied[2] and that reaches beyond his open-ended conclusion of Acts toward a contemporary mission of witness to Jesus.

The servant figure in Isaiah embodies the traditional biblical theme of the servant of the Lord commissioned by God to spread the knowledge of God's name. The biblical salvation narrative uses the expressions *servant* (Greek *pais*)[3] and *slave* (Greek *doulos*) in the Greek Bible for leaders of the people and representative figures like Moses, David, special kings and prophets, as well as for the people as a collective (as in "my servant Jacob").[4] These servant figures are commissioned to perform assigned tasks. On the one hand, they are to witness to God's presence with and care for the chosen people Israel. On the other, they are to witness to all nations that there exists only one God.

The multiple forms that witness to the Lord takes in Isaiah provide a context and background comprehensive enough to help integrate and show the relevance of apparently unrelated and seemingly novelistic stories and themes in Acts. Even humorous stories in Acts can be understood as contributing to this wide-ranging mission of the servant of the Lord in spreading faith in God.[5] Indeed such scenes as the burning of the magic books (Acts 19:19) and mocking pagan superstitions (14:11-18) can be read as related to the overall Lukan theology of witnessing about God to all nations.

Since in Isaiah the servant figure can refer to both individuals and to the people of Israel, it is easy for Luke to apply the mission of the servant of the Lord both to individuals like Jesus in his Gospel and Paul and Barnabas in Acts, as well as to collective groupings like the restored people of God and the church in Acts.[6] A significant task for the servant in Isaiah is to witness to the one God among polytheistic nations.[7] Not only does Jesus witness to God and his kingdom in Luke, and the apostles witness to God and to Jesus as Lord in Acts, but Israel as a people is also called to witness about God to all the Gentiles and to the ends of the earth, both in the Isaian Servant Songs and in Acts. In Acts, moreover, followers of Israel's Messiah, Jesus, carry on Israel's mission to witness about God (and Jesus as Lord) to all nations and to the ends of the earth.[8]

The Lukan Gospel depicts his intended readers as living in the "times of the Gentiles" before the final return of Jesus (Luke 21:24). The open-ended final pericope in Acts clearly invites Christian readers into the mission of the servant in Isaiah to witness to God to all nations, including Gentiles.[9] And is it not inappropriate to apply this servant witness to all nations to the "new evangelization" called for by the recent Pope John Paul II. For, all the nations to the ends of the earth today, including formerly Christian countries, can surely benefit from the biblical worldview of God's reality and love for the world to which we as servant figures can bear fresh witness.

EXEGESIS OF ACTS 1:8

Acts 1:8 is part of the risen Jesus' response to his disciples' question, "Lord, is this the time when you will restore the kingdom to Israel?" (v. 6).[10] After explicitly rejecting queries about "the times or periods that the Father has set" (v. 7), Jesus changes the focus of the disciples' question to their empowerment and subsequent mission. The mission charge that Jesus gives his apostles does not even mention restoring the kingdom to Israel. Instead, it emphasizes their witnessing to Jesus "to the ends of the earth," beginning from Jerusalem.

There has been considerable discussion about possible place referents for the phrase, "to the ends of the earth" (literally "to the end of the earth"). Most researchers acknowledge that it obviously has some geographical connotation, but there has been extensive debate over which locality is referenced—Spain, Ethiopia, Rome, a generalized farthest reach of the inhabited world, perhaps even more generally (but still stressing geography) to reaching the entire world.[11]

A strong argument, however, can be made that a non-geographical significance for the phrase, "to the end of the earth," is more important here than whatever allusion to a physical place it may also have.[12] An important clue to this additional sense is the fact that the phrase precisely echoes and alludes to identical wording in the Servant Song at Isaiah 49:6: "It is too light a thing that you should be my servant to raise up the tribes of Jacob and to restore the survivors of Israel; I will give you as a light to the nations, that my salvation may reach *to the end of the earth*" (NRSV, emphasis added). The Greek here (*heōs eschatou tēs gēs*, found also in LXX Isa 8:9; 48:20; and 62:11) is the identical phrasing used by Luke in Acts 1:8 and 13:47. Luke clearly echoes LXX Isaiah 49:6 in his choice of wording.[13]

The context in Isaiah 49:6 implies that the primary concern and referent of "to the end of the earth" for the servant in Isaiah is witness to all nations (obviously including Gentiles), wherever they may be, rather than any particular geographic location. The servant in Isaiah 49:6 had a mission that was broader in scope than merely to "raise up the tribes of Jacob and to restore the survivors of Israel." God had expanded the servant's mission: "I will give you as a light to the nations, that my salvation may reach to the end of the earth." The plural for *nations* here in both the biblical Hebrew and Greek translation (*goyim* and *ethnē*) can refer either to nations in general or to Gentiles as distinguished from Jews.

Acts 1:8 applies the mission of the servant to the nations to Jesus' disciples as it lays out the principal theme and plot of Acts. Like the servant of Second Isaiah, the disciples, when empowered by the Holy Spirit, will be witnesses to the Lord to the ends of the earth. Luke 2:29-32 had already applied this servant commission to Jesus in the words of Symeon's prayer, "Master, now you are dismissing your servant (*doulos*) in peace, according to your word; for my eyes have seen your salvation . . . a light for revelation to the Gentiles and for glory to your people Israel." Now Luke's second volume begins by applying the identical mission to the apostles here in Acts 1:8.[14]

This mission of witness to the nations is reiterated in the Pauline ministry narrated in the second half of Acts. In Acts 13:47, Paul and Barnabas cite Isaiah 49:6 directly. This citation is a response to Jewish resistance to their message in verse 46. Though Paul and Barnabas follow the biblical pattern of preaching first to Jews, they experience rejection from many of their own people. Thus they justify their turning also to the Gentiles by applying Isaiah 49:6 to their context, "For so the Lord has commanded us, saying, 'I have set you to be a light for the Gentiles, so that you may bring salvation to the ends of the earth.'"[15]

Also, the open-ended conclusion of Acts presents the prisoner Paul announcing that "this salvation of God has been sent to the Gentiles; they will listen" (Acts 28:28). Then for two years it shows Paul welcoming all who come to him (presumably both Jews and Gentiles) in his house arrest and "proclaiming the kingdom of God and teaching about the Lord Jesus Christ with all boldness and without hindrance" (v. 31). This finale implies that the bold witness of the biblical servant would continue without hindrance after the end of the Acts narrative and persist to the time of the writing and (when read canonically) even to the present time of us Christian readers. In a theological reading of the end of Acts, the Pauline servant mission of bold witness to the Lord has been passed on to contemporary Christians and cannot be prevented by persecution or even imprisonment.

INTERTEXTUAL OBSERVATIONS ON THE SERVANT MOTIF IN SEPTUAGINT ISAIAH

The Septuagint version of Isaiah 40–55 frequently mentions a servant figure, usually using *pais* but occasionally *doulos*. Sometimes the servant more evidently refers to an individual, at other times to a collective figure, the people as a whole. This alternation between an individual and corporate body is particularly facilitated by the biblical use of the name "Israel" both for the individual patriarch and for the people who bear his name. A quick survey of servant references in LXX Isaiah, which are concentrated mainly in Isaiah 40–55, can illustrate the main functions of servant figures in Second Isaiah and how these are applied in Luke and Acts as foundation for how they might be appropriated today.

The thematic use of "servant" (from either Greek word) in Isaiah is a feature primarily of Second Isaiah, chapters 40–55.[16] The first reference in LXX Isaiah 41:8-10 refers to Israel or Jacob as "offspring of Abraham" and "my servant." The emphasis of *pais* is more on its denotation as "servant" than on its other meaning as "son." Especially prominent is God's choice of Israel. The proper name denotes primarily the individual son of Abraham, but it is readily extended to refer to the people Israel as a whole. God assures both the individual Jacob and the people that they need not fear "for I am with you" (v. 10) and will strengthen and uphold you.

The "Servant Song" at Isaiah 42:1 refers to Jacob as "my servant," Israel as "my chosen," in whom the Lord delights and upon whom the Lord has given "my Spirit," that "he will bring forth justice to the nations." Though the verse immediately speaks of the individual Jacob or Israel, it is naturally applied also to the people named after him, so that this verse can readily support a theological application either to a particular person or to a corporate people. Both the individual servant and the people Israel have a divine mission to "bring forth justice to the nations."

Isaiah 42:6-7 emphasizes the Lord's election of this servant to be "a covenant to the people, a light to the nations, to open the eyes that are blind, to bring out the prisoners from the dungeon, from the prison those who sit in darkness." Luke and Acts directly apply this servant mission to those of Jesus and the apostles (esp. in Luke 2:31-32; Acts 13:47; 26:18). The servant's witness to both Jews and Gentiles in Isaiah 42 foreshadows the mission of witness to both in Acts.

The very next verse (Isa 42:8) insists that the Lord gives his glory to "no other, nor my praise to idols." This monotheistic emphasis will be a significant aspect of Paul's ministry in Acts. Repeatedly, as in Lycaonia (Acts 14:15-17), Paul will have to confront polytheistic or pagan Gentiles with the message that there is only one living God.

At first reading, the next reference to the servant (Isa 42:17-20) does not seem particularly helpful for a theological interpretation of the servant theme of witness in Luke-Acts or for appropriation today. The context is a sharp rebuke of God's servant Israel, accusing him of the same blindness which it has been the servant's mission to "heal." That is, even the servant whom the Lord wants to send as light to the nations who are living in the darkness of false worship is himself blind for lack of faith and fidelity to the Lord. The servant has consequently been plundered in punishment. But later in Isaiah 43 God will reassure Israel that they will be rescued.

When God restores Israel, they shall again function as witnesses to the Lord (Isaiah 43). After dwelling on the servant's punishment at the end of Isaiah 42, chapter 43 begins with strong reassurance that the Lord who created Israel has redeemed Israel. "I have called you by name, you are mine" (Isa 43:1). God claims that when Israel passes through waters or fire, "I will be with you" (v. 2) and "you shall not be burned" (v. 2). God will bring Israel's scattered exiled children back (vv. 5-7). The restored Israel will again function as God's servant witnesses: "You are my witnesses, says the LORD, and my servant whom I have chosen" (v. 10).

First, their own faith and awareness of God's reality will be deepened, "so that you may know and believe me and understand that I am he"

(v. 10). "I am he" is a literal translation of the Masoretic text, but the LXX simply has "I am." The Lord's self revelation goes on: "Before me no god was formed, nor shall there be any after me" (v. 10). The NRSV here is a literal translation of the Masoretic, whereas the LXX omits reference to a god being formed and translates the first clause, "before me there was no other god," focusing even more exclusively on the monotheistic claim that *only one* God exists.

Whereas the servant in Isaiah had become blind and been punished because of lack of faith, his renewed mission is to proclaim to all nations that "I am. Before me there was no other god, nor shall there be after me" (v. 10 LXX). There follows a warning to Israel against further backsliding, because if Israel strays again there is no god who can deliver him from God's hand (v.13).

Although Luke-Acts does not seem to have put much emphasis on this theme of the servant's own regression and consequent blindness as punishment, Dennis Johnson has suggested that the blindness theme in Isaiah may provide some background for the judgment miracles of Acts, which have caused so much puzzlement.[17] Two miracles of judgment are the deaths of Ananias and Sapphira, who lied to the Holy Spirit (Acts 5:3-4, 9-10), and of Herod Agrippa I, who arrogated to himself the glory due to God (Acts 12:21-23). The two judgment miracles that might relate more closely to our passage are the infliction of temporary blindness—on Saul, who persecuted Jesus (Acts 9:3-5, 8-9, 18; 22:6-8, 11-13), and on the Jewish sorcerer Elymas, who tried to turn the proconsul Sergius Paulus away from the faith (13:6-12).

Luke, however, does not emphasize that Saul's initial blindness is a punishment. Possibly a more appropriate biblical context for understanding Saul's blindness might be the blindness of the servants of the Lord in Isaiah 42:17-20, whom God will later make witnesses to him.[18] Acts, however, does not emphasize this aspect of Paul's blindness either. While the notion of the Isaianic servant as blind seems productive for contemporary application of the servant witness theme, Luke does not seem to have made much use of it.

The reminder of the servant's own sinful failure seems quite pertinent today to appropriating in a more humble manner the sense of being called to be servant witnesses to Christ. Evangelization today is done in a context of dialogue and openness to the insights of one's interlocutors. Focus both on new evangelization of post-Christian areas and on witnessing to Christ in places that have not known him postulates a good deal of listening to the other's experience and culture.[19]

The next Isaian mention of Israel as servant is in Isaiah 44:21-26, which immediately follows a prophetic satire on idolatry and idol makers, when God tells Israel to remember this lesson about the absurdity of idolatry. God addresses "O Jacob, and Israel," and offers reassurance, "for you are my servant; I formed you, you are my servant; O Israel, you will not be forgotten by me" (v. 21). God has forgiven Israel's sins and calls Israel to "return to me, for I have redeemed you" (v. 22). The call to reject all idolatry is immediately followed by a reassuring divine invitation to the Lord's servant Israel to repent.

The Lord goes on to recall that as Israel's redeemer God personally and lovingly formed Israel "in the womb." As Lord, God created all things, heavens and earth (v. 24). As Creator of all, the Lord "frustrates the omens of liars," but "confirms the word of his servant, and fulfills the prediction of his messengers" (vv. 25-26). The Lord reassures Israel that Jerusalem and Judah shall be rebuilt and inhabited again (v. 26). These prophecies seem to address first the nation Israel, but they do so in personal metaphors of forming an individual in the womb. Mention (in v. 26) of God confirming "the word of his servant" seems instead to relate to the word of an individual prophet. Here again the corporate body and individual both come into play in the same message.

The next Isaian mention of God's servant occurs in a word of the Lord to Cyrus in Isaiah 45. In the famous application of the term "anointed" (or "messiah") to a non-Israelite ruler (Cyrus who conquered Israel's enemy Babylon, which had exiled the inhabitants of Judah), the Lord reveals that he, the God of Israel, will subdue nations before him (Isa 45:1). For the sake of "my servant Jacob, and Israel my chosen," the Lord calls Cyrus by name "though you do not know me" (v. 4).

Then comes the self revelation of the Lord to Cyrus, "I am the LORD, and there is no other; besides me there is no god. I arm you, though you do not know me" (v. 5, translating the Hebrew; the Greek does not mention "I arm you"). The Lord's claim could hardly be more universal in scope or more insistent that there is no other God than the Lord: "so that they may know, from the rising of the sun and from the west, that there is no one besides me; I am the LORD, and there is no other" (v. 6). The next verse reemphasizes that God has created everything that exists: "I form light and create darkness, I make weal and create woe; I the LORD do all these things" (v. 7). Thus, one of the strongest monotheistic claims in Bible—that the Lord is the only God and is, indeed, God of all nations and not only of Israel—comes in this prophecy that is ostensibly directed to the foreign ruler Cyrus. This foreigner is given a commission usually reserved in the Hebrew Scriptures for a messianic figure from Israel.[20]

Another use of servant (this time *doulos*) comes after a strong indictment against Israel for not having heeded God's commandments. For, if they had obeyed, their "offspring would have been like the sand, . . . their name would never be cut off or destroyed from before me" (48:19). But now God brings to an end the punishment of their Babylonian exile, "Go out from Babylon, . . . proclaim it, send it forth to the end of the earth (*heōs eschatou tēs gēs*); say, 'The LORD has redeemed his servant Jacob!'" (v. 20). Here, too, the notion of servant is combined with reference to proclamation "to the end of the earth," as in Isaiah 49:6 as cited in Acts 1:8 and 13:47.

The "Servant Song" in Isaiah 49 has had the most direct Isaian influence on the servant imagery of Luke and Acts (Luke 2:32; Acts 1:8; 13:47). After God affirms the prophet with the words, "You are my servant, Israel, in whom I will be glorified" (v. 3), the prophet protests, "I have labored in vain" (v. 4). God first reassures the prophet regarding his prophetic vocation: "the LORD says, who formed me in the womb to be his servant, to bring Jacob back to him" (v. 5). The reference to the servant's being formed by the Lord "in the womb to be his servant" recalls the servant's own claim in Isaiah 49:1, "The LORD called me before I was born, while I was in my mother's womb he named me" (NRSV, whereas the Greek drops the Hebrew parallelism, simply saying, "from my mother's womb he called my name"). This claim of the servant echoes the prophet Jeremiah's call from the womb, "Before I formed you in the womb I knew you, and before you were born I consecrated you; I appointed you a prophet to the nations" (Jer 1:5), which was appropriated by Paul for himself as well (Gal 1:15).

The Lord also expands the mission of the prophet dramatically beyond his initial expectation of being a prophet to Israel. This extension made his vocation even more similar to the call of Jeremiah. "It is too light a thing that you should be my servant to raise up the tribes of Jacob and to restore the survivors of Israel; I will give you as a light to the nations, that my salvation may reach to the end of the earth" (Isa 49:6). The mission of the prophet Jeremiah to the nations is also given to the servant in Second Isaiah.[21]

The next mention of the servant is in the "Third Servant Song," Isaiah 50:4-11. The servant has been rejected by rebellious Israelites. After responding to them in law court terminology, he expresses confidence that God will vindicate him. He then turns to those who rejected him: "Who among you fears the LORD and obeys the voice of his servant, who walks in darkness and has no light, yet trusts in the name of the LORD and relies upon his God?" (Isa 50:10 NRSV). The Greek has imperatives rather than continuing the question: "Who is among you that fears the Lord? *Let him hearken* to the voice of his servant; ye that walk in darkness, and have no light, trust in the name of the Lord, and *stay* [rely] upon God" (LXX Isa 50:10, Brenton translation, emphasis added).[22] The servant's challenge has been rejected and is not being heeded, to the imminent punishment of those Israelites who refuse his message (vv. 10-11).

The last Isaian mention of the Lord's servant begins the "Fourth Servant Song" (Isa 52:13-53:12), part of which is cited in Acts 8:26-35 when the Ethiopian eunuch asks Philip about Isaiah 53:7-8 at Acts 8:32-33. While the Hebrew in Isaiah 52:13 reads "See, my servant shall prosper; he shall be exalted and lifted up, and shall be very high" (NRSV), the LXX translates the initial verb as *understand*—"See my servant shall *understand*" (emphasis added). Although this last "Servant Song" begins with promise of the servant's exaltation, in contrast most of the song itself focuses on the horribly disfiguring suffering the servant has to undergo first.

This suffering is what the eunuch asks Philip about in Acts 8:32-33. This Isaian view of suffering surely is part of the biblical basis for the repeated claim in Luke and Acts that the messiah had to suffer (see Luke 9:22; 17:25; 22:37 [which alludes to Isa 53:12]; 24:7, 26, 44; Acts 17:3). The suffering described in this servant passage, along with particulars of innocent suffering described in several psalms, helped fill out details of Jesus' suffering in the various New Testament passion narratives, as well as in other New Testament references to Jesus' passion. But Luke does not apply the Isaian view of the suffering servant only to Christ. It also helps support the claim in Acts 14:22, when Paul and Barnabas tell disciples, "It is through many persecutions that we must enter the kingdom of God." As Christ suffers, so will those who witness to Christ.

SUMMARY OF THE SERVANT ROLE AS WITNESS IN LUKE-ACTS AND ISAIAH

We have seen that the role of the Lord's servant goes back to God's servant Moses, receives a classic elaboration in Second Isaiah,[23] and is applied especially to Jesus and to his followers (then and now) in Luke and Acts. A pattern of theological characteristics of the servant's mission to witness to the end of the earth emerges from these scriptures.

First, it is God who calls someone as servant and witness. In Scripture individuals do not take this role on themselves. The notion of witness, especially in Isaiah, is also situated within a court setting.[24] In Isaiah God had with great mockery challenged the false gods and idols to present witnesses to their reality. Against the false gods who had no such witnesses, God called Israel to witness to God's existence and activity in human history. In Luke-Acts, Jesus and subsequently his followers are called by the Lord as witnesses to God's saving action in Jesus. Paul especially is lifted up as witness to the existence and actions of only one God against the non-reality and irrelevance of pagan gods and idols (as in Acts 17 at Athens).[25]

Second, Acts shows that servants and witnesses do not act from their own power or piety (Acts 3:12), but are first empowered by God who fills them with the Holy Spirit. The Spirit empowers the servant witnesses to speak (as do Peter and Stephen in Acts 4:8 and 6:10). The Spirit works healings and other signs and wonders through the apostles (as in Acts 2:43). The Spirit guides the directions that apostles travel to witness and prevents them from going in some directions they had personally chosen to go (Acts 16:6).

Third, servants are sent by God not only to the chosen people or to the church but also to all nations (Jews and Gentiles), "to the end of the earth." The servant commission is essentially a missionary one, to witness to God and to the good news of Jesus to everyone and to all peoples and nations, wherever God sends the servants, which is everywhere in the world.[26] Acts also makes clear that the witness of Christ's followers is expressed in language that is meaningful to the ethnic, religious, and cultural backgrounds of the listeners. Thus, Peter, Stephen, and Paul are shown speaking to Jewish audiences in Palestine and in the diaspora in biblical language and according to the biblical message of God's salvation, with distinctions between Jews in Jerusalem and Judea and Jews in the diaspora.[27] Paul, on the other hand, uses Hellenistic religious and philosophical language in witnessing to Gentiles at Athens and elsewhere.

Finally, even though followers of Christ witness in language understandable to their listeners, not all will be receptive to their message. In Christian history, the word *martyr*, from the Greek word for witness, *martys*, has a very strong connotation of not only witnessing to one's faith but suffering for it. Already in the Gospel Jesus had prepared his disciples not only for the necessity of his (the messiah's) suffering and death, but also for the probability that they too may have to take up their cross and follow him (Luke 14:27). Like Jesus himself, Christian witnesses may also have to share in the mission and destiny of the "Suffering Servant" of Isaiah.[28]

CONTEMPORARY MISSION AND WITNESS FOR THEOLOGICAL APPLICATION OF LUKAN MODELS

To be a genuine application of Scripture, and not a proof-texting misuse of the biblical evidence, theological application of biblical models should as much as possible be inspired and guided by the traditions, practices, goals, and approaches of the scriptural prototypes themselves. Thus, the characteristics of the servant mission of witness to God or Jesus that we have discovered especially in Luke-Acts, drawing upon Second Isaiah, will be part of the dialogue with contemporary conditions, issues, and concerns to which we attempt to apply that mission. Catholic discussion of these concerns has tended to focus more around a call to a "new evangelization" rather than starting from particular biblical passages. My Catholic contribution to this ecumenical volume will briefly relate some Catholic discussion of a new evangelization to this biblical call to witness to Jesus in the spirit of the servant in Second Isaiah.

The notion of a new evangelization has arisen especially from awareness of the radically different situation in which Catholics and other Christians find themselves in the twenty-first century from those described in Acts. Because Catholics since the Second Vatican Council (Vatican II) have stressed openness to the values of other religions and cultures, they have sometimes not emphasized evangelization. At times evangelization has also been identified with aggressive proselytizing, which Catholics reject. Popes Paul VI and John Paul II, however, reminded Catholics of the biblical commission from God to share our faith and witness out of love for our brothers and sisters.

Avery Dulles (now Cardinal) contributed to a 1995 collection of essays by Catholics on new evangelization with a clarification of the term "new evangelization."[29] He claims that to attract adherents in secularist and religiously pluralistic situations, Christianity again needs to be proclaimed, "as it had been in New Testament times, as a joyful message centered on Jesus Christ" (26). Although attention should be paid to the material needs of the poor, Dulles insists with Pope Paul VI in *Evangelii nuntiandi* [EN] that evangelization must include explicit proclamation of Jesus (no. 22) and not only sociopolitical development or liberation (nos. 31-33, cited on page 27).[30] John Paul II regarded evangelization as more urgent then ever, convinced that the number of people who do not know Christ had doubled since Vatican II (RM no. 3).[31]

Dulles provides a helpful overview list of ten characteristics of the new evangelization, which can serve as a good introduction and preparation for theological interpretation of the call in Acts 1:8 to be Spirit-filled witnesses to Jesus to the ends of the earth, from the perspective especially of the servant of the Lord in Second Isaiah.[32] The first characteristic of the new evangelization is the centrality of Christ: the Lordship of Christ, the Son of God, is at the top of the "hierarchy of truths" (Vatican II, *Unitatis redintegratio* [UR] on ecumenism, no. 11). There is no true evangelization if Jesus is not explicitly proclaimed (EN no. 22), and all missionary proclamation must be centered on Christ (RM no. 44).

Second, *ecumenism* is essential to the new evangelization, for church disunity undermines Christian witness (UR no. 1). Third, *interreligious dialogue* is intrinsic to the new evangelization. Though some see dialogue and evangelization as being at cross purposes, both are essential for contemporary evangelizing. Dialogue necessarily includes proclamation of one's own beliefs, but this proclamation must be done in a spirit of dialogue, respect for the other's conscience, and willingness to learn (RM no. 55-57).

Fourth, *religious freedom* is an indispensable presupposition for all evangelization, with no pressure to convert (*Dignitatis humanae* [DH], no. 1). The church avoids offensive proselytization (RM no. 8, 39). Fifth, evangelizing is a *continuous process*, with three phases. "First evangelization" is missionary proclamation where Christ is unknown or the church has not taken root; the second phase is pastoral care of evangelized Christians; the third process is *re-evangelization* of those who have fallen away (RM no. 33). In his 1995 essay Dulles adds that evangelization must go beyond initial proclamation to include "catechetical instruction, moral doctrine, and the social teaching of the Church." Its highest point will be intense liturgical life within vibrant church communities and should lead to "a civilization of love."[33]

Sixth, *social teaching* is an intrinsic element of contemporary evangelization, which includes commitment to the common good in that locality. Still, Paul VI warned against reducing the church's mission to a purely temporal project. Social structures cannot ensure truly human culture without conversion of mind and heart (EN no. 32-36). Nevertheless, evangelization includes efforts to promote a civilization of peace, solidarity, love, and human rights.

Seventh, *evangelization of cultures* and not merely of individuals is important. It is urgent that faith interact with and elevate cultures (*EN* no. 20). Eighth, employment of *new media* is part of proclamation today. John Paul II sees the media as a contemporary Areopagus needing the Christian message (as in Paul's address in Athens in Acts 17). Ninth, evangelization *involves all Christians*, not merely clerics and missionary orders. It is a basic duty of the whole People of God (*Ad gentes* on missions [AG], no. 35).

Tenth and finally and of utmost importance is the *primacy of the Holy Spirit* in all evangelizing, versus any crypto-Pelagianism. It is the Spirit who both impels the gospel to be proclaimed and the word of salvation to be accepted (*EN* no. 75). It is the Spirit who guides the growth of the church (as the Acts of the Apostles had clearly demonstrated).[34]

Roch Kereszty also lists several ways in which evangelization today is a "new evangelization." First, it proclaims Christ as a light for the nations, without imposing itself as a power structure between Christ and its people. While maintaining the church's visible institutions, the new evangelization strives to eliminate cultivating "institutional elements for their own sake (servility, papolatry, ritualism, clericalism, or more recently, the self-celebration of local communities)," but to treat institutional elements as signs leading to encounter with Jesus himself.[35]

Second, according to Kereszty, martyrs are the most perfect images of Jesus. In following Jesus, Christians must be willing to face rejection or worse in fidelity to their witness to the truth of the gospel (608).

Third, evangelization has to be inculturated in new cultures, incubating "*the Christian mystery in the genius of a people*" (citing Paul VI with *RM*, no. 54, 608–9, Kereszty's emphasis). Although inculturation enriches the church with the new culture's values, it also transforms the culture "from within" (citing *RM*, no. 52; *Evangelii nuntiandi*, no. 20, 609).

Fourth, through interreligious dialogue the new evangelization seeks to uncover "seeds of the word" and their rays of truth in non-Christian cultures and religious traditions. Patristic authors did not deny that in Hellenistic religious philosophies truth was sometimes mixed with error. As they learned from Hellenistic philosophies, so we should learn from dialogue with other religious traditions today. By learning both from other religions and secular movements, the church actualizes more fully its catholicity, without distorting its message (609–10).

Fifth, church members need to be aware of their responsibility for the salvation of all, with a love like God's for all humans and a desire for their salvation. Such a universal love is needed to heed God's call if he leads individuals to an explicit missionary vocation, to be Christ's "witness to all nations." Rejecting a missionary vocation is an act of resisting the Holy Spirit, who desires all humans to embrace the fullness of Christ in the church.

Cardinal George of Chicago discusses new evangelization in the postmodern context of interreligious dialogue and recommends an evangelization that does justice both to the apostolic and catholic aspects of our mission, both to the subjective and objective aspects of the person, and to truth and universal charity.[36] He recalls Pope John Paul II's list of dynamics of the new evangelization as "encounter, conversion, communion, and solidarity" (342).

George sees the need for a new Catholic apologetics to be a part of any new evangelization. Such apologetics has to be "philosophically rigorous so we may talk to secularists but also biblically enriched, with an attendant focus on history, languages, and interpretive methods, along with a deep respect for the faith that enables fundamentalist Christians to walk with the Lord and to love him" (349). The new apologetic has to have four characteristics.

First, it must understand Catholic faith in Catholicism's own terms, not only what is taught but also why, and in what historical contexts. Second, it must understand the positions of one's dialogue partners. Catholics must be as "scientifically and philosophically sophisticated as secularists and as biblically knowledgeable as Christian fundamentalists" (349). It presupposes openness to others' positions and willingness to learn from them. Third, apologists must use language understood by our interlocutors without diminishing the content of the faith. We have a right to our own vocabulary but also an obligation to translate or use it in ways that are not off-putting (350). Fourth, the new apologetics must be a "personal, non-defensive, loving response to arguments against the Catholic faith," even when coming from those who hate the church. It must be "permeated by humility and respect."

We must love enemies of the faith, but we must also love Scripture more than fundamentalists do and love the world more than secularists do. Apologetics needs to combine Jesus' respect for persons with respect for truth. It must presuppose the good will and respect the dignity of all in the conversation, even if good will in fact happens to be lacking. But, it is also grounded in the faith received from the apostles and proclaimed without compromise. Such forms of new evangelization will contribute to uniting the human family today (350).

CONCLUSION: THEOLOGICAL APPROPRIATION OF LUKAN SERVANT WITNESS

Jesus' promise and call of his disciples to be filled with the Holy Spirit and to be his witnesses to the ends of the earth (Acts 1:8) retains its significance for contemporary Christians. A Catholic form of appropriating the Lukan servant witness to the "new evangelization" interprets the biblical evidence in relation to the radically changed situation for Christian witness in the twenty-first century. Despite the necessity of interreligious dialogue, ecumenism, and inculturation, Christians believe that God continues to call them to witness to the good news of God and Jesus. If God's Son has become incarnate and has acted as suffering servant to reconcile alienated humans to his Father, Christians have a responsibility to share this truth and good news with the large numbers of people who do not sufficiently know God nor Jesus. The bold and unhindered servant witness of Paul, even within his house arrest with which Acts closes, is meant to be continued by Christians today.

Acts, however, makes it clear that the power of the Holy Spirit is required to be God's servants and witnesses to Jesus. Servants and witnesses do not act from their own power or piety (Acts 3:12), but from the power of God. The more Christians personally know and love Jesus, the more convincingly are they able to witness to others concerning Christ. The more Christians see themselves as God's servants obeying the guidance of the Holy Spirit in their lives and missions, the more effective they will be. Christians also need to be aware of their own blindness (as with God's servants in Isa 42:17-20), and the fact that, despite their own shortcomings, God chooses them as servant witnesses to others. Their sharing with others is a humble sharing that is open to listening and learning from the insights of one's interlocutors in a respectful conversation, and not just "preaching at" them.

Already in the Jewish Scriptures, God's servants (whether individuals or the people as a whole) were sent by God not only to the chosen people (or to the church in the New Testament) but also to all nations. Isaiah could not be clearer that there exists only one God, and that the Lord's servants were to witness to this true God amidst all nations and people, no matter how polytheistic or irreligious they were. Acts demonstrates Paul exercising a similar ministry of witness to the true God among polytheistic pagans and Greek philosophers.

Although the new evangelization demands respect for the religions, natural insights, and cultures of the peoples being addressed, contemporary Christians have to regard the apostolic message and witness to God's reconciliation of all humans in Jesus as a priceless truth to be shared lovingly and humbly but openly and fearlessly. They cannot allow themselves to be immobilized by modern and post-modern skepticism and relativism. Yet, even when followers of Christ witness in language understandable to their listeners, not all will be receptive to their message.

The ultimate form of witness remains that of the "martyr," who is willing to shed his or her blood in giving witness to Jesus. This, however, is a martyrdom not of homicidal suicide bombers but of a love for Jesus and for one's listeners so intense that nothing can deter one from speaking the truth in love, not even persecution or martyrdom by those who reject one's witness. Pope Benedict XVI's first and only encyclical to date has grounded such evangelizing love in the very being of God as love. "The Spirit is also the energy which transforms the heart of the ecclesial community, so that it becomes a witness before the world to the love of the Father, who wishes to make humanity a single family in his Son."[37]

SWALLOWING JONAH: SCRIPTURE AND IDENTITY IN EARLY CHRISTIANITY

WAYNE A. MEEKS

The early Christians discovered their identity, in part, by reading themselves into the scriptures of Israel. Their reading was not a clear and simple process. It was the beginning of that complex dialectic—often messy, convoluted, conflictual, and experimental—between the "texts of human lives" and the multiple and malleable texts of Scripture, which Luke Timothy Johnson has described so eloquently.[1] Throughout the history of that dialectic, various practices of reading established themselves, and often there were certain tensions between them. The readings by the clerical élites of the church, trained in the rhetorical habits so prized in the larger culture, were not always congruent with the less systematic readings that grew up among the lay people of the communities, readings that are only rarely visible to us.

Among the things the early Christians found in Scripture were a number of images that could encapsulate their experiences and their hopes, either as parts of an emerging master narrative or individually, resonating with common human yearnings expressed in iconic traditions familiar already in the visual culture that surrounded them.[2]

When they were able, the Christians, too, had some of those images produced in paint and sculpture, either in their burial places or, rarely at first, in the houses where they met. Naturally it is mostly the former that have survived for us to see, beginning with third-century sarcophagi and wall paintings in the Roman catacombs.[3] Their choices are not always what we might have expected, though understandable if we know something about the typological interpretations that would become common in patristic authors: Moses striking water from the rock, Daniel in the lion's den, the three boys in the fiery furnace, Balaam pointing to the star that would arise from Jacob, and a few others. Even knowing the commentary tradition, however, we would not have guessed that the overwhelming favorite would be the prophet Jonah. What was it about this "strange book in the Bible"[4] that so captured the imagination of those third-century Christians?

THE JONAH CYCLE IN EARLY CHRISTIAN ART

In the earliest examples in Christian funerary art, Jonah's story is presented in just three scenes: Jonah thrown overboard, often directly into the mouth of a dragon-like sea monster (*kētos*, as the LXX translators already interpreted the "great fish" of the Hebrew); Jonah vomited headfirst onto the land; and Jonah sleeping peacefully under the canopy of a gourd vine. Later another scene or two might be added—Jonah praying or Jonah angered by the gourd's wilting—or one of the original scenes might be divided, or all compressed into one.[5] In all cases it is remarkable that so little of the biblical story is presented. There is no hint of Jonah's mission to Nineveh or of the dramatic repentance of Nineveh's people, cattle, and king. We would never surmise from the images that the story's central theme was Jonah's prophetic call and his flight from it and the climactic confrontation between the merciful God and his disgruntled prophet. The Christians who commissioned these carvings or paintings were not looking for illustrations of their Bible, but for scenes appropriate for the resting places of their dead.

Jonah Sarcophagus, inventory no. 0857 in the Ny Carlsberg Glyptotek in Copenhagen, Denmark. Used by permission.

In that context it is not Jonah the reluctant prophet but Jonah the hero saved from death that resonates. The drama of the middle portion of the Book of Jonah, read without irony, readily qualified this obscure figure to join the other examples of miraculous rescue that the Christians found in their Bibles and depicted on the walls of the catacombs. Jews before them had already singled out Jonah along with Daniel and the three boys as models not only of individual salvation but of God's protection of the people from its enemies. Thus, in the apocryphon misnamed Third Maccabees, the priest Eleazar prays for the Jews of Egypt, threatened by King Ptolemy:

> The three companions in Babylon who had voluntarily surrendered their lives to the flames so as not to serve vain things, you rescued unharmed, even to a hair, moistening the fiery furnace with dew and turning the flame against all their enemies. Daniel, who through envious slanders was thrown down into the ground to lions as food for wild animals, you brought up to the light unharmed. And Jonah, wasting away in the belly of a huge, sea-born monster, you, Father, watched over and restored unharmed to all his family. And now, you who hate insolence, all-merciful and protector of all, reveal yourself quickly to those of the nation of Israel—who are being outrageously treated by the abominable and lawless Gentiles. (3 Macc 6:6-9)[6]

As we shall see, some of the more learned interpreters of Jonah among the early Christians precisely reversed Eleazar's sentiment and turned the point of the prophecy against the Jews, but that was far from the issue foremost in the minds of those who decorated the catacombs. The miracle-working God who could save a hero even from a "huge, sea-born monster" could save these faithful dead, buried under that hero's image, and all the living faithful from the threats of a hostile world.

The wealthier Christians who ordered the art, and the artisans they hired to make it, were sufficiently at home in that larger world of Greco-Roman culture that they knew exactly how the rescue of a hero from death and his happy life in the hereafter could be depicted.[7] Rescue from a sea-monster, after all, was a familiar motif in Greek mythology, and consequently, as Marion Lawrence has demonstrated, "Jonah's *kētos* has a long history in Greek art."[8] It is exactly such a monster who threatens Andromeda before she is saved by Perseus, or Hesione as Herakles rushes to the rescue. Even Jason can appear in Greek art lifelessly drooping from the jaws of a *kētos*, as Athena sternly bids the monster to give him up, though no literary source of the scene survives.[9] The rescued Jonah, too, sleeping peacefully under his gourd vine, strikes a pose well known from the pictured story of Endymion, sleeping immortally in the love of the moon-goddess, or of Dionysus, resting among vines in the bliss of a pastoral landscape. Endymion, especially, had become a favorite motif on Roman sarcophagi, and that image for the hope of immortality has long been recognized by art historians as the primary prototype of the reclining Jonah.[10]

The *mise en scène* of the rescued Jonah's repose is also built of many motifs familiar in Greek and Roman funerary art. The shading bower, its vine sometimes echoed in tendrils that curl across walls and ceilings, separating scenes in the wall paintings of the catacombs, is at home in scenes of pastoral bliss. Not surprisingly, the "Good Shepherd," the Christians' version of the soul-protecting *kriophoros*, is often nearby. Earlier in the sequence, the boat from which Jonah is cast is modeled on the boat of Erotes, familiar transport to the Isles of the Blessed. Despite the raging waves in the first panel, the combined scenes convey a reign of peace on both land and sea.[11] As we have seen above, Jews living in the Greco-Roman world also found in the Jonah story a symbol of peace in the face of threat, of rescue from peril of death, and their traditions undoubtedly found their way into the church's interpretations as well. Indeed, it has been suggested that a selective reading of the Jonah story in Jewish tradition helped to shape the story of Jesus' stilling the storm in Mark 4:35-41.[12] It is perhaps only because of accidents of survival that Jonah is almost entirely lacking from extant Jewish art from antiquity.[13]

In the Christian piety revealed in third-century burial places, Jonah is neither the reluctant prophet nor the successful preacher of repentance. He is the death-defying hero, rescued by God and resting forever in a peaceful paradise. Thus the Christians have found in their Bibles and in the traditional interpretations of the Jews a hero fully the equal of the Herakles or the Perseus of their pagan neighbors. With this immortal hero the blessed dead laid to rest under his image could be identified, and the peace of the Isles of the Blessed would belong to those to whom the resurrection was promised. But of course, for those who actually read the biblical account of Jonah, or remembered it from hearing it read in church (most likely during Lent or Holy Week), there were other odd and even disturbing lessons to be learnt. The literate fathers of the church addressed those other issues; Jonah the hero was of very much less significance in their commentaries.[14]

THE COMMENTARIES

The two earliest full commentaries on Jonah that survive are by Theodore of Mopsuestia and Jerome. They both used an earlier commentary by Origen, but it is lost and cannot be reconstructed. For the sake of simplicity, I limit the following discussion to the main points in Theodore's and Jerome's commentaries.[15]

The commentators pay little attention to the pictorial representations of Jonah, but they do not neglect the central concern expressed in those, the miraculous preservation of the castaway. The emphasis on Jonah's being entirely unscathed, a motif fancifully expanded in ancient Jewish preaching in both Greek and rabbinic sources and suggested in some of the later images by Jonah's emergence from the monster bearded and fully clothed, appears also in the patristic commentaries. Indeed it was not to punish Jonah that God prepared the *kētos*, according to Theodore, but to demonstrate God's providential care. "The result was that he [Jonah] marveled at being kept unharmed and quite unaffected in the sea monster, as though finding himself in some small room in complete security."[16]

Naturally, too, the commentators take this preservation and deliverance of Jonah from the dangers of sea and sea monster as a sign of protection of the soul from death and hell. Thus when Jerome comes to Jonah 2:8a, which the LXX renders "When my soul abandoned me, I remembered the Lord," he comments: "From this we learn . . . that in that time when our 'soul abandons us' and is torn away from our bodily frame, we must not turn our thought to another but to him who is our Lord both in the body and outside of the body" (Duval 250, Risse 166, trans. Hegedus 41f.).

However, there is a further step that is not clearly implied in the works of art. Jerome quickly adds that it is "not difficult" to apply the verse to the Savior, in light of sayings in the Gospels such as "My soul is sorrowful unto death" (Matt 26:38; Mark 14:34), "Father, if it is possible, may this cup pass from me" (Matt 26:39), and "Into your hands I commend my spirit" (Luke 23:46). That christological interpretation predominates in Jerome's comments on the whole psalm of Jonah 2: it is "in the persona of Christ" that Jonah prays, and Jerome is at pains to draw the parallels to the New Testament's presentations of the Savior's mission. That Jonah, "tropologically," represents the Savior is assured for Jerome even by his name, which he tells us means both "dove" and "sufferer" (*dolens*). By further etymological plays, Jerome makes Amittai to mean "truth" (*veritas*) and both Jaffa and Nineveh to mean "the beautiful" (*speciosâ pulchra*):

> According to tropology, however, our Lord, that is Jonah—the "dove" or the "sufferer"—for he can be understood as both, whether it be because the Holy Spirit descended in the form of a dove and rested on him, or because he suffered for our wounds, wept over Jerusalem, and "by his bruises we are healed"—he who is truly the Son of Truth, for God is Truth, is sent to Nineveh the beautiful, that is, to the world, than which with our bodily eyes we see nothing more beautiful. Among the Greeks as well the *kosmos* receives its name from the idea of ornament. (On 1:1f., Duval 170, Risse 96; trans. Hegedus 5)[17]

The casting of Jonah into the sea signifies the Savior's descent from heaven to earth; the flood that washes over him, the temptations that he withstood "without sin"; the abyss and the belly of the sea monster, his voluntary descent to hell:

> I who have descended of my own will shall ascend of my own will. I who came as a voluntary captive, am bound to free the captives, so that this might be fulfilled: "Ascending to the heights he led captivity captive" (Ps 67:19; Eph 4:8)—for those who had before been captives in death he has led to life. (Duval 242, Risse 158, trans. Hegedus 37f.)

Even Theodore, who strives in proper Antiochene fashion to make the story historically and psychologically plausible, argues from the outset that the very excess of God's actions was designed precisely to make the story into a prototype of Christ's appearance. The cases of other reluctant prophets, like Moses and Jeremiah, show that God could easily enforce their obedience without the extreme measures he deploys against Jonah. The miracles, then, served the dual purpose of consoling and instructing all the prophets and, above all, foreshadowing the events of Christ's mission and sacrifice (Preface, cols. 318–28).

Thus in the commentary tradition, in contrast to the artistic conventions, it is not identification with the hero Jonah that promises safety against the storm of death, but the resurrection of Christ, which is figured in the story of Jonah. Small wonder that the resurrection would be the pivot around which the commentaries would revolve, for Matthew's Gospel had already wrested the Q saying about Jonah as sign in that direction: "For just as Jonah was three days and three nights in the belly of the sea monster, so for three days and three nights the Son of Man will be in the heart of the earth" (Matt 12:40).

Nevertheless the Lukan form of the saying is not forgotten:

> For just as Jonah became a sign to the people of Nineveh, so the Son of Man will be to this generation. . . . The people of Nineveh will rise up

at the judgment with this generation and condemn it, because they repented at the proclamation of Jonah, and see, something greater than Jonah is here! (Luke 11:30, 32)

It is as the preacher of repentance that Jonah first appears outside the New Testament as well (1 Clement 7:7), though that motif does not appear in the artistic tradition until Byzantine times.[18] Both Jonah, preaching repentance to the Gentile world "in the persona of the Savior," and the penitent Ninevites become important types in the Christian commentary tradition. This was already true in Jewish interpretation, undoubtedly known to Origen and either through him or independently by Theodore and Jerome. It was on Yom Kippur, according to the Talmud (b. Megilla 31a), that Jonah was read; its relevance for that penitential season was evident. The fact that the Ninevites, arch-enemies of Israel, were the objects of Jonah's preaching was of course not lost on the Jewish interpreters. If even the Ninevites could be forgiven, the depths and power of God's mercy were vividly demonstrated. So the leitmotif of the early Greek-language homily on Jonah is God's *philanthrōpia*. The opening remarks of the homilist suggest that the lesson to be learnt from the story is the superiority of God the merciful, not only to the world, but also to the strict judicial construal of God's righteousness. God, by a very familiar rhetorical *syn crisis*, is as much superior to his creation as the lutenist to the lute, the architect to the house, the steersman to the ship, the soul to the body. The application, however, is surprising: God's lawgiving is like a "well crafted ship"—to which, of course, the Steersman of the whole world is superior (Ps-Philo, *De Iona*, 2–4). Before Jonah could heal the Ninevites, first God must heal and educate the physician. Jonah must learn that God's mercy trumps his judgment. Thus the central theme of the homily is related to the discussion, known from both Greek Jewish sources and rabbinic literature, about God's two "powers" or *middot*, mercy and judgment. The same motifs appear in the surviving rabbinic midrash on Jonah: When the Holy One, Blessed be He, saw the Ninevites' penitence, "he stood up from the throne of righteousness and sat down on the throne of mercy, and he was mollified, and he said, 'I forgive.'"[19]

The Jonah story was a worthy example of the power of repentance also in the patristic Christian commentaries. The ascetic Jerome especially emphasized the extreme measures by which the Ninevites shrived themselves and commended themselves to God's mercy. For the church fathers, however, the repentance precisely of Gentiles had a special significance: the Gentiles were—ourselves, the converts who have become the church. "But the great and most beautiful city of Nineveh prefigures the Church, in which there is a greater number than the ten tribes of Israel" (Duval 314, Risse 218, trans. Hegedus 68). So, as Jonah represents the Savior, his preaching signifies Christ's preaching—and that of the Apostles:

> But our Lord is properly said to have risen after the descent into hell, and to have preached the word of the Lord when he sent the apostles to baptize those who were in Nineveh in the name of the Father and of the Son and of the Holy Spirit, that is, in a "three days' journey." (comment on Jonah 3:3–4a, Duval 262, Risse 176; trans. Hegedus 47)

That self-identification with the Ninevites had a further negative implication, setting in motion a tradition of contrast between the repentant Gentiles and the unrepentant Jews that would have baleful consequences throughout the Middle Ages and into modernity.

Theodore already sounds the theme that will become almost the leitmotif of subsequent patristic comment on Jonah. On the historical level, Theodore explains Jonah's dejection, and indeed even his first flight from his prophetic calling (col. 328), as due to his realization "that Jews would be shown to be deserving of extreme punishment for exhibiting no correction despite so much instruction, while Ninevites, who were addicted to godlessness and perversity, all of a sudden at the mere disclosure of the future proved to have a change of heart for the better" (col. 325, trans. Hill 191). Moreover, Jonah recognized this as a sign of the future, "when the nations were called by divine grace and moved en masse to godliness, whereas Jews remained unresponsive and resistant to Christ the Lord, despite having in their midst from the beginning prophecy and teaching about him" (col. 325, trans. Hill 191). Theodore can speak of Israel's "complete rejection" and compares Jonah's unhappiness with Paul's lament in Romans 9:1-5 (col. 328).

Jerome introduces the same theme already at the conclusion of his preface. After citing Matthew 12:41 and Luke 11:32, he takes "this generation" to refer to all unconverted Jews:

> The generation of the Jews is condemned by the believing world, and while Nineveh repented, unbelieving Israel perishes. They have the books, we have the Lord of the books; they have the prophets, we have the understanding of the prophets; "the letter kills" them, us "the Spirit makes alive" (2 Cor 3:6); among them Barabbas the robber is let loose, for us Christ the son of God is set free." (Duval 168, Risse 94, trans. Hegedus 4)

The theme runs throughout Jerome's commentary: "The repentance of the Gentiles is the ruin of the Jews" (*paenitentia gentium, ruina sit Iudaeorum*).[20] Jerome cannot resist contrasting the prayer of the sailors, "Do not hold over us the blood of a just man," which he equates with Pilate's washing his hands, with the cry of the Jews in Matthew 27:25, "His blood be on us and on our children" (comment on 1:14; Duval 214, Risse 134, trans. Hegedus 24). Jerome manages to make even Jonah 2:9, which Jewish interpreters quite naturally take to refer to pagans, apply to disbelieving Jews. First he gives an "historical" comment, describing Jonah as a philosopher reflecting on the general ways of the merciful God who "does not forsake those who guard vain things, he does not hate them, but waits for them to return; but they of their very own accord 'forsake the mercy.'" Then he proceeds to a tropological interpretation: "This also can be prophesied from the person of the Lord concerning the faithlessness of the Jews" (*de Iudaeorum perfidia*) (Duval 184, Risse 170, trans. Hegedus 12).

READING REPENTANCE OR REPENTING OF READING?

After the Holocaust, we can hardly read these remarks of Theodore and Jerome without pain. And they are not exceptions, but early representatives of a long and powerful tradition of reading Jonah—and not only Jonah, but Scripture as a whole taken to be the history of salvation, neatly illuminated against its shadow side, the *Unheilsgeschichte* of the Jews, the history of their sin and rejection. When a way of reading is so deeply woven into the fabric of western Christian thought, liturgy, and habit, and when that way of reading has implicated itself in practices productive of such evil, we have every reason to ask whether Christians ought to trust the Bible to reprove and correct us. Can Jonah, the book, become for us, as Jerome would name him, "the son of truth"? Can the prophet of our repentance be disgorged from the monsters of our own making?

In the midrash, Jonah's big fish takes him to a confrontation with the primaeval sea monster, Leviathan. When we ask questions like those above of this little book, we risk a similar confrontation, with the hermeneutical Leviathan that presently threatens all serious conversation about the use of the Bible in the church. I cannot seriously enter that fray in these few pages, but perhaps the conundrums posed by our reading of Jonah may serve as a small test case of some of the principles that Luke Johnson has proposed to guide the process of "scripture and discernment."

THE CANON

The first principle has to do with reading individual texts within their canonical context. Johnson's reflections on biblical interpretation all take for granted that the church reads each part within the whole, and that it is the canonical form of each text that is, in whatever sense, normative. In that respect he shares a concern, expressed often over the past half-century, that the very successes of modernist historicism threatened to dismantle the canon. The historical-critical method, as it evolved from the eighteenth to the mid-twentieth century, tended to privilege the sources or the antecedent oral traditions over the final stages of composition, historically reconstructed facts over the texts' representations, "original" meanings over meanings attributed by later readers. The result, some warned, was a fragmentation of the biblical witnesses, tearing asunder the unity of the Bible and substituting for the authority invested in Scripture the continually changing judgments of historical probability.[21]

Johnson's concern, however, is less with the unity of the canon than with the *variety* of different witnesses that it shelters within its frame—not the exclusions that constituted its formal definitions, but the de facto inclusiveness that the long history of its reading and writing communities had created. That diversity, far from being something to be feared, calls us "to embrace the freedom God gives us." Recognition of it "could not ... be more in tune with the implicit logic of the canonizers."[22] From this perspective, reading Jonah within the Christian canon of Scripture would, counter-intuitively, liberate the story itself from the constraints of any all-embracing master narrative or theological system. Trusting the canon, we could trust the individual composition's own integrity. The text, performed within the practice that constitutes a community acknowledging the text as part of its canon, could be trusted to do what it is meant to do. (Meant—by whom or what? By the author? By the community? By God? A worrying question that I must perforce leave unpursued here.) Tantalizingly, this way of construing a canonical reading points toward a way in which it might be possible to heal the modern breach between critical practice, which attempts to rediscover the way the individual text would have worked within its historical context, and faithful appropriation, which wants to hear what the text can be made to say in the here and now. Easier said than done. Johnson's proposals, however, do offer a provocative starting point for attempts to effect that reconciliation.

The crucial question is how we are to construe that dialectic between the internal integrity of the text and the larger field of reading that is constructed, however malleably and open-endedly, by the fact of the canon and the history of its practical use. Johnson is right that we ought to renounce the attempts "to suppress the complexities, ambiguities, and contradictions in Scripture by means of a univocal reading," whether by means of a "biblical theology" or by means of an historicist construction of Jesus or other biblical events.[23] We have seen how the master narrative that we label *Heilsgeschichte* entailed the church's swallowing Jonah, as it swallowed the whole of Jewish Scripture into its "Old Testament," in the process transforming rejected Israel into its own primary anti-self, the unrepentant Other. If we looked at the history of the church's reading of other texts, we could multiply examples of mischief wrought by the quest for a single master narrative to explain the Bible, reality, and ourselves.

Yet to recognize all this does not require us to conclude that we ought to eschew every constructed narrative that offers a story of the Bible as a whole. There would be no canon at all—that is to say, the practice that eventually was codified as canon would not have evolved—had there not been, from the beginning of the Christian movement, manifold attempts to make sense of what God was doing by saying, through the texts of Scripture, what God had done before. And those attempts at sense-making continued and adapted modes of reading and misreading that generations of Jewish readers, in constantly changing historical and cultural settings, had learned.

There is no saying of Jesus that is comprehensible without hearing resonances of the Law and the Prophets, no New Testament document in which the "echoes of Scripture" do not resound.[24] The Jonah story would make no sense if we did not know what a prophet is, characteristics of the call narratives of Israel's prophets, and certain key phrases in earlier reflections on the character of Israel's God.

In a sense, then, the emergence of a canon recognizes and formalizes a practice of intertextual hearing, reading, and writing that implied a drive toward making some comprehensive story. The key word in Johnson's description of the mistake to be avoided is "univocal." It is the quest for a single, unambiguous narrative, or theological system, or moral program that runs counter both to the history of human experience and to the multiple, often contradictory witnesses contained within the ample boundaries of the canon. It is the "imperialism of the single vision" that must be resisted.[25]

THE COMMUNITY

Central to Johnson's conviction that the canon authorizes freedom at least as much as it constrains heresy is his understanding, shared with a growing company of theologians, philosophers, and literary theorists, that meaning does not reside in a text but in the dialectic between a text and a reading community. To describe this dialectic, Johnson has undertaken to rehabilitate for theological interpretation the category of religious experience, so dear to modernist theology of a century ago and so disfavored by more recent biblical theology.[26] Theology, then, becomes "a reading of the *texts of human lives* in a continuing process of self-revelation by the Living God, rather than as, first of all, a reading of the *texts of scripture* as a record of a past and finished revelation." "Neither the experience of God in the community as expressed through narratives of faith, nor the text of scripture is a *norma non normata*; both are essential moments in a dialectic of experience and interpretation that constantly characterizes the living faith community."[27]

The instantiation of that community that Johnson has principally in view is a small group engaged in moral decision-making.[28] It is important to recognize, however, that the particular group participates in a much larger field of discourse. That larger field has both cultural and historical dimensions. In the decision-making process, not only the larger ecclesiastical context, but also the embeddedness of that context in the culture of the wider, non-Christian society must be taken into account. And the history of the community, including the history of the effects of its construal of scripture, must also be reckoned with.

The effective context of interpretation is thus hugely complex, but not daunting for Johnson:

> Within a reading community dedicated to the practices of Christian piety, neither the complexities of the biblical text nor the ambiguities of human experience need be feared or suppressed. A community so grounded in practice and so nurtured by Scripture's wisdom can be trusted to read with discrimination and discernment according to the Mind of Christ.[29]

That sounds a trifle too optimistic. The history of the community and the *Wirkungsgeschichte* of the Christian Bible are unfortunately punctuated by countless instances of evil practiced in the name of God and revealed truth. The process of discernment has too often gone horribly, destructively wrong, as of course Johnson knows quite well. "In the end," as Dale Martin observes, "there are no guarantees that we or anyone else will not use the text unethically."[30] There are no guarantees, but awareness of the ways previous interpretations have gone astray is at least a prerequisite for trying to avoid really pernicious readings.

Returning to our paradigm, the little book of Jonah, what may we learn from the role of the community in its interpretation by early Christians? For one thing, the patterns we saw in the deployment of the Jonah cycle in early Christian burial art demonstrate a certain tenacity on the part of circles of Christians not represented in the literary tradition, a consistent extraction of the fish story from the main narrative and a rich incorporation into it of iconic traditions familiar in the "pagan" world around. Johnson, inveighing against "the academic captivity of theology," should be pleased, for the academic theologians like Theodore and Jerome seem to have had little effect on the way their parishioners buried their dead, nor did the artistic traditions often influence the academics, for all we can see.

So on the one hand we see the community—or at least those representatives of it who could afford to buy the artistic productions that remain for us to see—plucking out of the text just those elements that were useful for a particular setting, and easily fusing them with elements from the larger culture, with minimal "conversion." On the other hand, we find learned commentators whose "historical" or "literal" reading seems at our distance often tone deaf, while their tropological reading dismembers the story line in order to impose on the parts a theological straitjacket. Does the text itself have any latent power to reassert itself against bad or dangerous readings?

THE TEXT

Johnson stresses the importance of hearing the texts in their "literal" sense, by which he means "the text in its most publicly available form, the text as it comes to us most as 'other,' and [as] least shaped by our individual preconceptions and preconstruals."[31] This is a careful formulation, but it only hints at one of the central problems: the literal sense is a social construct (perhaps implied by "publicly available," though I believe Johnson intends the weight of this phrase to be nearly the opposite). Consequently that corrective dialectic between community and text, on which we have placed our hope for readings that would heal our sinful errors, might turn out to be an illusion, the self-congratulatory dialectic of the community with its own "preconceptions and preconstruals" mirrored in the domesticated text.

The modernist project in biblical interpretation sought to expose and reverse that fiction by, in effect, estranging the text from the community. Plucked from its traditional and comfortable setting and restored, by the magic of historical science, to its original context and meaning, the text could stand over against the community as a reformative force. It is now fashionable to sneer, from our postmodernist tower, at the presumption of that project, but in fact the historian's role in trying to discover the probable force of a given literary production or rhetorical composition, within the cultural setting or settings in which it was heard when it came to be so valued that eventually it became part of Jewish or Christian Scripture, remains useful and necessary. It is one step in trying to preserve the "otherness" of the text. To be sure, we discover, ironically, that the historian, too, is not immune from projection. (Those of us who once read Augustine, Calvin, or Barth, never mind Freud, should hardly be surprised.) If the attempt to make historiography scientific sometimes occasions a pseudoscientific arrogance, it is correctible by better science.

Historical criticism has disappointed those who sought certainty. The attempt to redefine the literal sense as the historical sense, and thus implicitly to give to the historical critic the last word in the polyphony of interpretation, failed, as it deserved to fail. Yet the very open-endedness of historical judgments, unable to leap from probability to certainty, reflects the genius of real science, which restlessly pursues new data and new construals of the old, and builds self-corrective measures into its own practice and its own social forms. Historical criticism, self-reflective and chastened, has an important role still to play in liberating that integrity of the individual text and that polyphony of the canon (and of the community's reading) that Johnson advocates.

What is most frightening to those religious people, whether "conservatives" or "liberals," who confuse confidence with certainty[32] is the collapse of the distinction between fact and fiction and, with it, the distinction between reality and imagination. With the end of Cartesian foundationalism, the bugbear of "historical relativism" appears to have conquered—but in fact it turns out to be a friendly ghost. All our perceptions of reality are indeed inescapably relative. However, that does not mean that there is no truth of the matter—only that we do not and never shall (in this life) possess it.

A quiet revolution has taken place in late modern epistemology. Garrett Green has brilliantly summed up some of the most important implications for theology. It was Feuerbach, the quintessential modernist, who taught us that "'imagination' is the diametric opposite of 'reality'; it is the organ of fiction and error."

As soon as one makes the postmodern turn, however, the first thing to go is the foundational confidence that we have reliable access to a "reality" against which imagination might be judged "illusory." Imagination now becomes the unavoidable means of apprehending "reality," though there is, of course, no guarantee that it will succeed.[33]

"The new place of imagination," says Green, "is nowhere more evident than in recent philosophy of science, which one might summarize by saying that the history of science is the history of the scientific imagination." So Green urges Christians to welcome the Feuerbachian thesis that religion "is a product of human imagination." There is no escape from the obligation to interpret, and there is no interpretation without imagination. "In other words, right interpretation depends on right imagination."[34] Obviously this perspective has direct and important implications for interpreting Scripture—perhaps most easily seen in a text like Jonah, which (at least to our modern ears and, we suspect, to its intended audience in ancient Israel) is transparently fiction.[35]

While Johnson's definition of the "literal sense" is rather unspecific, we know from hints in his essays and from his interpretive practice exhibited in many pages of commentary that the "literal" is for him very close to the "literary." That is, the beginning point for interpretation is to hear the rhetorical wholeness of a given text. So we come round again to listen to Jonah's quirky story. To be sure, I can single out here only a few of the more salient features of the narrative, but they are sufficient to suggest the power still inherent in such a text.[36]

The story begins with familiar words: "The word of YHWH came to Jonah, son of Amittai, 'Arise, go. . . .'" We know at once, if we know Israel's scriptures at all, that we are being told about a prophet—though Jonah is never called a prophet in this story. The very knowledgeable reader may recall, however, a small footnote in the account of the doings of King Jeroboam II of Israel, to the effect that Jeroboam's expansionist policies were at the behest of "the word of YHWH God of Israel, which he spoke by the hand of his servant Jonah, son of Amittai, the prophet"

(2 Kgs 14:25). The editor of that earlier narrative comments that God chose to save Israel by Jeroboam's hand, despite Jeroboam's and Israel's great sin, because the Lord saw Israel's distress (vv. 26 f.). The writer of the Book of Jonah can hardly have expected his audience to hear an echo of that deuteronomistic note, but, as we shall see, it is rather apposite.

"Arise, go to Nineveh, . . ." and the next line begins as expected, "And Jonah arose. . . ." But then the spell is broken, and we have the first hint that we are hearing a parody of a prophet's story: "And Jonah arose to flee to Tarshish [wherever that was, certainly in the opposite direction from Nineveh] away from the presence of YHWH; and he went down. . . ." He went down to Joppa, and then down, down, down: as every commentator points out, the verb *yrd* echoes like a dirge through the first chapter, even comically in the *wayêrdam* of verse 5, his deep sleep that the LXX renders even more comically as "he snored."

Of course reluctant prophets were not new to Israel's story: Moses, the *Urprophet*, already establishes the theme (Exod 3–4), and it reaches its eloquent climax in the anguish of Jeremiah's complaints. Especially interesting is the case of Elijah, who also ran away—to be sure, after beginning to obey his prophetic call, not before, and only after receiving a quite credible death threat from the queen herself (1 Kgs 19:3). Sitting under a broom tree in the wilderness, he pleads for death: "Now, YHWH, take my life from me" (v. 4). It is hard to think that the almost identical language in Jonah 4:3, *weʿatah yhwh qaḥ-naʾ ʾet-nafšî mimmenî*, is not a deliberate echo, then echoed twice in turn. We might even fancy that the castor oil bush so important in the final verses of Jonah is a vastly amplified echo of Elijah's broom tree.[37] Be that as it may, the implied reader of Jonah is well versed in Israel's scriptures and traditions. No one has to tell this reader that Nineveh, that "by-God big city" (3:3), is Israel's stereotypical enemy, the personification of wickedness.

Of all the echoes in this story, none is more vivid and none more fundamental than the quotation in 4:2. Yahweh himself has revealed to Moses on Sinai that he is "a God merciful and gracious, slow to anger, and abounding in steadfast love [*ḥesed*]" (Exod 34:6). It is a line that the writers and singers of Israel had loved to quote, with multiple variations: Numbers 14:18; Nehemiah 9:17; Psalms 85:15; 103:8; 145:8; Joel 2:13, though some, like Jonah, prefer the subsequent line, "yet by no means clearing the guilty" (Exod 34:7c).

Here the irony of the anonymous satirist reaches its climax. Jonah rages against God's mercy: it was precisely because he *knew* that Yahweh was a merciful God and, therefore, that his preaching might lead not to God's punishing wicked Nineveh but to God's forgiving those sinners, that Jonah fled in the beginning (Jonah 4:2). Then follows the delightful, half-comical episode of the bush and the worm, the object lesson that leaves Jonah unrepentant, "angry enough to die" (v. 9). The last word, however, is neither Jonah's nor the narrators, but Yahweh's:

> You are concerned about the bush, for which you did not labor and which you did not grow; it came into being in a night and perished in a night. And should I not be concerned about Nineveh, that great city, in which there are more than a hundred and twenty thousand persons who do not know their right hand from their left, and also many animals? (vv. 10-11)

The satiric novella of Jonah has had several lives in the history of its reading by both Jews and Christians. Some have had good effects, some bad. Reading the story with our own particular histories, we are sometimes astonished, sometimes appalled by the early traditions. We must then acknowledge the risk of reading texts that count as sacred: we, too, will project our own prejudices and our own hopes into the text. The metaphor of the text "speaking" or "teaching" may conceal many kinds of bad faith. Yet the tradition, the community, the canon, and the text itself each have a grain that resists our manipulations.

The catacomb painters and carvers understood one thing: to hear this story aright, one must identify with Jonah. And to identify with him is to be able to pray with him that psalm—which seems so ill fitting in its context that many modern commentators have thought it an alien intrusion—the psalm of rejoicing in the God who saves even the unworthy faithful from the maw of death. But of course they were wrong to stop there. It is that final, long question from God, addressed to Jonah and to every reader, that demands the most troubling identification. The story demands (the agential metaphor again) that we recognize ourselves in the prophet who resists the mercy of God, who says, "See, I knew you were a God of mercy and grace, but really—forgiving *those* people? I'd rather die than see them live." The anonymous ancient preacher in a Greek synagogue came closest to a proper summary: the story is about God's *philanthrōpia*, his embarrassingly universal love of humanity (and, don't forget, the animals). Yet the philosophical term, however apt, remains an abstraction. What the story itself does for us when we let it, when we hear it within a community shaped by the polyphony of the multitude of often conflicting voices from this text and the others, with the echoes of centuries of good and bad readings ringing in our ears, is more powerful than any abstraction. The job of the interpreter is to help that complicated hearing happen.

NOTES

Introduction

1. Luke Timothy Johnson, with the assistance of Todd C. Penner, *The Writings of the New Testament: An Interpretation*, rev. ed. (Minneapolis: Augsburg Fortress, 1999), 16.

Religious Experience in the New Testament

1. Luke Timothy Johnson, *Religious Experience in Earliest Christianity: A Missing Dimension in New Testament Studies* (Minneapolis: Augsburg Fortress, 1998).
2. See particularly my *Jesus and the Spirit: A Study of the Religious and Charismatic Experience of Jesus and the First Christians as Reflected in the New Testament* (London: SCM, 1975; Grand Rapids, Mich.: Eerdmans, 1997).
3. *Institutes*, 1.7.4–5.
4. "The Witness of the Spirit," *Forty-four Sermons* (London: Epworth, 1944), 115. The language echoes Wesley's own account of his Aldersgate experience in his Journal for May 24, 1738: "In the evening I went very unwillingly to a society in Aldersgate Street, where one was reading Luther's preface to the *Epistle to the Romans*. About a quarter before nine, while he was describing the change that God works in the heart through faith in Christ, I felt my heart strangely warmed. I felt I did trust in Christ, Christ alone for salvation; and an assurance was given me that He had taken away *my* sins, even *mine*, and saved *me* from the law of sin and death."
5. Examples from the hymns of Charles Wesley include, as found in *Hymns and Psalms*, 325 v.4—"Inspire the living faith, Which whosoe'er receives, The witness in himself he hath, and consciously believes;" 728 v.1—"How can we sinners know Our sins on earth forgiven?" 740 v.1—"My God! I know, I feel thee mine, And will not quit the claim."
6. *Religious Experience*, 12–22; he then begins a critique of J. Z. Smith, which runs through the book.
7. It was always a matter of surprise to me that the great study of *Enthusiasm* by R. A. Knox (Oxford: Clarendon, 1950) assumed that the phenomenon had more or less ceased with the eighteenth century, when already the latest

manifestation of Christian enthusiasm (Pentecostalism) was burgeoning almost under Knox's very nose.

8. H. Gunkel, *Die Wirkungen des heiligen Geistes* (Göttingen, 1888), 83–91 (here 86).

9. *TDNT*, 6.396.

10. G. D. Fee, *God's Empowering Presence: The Holy Spirit in the Letters of Paul* (Peabody, Mass.: Hendrickson, 1994).

11. *Religious Experience*, 9.

12. Gen 8:1; Exod 10:13, 19; Num 11:31; 1 Kgs 18:45; Prov 25:23; Jer 10:13; Hos 13:15; Jonah 4:8.

13. Exod 14:21; 1 Kgs 19:11; Pss 48:7; 55:8; Isa 7:2; Ezek 27:26; Jonah 1:4.

14. Gen 6:17; 7:15, 22; Pss 31:5; 32:2; Eccles 3:19, 21; Jer 10:14; 51:17; Ezek 11:5.

15. Gen 41:8; Num 5:14, 30; Judg 8:3; 1 Kgs 21:5; 1 Chron 5:26; Job 21:4; Prov 29:11; Jer 51:17; Dan 2:1, 3.

16. Gen 45:27; Josh 5:1; Judg 15:19; 1 Sam 30:12; 1 Kgs 10:5; Ps 143:7; Isa 19:3.

17. Judg 3:10; 6:34; 11:29; 13:25; 14:6, 19; 15:14-15; 1 Sam 11:6.

18. Num 24:2; 1 Sam 10:6, 10; 19:20, 23-24; Neh 9:20, 30; Prov 1:23; Ezek 2:2; 3:1-4, 22-24; etc. Zech 7:12.

19. "Prophesy to the *ruach*, prophesy son of man, and say to the *ruach*: 'Thus says the Lord GOD: Come from the four winds (*ruchoth*), O *ruach*, and breathe upon these slain, that they may live.' I prophesied as he commanded me, and the *ruach* came into them, and they lived, and stood on their feet, a vast multitude."

20. "The *pneuma* blows where it will, and you hear the sound of it, but you do not know where it comes from or where it goes. So is everyone who is born of the *pneuma*."

21. Fee resolves the issue by translating the ambiguous references by the inelegant "S/spirit" (*God's Empowering Presence*, 24–26).

22. John 6:63; Rom 8:11; 1 Cor 15:45; 2 Cor 3:6; 1 Pet 3:18.

23. Luke is explicit that Jesus' baptism had been completed before the Spirit descended on him, while he was praying (Luke 3:21-22); and John does not even mention Jesus' baptism by John (John 1:33). See further my *Jesus Remembered* (Grand Rapids, Mich.: Eerdmans, 2003), 372–74.

24. *Jesus and the Spirit*, ch. 3.

25. See further F. Philip, *The Origins of Pauline Pneumatology*, WUNT 2.194 (Tübingen, Germany: Mohr Siebeck, 2005).

26. L. Newbigin, *The Household of God* (London: SCM, 1953), 95.

27. I suggest this criticism of Luke in *Unity and Diversity in the New Testament* (London: SCM, 1977; 2006), #44.

28. In what follows I take off from and develop the much fuller discussion of *Jesus and the Spirit* ch. 8 and particularly 293-97.

29. So the majority of commentators on 1 Corinthians.

30. See further my "Discernment of Spirits—A Neglected Gift," *The Christ and the Spirit: Vol. 2 Pneumatology* (Grand Rapids, Mich.: Eerdmans, 1998), 311-28.

31. See my *The Theology of Paul the Apostle* (Grand Rapids, Mich.: Eerdmans; Edinburgh, Scotland: T & T Clark, 1998), 55-61.

32. For charisma as the result or effect or expression of *charis* ("grace") see my *Jesus and the Spirit*, 205-7, and *Theology of Paul*, 553-60.

33. I thus summarily refer to major emphases of *Jesus and the Spirit*, ch. 10, and *Theology of Paul*, #18.

34. See further M. J. Gorman, *Cruciformity: Paul's Narrative Spirituality of the Cross* (Grand Rapids, Mich.: Eerdmans, 2001).

Spiritual Sacrifices in Early Christianity

1. Jeffrey Carter, ed., *Understanding Religious Sacrifice: A Reader* (London: Continuum, 2003).

2. Gerd Theissen, *The Religion of the Earliest Churches: Creating a Symbolic World* (Minneapolis: Augsburg Fortress, 1999), 139-60.

3. Luke Timothy Johnson, *Religious Experience in Earliest Christianity: A Missing Dimension in New Testament Studies* (Minneapolis: Augsburg Fortress, 1998).

4. Johnson, *The Gospel of Luke*, SP 3 (Collegeville, Minn.: Liturgical Press, 1991); and *The Acts of the Apostles*, SP 5 (Collegeville, Minn.: Liturgical Press, 1992).

5. For a classic treatment, see Roland de Vaux, *Ancient Israel: Its Life and Institutions* (New York: McGraw Hill, 1961), 415-56. For a recent discussion, see Jonathan Klawans, *Purity, Sacrifice, and the Temple: Symbolism and Supersessionism in the Study of Ancient Judaism* (New York: Oxford University Press, 2006).

6. See Martin Nilsson, *A History of Greek Religion* (Oxford: Clarendon Press, 1949); and Walter Burkert, *Greek Religion* (Cambridge, Mass.: Harvard University Press, 1985).

7. See Jacob Milgrom, *Leviticus 1-16*, AB 3 (New York: Doubleday, 1991).

8. For translations, see Geza Vermes, *The Complete Dead Sea Scrolls in English* (London: Penguin, 2004).

9. See E. P. Sanders, *Jesus and Judaism* (Philadelphia: Fortress Press, 1985); and N. T. Wright, *Jesus and the Victory of God* (Minneapolis: Augsburg Fortress, 1996).

10. See Raymond F. Collins, *First Corinthians*, SP 7 (Collegeville, Minn.: Liturgical Press, 1999), 304–91.

11. For translations, see Jacob Neusner, *The Mishnah: A New Translation* (New Haven: Yale University Press, 1991).

12. Neusner, "Map without Territory: Mishnah's System of Sacrifice and Sanctuary," *HR* 19 (1979): 103–27.

13. Klawans, *Purity, Sacrifice, and the Temple*, 211.

14. For major commentaries, see Brendan Byrne, *Romans*, SP 6 (Collegeville, Minn.: Liturgical Press, 1996); James D. G. Dunn, *Romans*, WBC 38 (Dallas: Word, 1988); and Joseph A. Fitzmyer, *Romans*, AB 33 (New York: Doubleday, 1993).

15. See Xavier Paul Viagulamuthu, *Offering Our Bodies as a Living Sacrifice to God: A Study in Pauline Spirituality Based on Romans 12,1* (Rome: Pontifical Gregorian University Press, 2002).

16. For major commentaries, see Paul Achtemeier, *1 Peter: A Commentary* (Hermeneia; Minneapolis: Augsburg Fortress, 1996); John H. Elliott, *1 Peter*, AB 37B (New York: Doubleday, 2000); and Donald Senior, *1 Peter*, SP 15 (Collegeville, Minn.: Liturgical Press, 2003).

17. Elliott, *A Home for the Homeless: A Social-Scientific Criticism of 1 Peter, Its Situation and Strategy* (Minneapolis: Augsburg Fortress, 1990).

18. Martin Albl, *"And Scripture Cannot Be Broken": The Form and Function of the Early Christian Testimonia*, NovTSup 96 (Leiden, Netherlands: Brill, 1999).

19. See Pliny's "Letter to Trajan," *Epistles* 10.96.

20. Thomas G. Long, *Hebrews* (Louisville: John Knox, 1997).

21. Daniel J. Harrington, *What Are They Saying About the Letter to the Hebrews?* (New York: Paulist, 2005).

22. George H. Guthrie, *Hebrews*, NIV Application Commentary (Grand Rapids: Zondervan, 1998).

23. For major commentaries, see Harold W. Attridge, *The Epistle to the Hebrews*, Hermeneia (Philadelphia: Fortress Press, 1989); Craig R. Koester, *Hebrews*, AB 36 (New York: Doubleday, 2001); and William L. Lane, *Hebrews*, WBC 47 (Dallas; Word, 1991).

24. Robert J. Daly, *Christian Sacrifice: The Judaeo-Christian Background before Origen* (Washington, D.C.: Catholic University of America Press, 1978); and *The Origin of the Christian Doctrine of Sacrifice* (Philadelphia: Fortress Press, 1977).

"Speaking the Very Words of God": New Testament Perspectives on the Characteristics of Christian Speech

1. See Luke Timothy Johnson, *The Letter of James*, AB 37A (New York: Doubleday, 1995); also his collected essays on James found in *Brother of Jesus, Friend of God: Studies in the Letter of James* (Grand Rapids, Mich.: Eerdmans, 2004).

2. See the classical references amassed by L. T. Johnson in "Taciturnity and True Religion," in *Brother of Jesus, Friend of God*, 155-67. Dibelius' commentary on James is particularly useful for noting the classical parallels in James; see Martin Dibelius, *James: A Commentary on the Epistle of James*, Hermeneia (Philadelphia: Fortress Press, 1976).

3. See L. T. Johnson, "Taciturnity and True Religion," esp. 157–64.

4. The Greek text of 3:6b is quite difficult here, leading some commentators to suggest the text is corrupted. However, while the grammar is complex there is no need to alter the wording, and the basic meaning is clear. James asserts at the beginning of the verse (which is not in dispute) that the "tongue is a fire"; in the latter half of the verse James seems to use one verb ("to be placed," *kathistatai*) with several nominatives. The literal meaning can be translated as Hartin suggests in his recent commentary: "the tongue is the world of iniquity placed among our members"; see Patrick J. Hartin, *James*, Sacra Pagina (Collegeville, Minn.: Liturgical Press, 2003), 176–77.

5. See L. T. Johnson, *The Letter of James*, 264.

6. In her commentary Sophie Laws suggests that in 3:15 James means that the kind of twisted wisdom that leads to evil speech is "devilish" but not truly "demonic," suggesting "similarity rather than origin" (see Sophie Laws, *The Epistle of James*, Harpers New Testament Commentaries [New York: Harper & Row, 1980], 161). However, most commentators believe that, given James's overall dualistic view, he does intend to see such evil as demonic in origin; see, the discussion in P. Hartin, *James*, 193–94.

7. Paul, of course, is concerned about false teaching, particularly that of opponents who undermine his own preaching of a law-free gospel; see, for example, Gal 1:6-9; 5:7-12.

8. The Pauline authorship of Colossians is still debated; for the purposes of this article I am listing it under the deutero-Pauline category.

9. See Margaret Y. MacDonald, *Colossians and Ephesians*, Sacra Pagina (Collegeville, Minn.: Liturgical Press, 2000), 173, who refers to Plutarch's use of the same metaphor; also James D. G. Dunn, *The Epistles to the Colossians and to Philemon*, New International Greek Testament Commentary (Grand Rapids, Mich.: Eerdmans, 1996), 266–67.

10. See M. Y. MacDonald, *Colossians and Ephesians*, 306.

11. References to "grace" (*charis*) as an expression of God's gift of salvation are frequent in Ephesians: see 1:2, 6, 7; 2:5, 7, 8; 3:2,7, 8; 4:7, 29; 6:24; concern for the unity of the church is a persistent motif throughout the letter; see, for example, 2:11-22; 4:1-16, 25-32.

12. See the discussion in Donald Senior and Daniel Harrington, *1 Peter, Jude and 2 Peter*, Sacra Pagina (Collegeville, Minn.: Liturgical Press, 2003), 7–10; also, Paul J. Achtemeier, *1 Peter*, Hermeneia (Minneapolis: Augsburg Fortress, 1996), 23–35; John H. Elliott, *1 Peter*, AB37B (New York: Doubleday, 2000), 87–117.

13. Cf. D. Senior, *1 Peter*, 95–96.

14. See I. Howard Marshall, *The Pastoral Epistles*, ICC (Edinburgh, Scotland: T & T Clark, 1999), 489.

15. On this, see I. H. Marshall, *The Pastoral Epistles*, 766.

16. John Coffey, "The Myth of Secular Tolerance," *Cambridge Papers* 12 (2003): 1–4.

"For the Glory of God": Theology and Experience in Paul's Letter to the Romans

1. *Religious Experience in Earliest Christianity: A Missing Dimension in New Testament Studies* (Minneapolis: Augsburg Fortress, 1998), 1. It is gratifying to recall that this volume began as Johnson's 1997 Stone Lectures at Princeton Theological Seminary, and it is a pleasure to offer this essay in his honor.

2. Ibid., 2.

3. Ibid.

4. See John M. G. Barclay, "'Do We Undermine the Law?' A Study of Romans 14.1–15.6," *Paul and the Mosaic Law*, ed. James D. G. Dunn (Grand Rapids, Mich.: Eerdmans, 1996), 287–308.

5. *Reading Romans: A Literary and Theological Commentary* (New York: Crossroad Publishing, 1997), 10.

6. *Romans*, ANTC (Nashville: Abingdon Press, 2005), 385.

7. *Romans*, Hermeneia (Minneapolis: Augsburg Fortress, 2006), 157.

8. On the concluding doxology, see the discussion and bibliography below. Two brief treatments of doxology and thanksgiving appear in Paul S. Minear, "Gratitude and Mission in the Epistle to the Romans," *Basileia: Walter Freytag zum 60. Geburtstag*, eds. Jan Hermelink and Hans Jochen Margull (Stuttgart: Evang. Missionsverglad GMBH, 1959), 42–48; and A. B. du Toit, "Die Kirche als Doxologische Gemeinschaft im Römerbrief," *Neotestamentica* 27 (1993): 69–77.

9. Translations are my own unless otherwise noted.

10. The exegetical argument in support of this connection between the "desires" and enslavement to Sin and Death may be found in Beverly Roberts Gaventa, *Our Mother Saint Paul* (Louisville: Westminster John Knox, 2006), 113–23.

11. "Gratitude and Mission in the Epistle to the Romans," 46.

12. This understanding is adopted by a number of commentators, of course, but in my judgment the rhetorical situation is somewhat more complex, with verses 18-32 explicitly attacking Gentile sinfulness while implicitly including Jews in its purview. Among Jews, Gentiles are notorious for their idolatry and sexual immorality, but Jews may also be said to withhold praise and thanksgiving from God, as 2:1–3:19 makes clear.

13. See Gaventa, "From Toxic Speech to the Redemption of Doxology in Paul's Letter to the Romans," *The Word Leaps the Gap: Essays in Scripture and Theology in Honor of Richard Hays*, eds. A. Katherine Grieb, C. Kavin Rowe, and J. Ross Wagner (Grand Rapids, Mich.: Eerdmans, 2008).

14. On this passage, see Edward Adams, "Abraham's Faith and Gentile Disobedience: Textual Links between Romans 1 and 4," *JSNT* 65 (1997): 47–66.

15. As in Heikki Räisänen, *Paul and the Law*, WUNT 29 (Tübingen, Germany: J. C. B. Mohr, 1983); and E. P. Sanders, *Paul, the Law, and the Jewish People* (Philadelphia: Fortress Press, 1983).

16. *Commentary on Romans* (Grand Rapids, Mich.: Eerdmans, 1980), 47, 49.

17. Numerous questions attend verse 17b, but I am not convinced by the argument that it is a gloss, since there is no manuscript evidence to support that thesis (see the discussion of this problem in Jewett, *Romans*, 417–19). Admittedly, the reference to a "type of teaching" is peculiar, but Paul's repeated use of *paradidōmi* in Romans also needs to be factored into this discussion (1:24, 26, 28; 4:25; and 8:32); see the discussion in Gaventa, *Our Mother Saint Paul*, 113–23, 194–97; Idem, "Interpreting the Death of Jesus Apocalyptically: Reconsidering Romans 8:32," in *Jesus and Paul Reconnected: Fresh Pathways into*

an Old Debate, ed. Todd D. Still (Grand Rapids, Mich.: Eerdmans, 2007), 125–45.

18. "What Makes Romans Tick?" *Pauline Theology. Volume III: Romans*, eds. David M. Hay and E. Elizabeth Johnson (Minneapolis: Augsburg Fortress, 1995), 25.

19. On the role of sin in Romans 7, see especially Paul W. Meyer, "The Worm at the Core of the Apple: Exegetical Reflections on Romans 7," *The Word in this World: Essays in New Testament Exegesis and Theology* NTL, ed. John T. Carroll (Louisville: Westminster John Knox Press, 2004), 57–77.

20. *Romans*, 417.

21. One suspects that the movement runs in both directions: *from* upbuilding of the community *to* gratitude to God and also *from* gratitude *to* upbuilding. In his remarkable volume *The Beloved Community: How Faith Shapes Social Justice, From the Civil Rights Movement to Today*, Charles Marsh writes what might be regarded as a contemporary gloss on Romans 14: "Gratitude lifts us out of our natural instinct to find fault and to belittle others. Gratitude is more than thanks to God for the good things. Gratitude reshapes the self in relation to others by releasing the other from our compulsions of truth" (New York: Basic Books, 2005), 214. Yet it is significant that Romans points again and again toward God's glory.

22. Leander Keck comments that "the horizon of 15:7-13 is nothing short of the entire argument" ("Christology, Soteriology, and the Praise of God [Romans 15:7-13]," *The Conversation Continues: Studies in Paul and John in Honor of J. Louis Martyn*, eds. Robert T. Fortna and Beverly R. Gaventa [Nashville: Abingdon Press, 1990], 85). Johnson identifies 15:1-13 as "the climax of Paul's theological argument" (*Reading Romans*, 203). N. T. Wright regards it as a "triple conclusion" to 14:1–15:13, to 12:1–15:13, and to the entirety of the letter ("Romans," *The New Interpreter's Bible*: Volume X [Nashville: Abingdon Press, 2002], 744). Jewett refers to 15:7-13 as the "coda" for "the entire preceding argument of the letter" (*Romans*, 887).

23. Keck rightly notes that all of the Scripture quotations "paraphrase the theme of glorifying God" ("Christology, Soteriology, and the Praise of God," 88).

24. On this translation, see J. Ross Wagner, "The Christ, Servant of Jew and Gentile: A Fresh Approach to Romans 15:8-9," *JBL* 116 (1997): 473–85.

25. Brendan Byrne, *Romans*, Sacra Pagina (Collegeville, Minn.: Liturgical Press, 1996), 428. By contrast, Keck regards the "universal praise of God" anticipated in Romans 15 as "the actual material soteriological alternative to the root

problem of humanity: not giving praise to God or honoring God" (as in 1:21; "Christology, Soteriology, and the Praise of God," 94).

26. C. K. Barrett, for example, writes that "the great theme" in this passage "is the union of Jew and Gentile in Christ" that "marks the full end of God's purposes" (*The Epistle to the Romans,* HNTC; New York: Harper and Bros., 1957], 272).

27. "Christ Prays the Psalms: Paul's Use of an Early Christian Exegetical Convention," *The Future of Christology: Essays in Honor of Leander E. Keck,* eds. Abraham J. Malherbe and Wayne A. Meeks (Minneapolis: Augsburg Fortress, 1993), 137–52.

28. See the discussion in James L. Bailey and Lyle D. Vander Broek, *Literary Forms in the New Testament: A Handbook* (Louisville: Westminster John Knox Press, 1992), 72, and the literature cited there.

29. *Romans,* AB 33 (New York: Doubleday, 1993), 285.

30. *Romans 1-8,* WBC 38A (Dallas: Word Books, 1988) 64, 73.

31. The debate is reviewed at length in C. E. B. Cranfield, *The Epistle to the Romans. Volume II,* ICC (Edinburgh, Scotland: T & T Clark, 1979), 464–70.

32. N. T. Wright characterizes 9:5 as "a kind of heading for what is to come" (*Romans,* 630).

33. The "amen" is omitted in P^{46}, presumably because that manuscript adds the doxology in 16:25-27 at this point. It is also omitted in A, F, G, and a few other manuscripts, but is included in B, C, D, ψ, and elsewhere. Given that the letter continues in chapter 16, the omission in some manuscripts may reflect a scribal sense that an "amen" should not appear just prior to the greetings and benediction of 16:1-23.

34. Contra Byrne, *Romans,* 462. See Douglas Moo's helpful review of the evidence and the scholarly judgments in *Romans,* NICNT (Grand Rapids, Mich.: Eerdmans, 1996), 936–37. Johnson notes the large number of textual variants in chapter 16, especially regarding 16:25-27, but eventually comments that the doxology "magnificently summarizes" the letter as a whole (*Reading Romans,* 223). One of the arguments frequently adduced *against* Pauline authorship of the doxology is that Paul does not elsewhere conclude a letter with a doxology. Given the many ways in which Romans is distinctive and the recurrent attention here to elements of praise and thanksgiving, that strikes me as a particularly weak argument (for further problems with arguing from the conclusions to other Pauline letters, see Larry Hurtado, "The Doxology at the End of Romans," *New Testament Textual Criticism: Its Significance for Exegesis: Essays in Honour of Bruce*

M. Metzger, eds. Eldon Jay Epp and Gordon D. Fee (Oxford: Clarendon Press, 1989), 185–99, especially 189–90.

35. Meyer, "Romans," *The Word in This World*, 217.

36. The argumentation that supports this paragraph may be found in Gaventa, "'To Preach the Gospel': Romans 1, 15 and the Purposes of Romans," *The Letter to the Romans*, BETL, ed. Udo Schnelle (Leuven, Belgium: Peeters, forthcoming).

37. See Bruce N. Chilton, "Amen," *ABD* 1:184-86; also Heinrich Schlier, "amēn," *TDNT* 1:335-38. It should be noted, however, that in the LXX, "amēn" appears only at 1 Chr 16:36; Neh 5:13; 8:6.

38. Jewett contends that Tertius is the reader of the letter, since "a person of [Phoebe's] social class would have her scribe read the letter aloud in her behalf" (*Romans*, 22), but it is hard to understand the greeting *from* Tertius in 16:22 if he is among those who presumably accompany Phoebe on her mission. In addition, it is odd to reconcile the argument based on Phoebe's social class with Jewett's insistence elsewhere that Paul interprets the gospel as a radical overturning of "the pyramid of honor" (ibid., 49–51 and *passim*).

39. Here Jewett is right: the Romans "are expected to reply to Paul's 'amen' with an 'amen' of their own" (ibid., 941). See also the suggestive comments in Bailey and Vander Broek, *Literary Forms of the New Testament*, 78.

40. *Religious Experience in Earliest Christianity*, 184.

Ecstasy and Exousia: Religious Experience and the Negotiation of Social Power in Paul's Letter to the Galatians

1. Luke T. Johnson, *The Writings of the New Testament: An Interpretation*, rev. ed. (Minneapolis: Augsburg Fortress, 1999), 335; compare also 330–31.

2. Ibid., 335.

3. Religious experience has occupied the study of religion for some time now, but has yet to take center stage in biblical studies. It is revealing that for the construction of his experience-interpretation model, Johnson relies almost exclusively on scholars of comparative religions. The influence of Joachim Wach, in particular his *Comparative Study of Religions*, ed. J. Kitagawa (New York: Columbia University Press, 1958), and the Chicago School is readily acknowledged, while few if any biblical scholars are cited. In this regard Johnson's overall contribution is even more appreciated.

4. Luke T. Johnson, *Religious Experience in Earliest Christianity: A Missing Dimension in New Testament Studies* (Minneapolis: Augsburg Fortress, 1998), 49; emphasis supplied.

5. Ibid., 50; see also his *Writings*, 10–16.

6. Ibid., 60. His commentary on this definition is found on 61–67.

7. I am responsible for all translations except where noted.

8. John L. White, "Introductory Formulae in the Body of the Pauline Letter," *JBL* 90 (1971): 96; citation of text on page 94.

9. Hans D. Betz, *Galatians: A Commentary on Paul's Letter to the Churches in Galatia*, Hermeneia (Philadelphia: Fortress Press, 1979), 47n39–40. For parallel usages in legal and political rhetoric, see Franz Mußner, *Der Galaterbrief: Auslegung*, 5th ed. (Freiburg im Breisgau, Germany: Herder, 1988), 53n53–54; J. Louis Martyn, *Galatians: A New Translation with Introduction and Commentary*, Anchor Bible (New York: Doubleday, 1997), 107.

10. Georg Betram, "*thauma*, etc.," *TDNT* 3.29.

11. Ibid., 31.

12. Ibid., 37.

13. Martyn, *Galatians*, 108, thinks the Galatians might have heard the middle voice as suggesting some form of conversion from one school of thought to another, whereas Paul might have intended it as "foot soldiers defecting from the ranks of an apocalyptic army." But see next note.

14. Mußner, *Galaterbrief*, 53.

15. Acts 9:2; 19:9, 23; etc. See Longenecker, *Galatians*, 14.

16. Betram, "*thauma*," 33–34.

17. For more on the negative sense of *thaumazein*, see Betram, "*thauma*," 34–35; Terence Y. Mullins, "Formulas in New Testament Epistles," *JBL* 91 (1972): 385–86, who suggests that if *thaumazō* with *hoti* is used as a formula, it is used ironically or sarcastically, "[The letter writer] is not really astonished; he is irritated" (385). But for *thaumazein* to mean "to be irritated" does not require irony or sarcasm. Thus Longenecker suggests, rightly, that a broader survey of evidence warrants taking *thaumazō hoti* as an "astonishment-rebuke" formula; *Galatians*, 14.

18. So, disapprovingly, according to Ronald Knox, *Enthusiasm: A Chapter in the History of Religion, with Special Reference to the XVII and XVIII Centuries* (Oxford: Oxford University Press, 1950), 1–3, who sees enthusiasm or what he calls "ultrasupernaturalism" lying at the root of schisms throughout the history of the Christian church. His sardonic if also witty remark is illustrative: "You have

clique, an *elite*, of Christian men and (more importantly) women, who are trying to live less worldly life than their neighbours; to be more attentive to the guidance (directly felt, they would tell you) of the Holy Spirit. More and more, by a kind of fatality, you see them draw apart from their co-religionists, a hive ready to swarm" (1).

19. I. M. Lewis, *Ecstatic Religion: An Anthropological Study of Spirit Possession and Shamanism* (Harmondsworth, England: Penguin Books, 1978), 34.

20. Lewis, *Ecstatic Religion*, 35; see also 205.

21. For a more detailed discussion of the power dynamics between Paul and the Jerusalem church, see my "The Letter to the Galatians," *A Postcolonial Commentary on the New Testament Writings*, The Bible and Postcolonialism 13, eds. F. F. Segovia and R. S. Sugirtharajah (London: T & T Clark, 2007), 246–64.

22. BDAG, 171.

23. Spiq, "*baskainō*," TLNT 1.273–74.

24. So Gerhard Delling, "*baskainō*," TDNT 1.595 ("This is certainly not to be understood in a naively realistic way as mechanical magic"); Betz, *Galatians*, 131 and also notes 31–34; Spiq, "*baskainō*," 272–76 ("Who beclouded your mind?"); Longenecker, *Galatians*, 100; Martyn, *Galatians*, 282–83 ("Given Gentile aversion to circumcision, the Teachers must indeed have been *virtual* magicians to have made the Galatians long to come under the Law." Emphasis supplied). These scholars have good ancient evidence on their side: Philo, *Agr.* 112; Josephus, *Ant.* 10.250, 257.

25. Ernest Burton, *A Critical and Exegetical Commentary on the Epistle to the Galatians*, International Critical Commentary (Edinburgh, Scotland: T & T Clark, 1921), 144. I must confess I find his rather dismissive comment betrays a modernist prejudice towards magic and sorcery. A subtle critique might be found in Jerome Neyrey, "Bewitched in Galatia: Paula and Cultural Anthropology," CBQ 50 (1988), 73.

26. Heinrich Schlier, *Der Briefe an die Galater*, 13th ed. (Göttingen, Germany: Vandenhoech & Ruprecht, 1965), 119.

27. See M. Dickie, "Heliodorus and Plutarch on the Evil Eye," *Classical Philology* 86 (1991): 17–29.

28. John H. Elliott, "Paul, Galatians, and the Evil Eye," *Currents in Theology and Mission* 17 (1990): 264; see pages 267–69 for full discussion of the evil eye ethos of Galatians and pages 272–73 for full bibliography.

29. So Neyrey, "Bewitched," 96–99; Elliott, "Evil Eye," 70–71.

30. Mary Douglas, *Natural Symbols* (New York: Pantheon, 1982); cited in Neyrey, "Bewitched," 75–76.

31. Neyrey, "Bewitched," 97, depending in part on Mary Douglas, *Witchcraft Confessions and Accusations* (New York: Tavistock, 1970).

32. Lewis, *Ecstatic Religion*, 120.

33. Ibid., 117.

34. Ibid., 120.

35. Ibid., 121. Furthermore, according to Lewis, "the rare exceptions to this generalization prove the rule. For where witchcraft charges are brought against a superior by an inferior, the explicit intention is to question the legitimacy of this status difference and ultimately to assert equality" (120).

36. A similar accusation is attempted in 2 Corinthians 11:13-15, where Paul calls the Superapostles "deacons of Satan" (v. 15).

37. For more detailed analysis, see Wan, "Galatians," 246–64.

38. See J. Louis Martyn, "A Law-Observant Mission to Gentiles: The Background of Galatians," *SJT* 38 (1985): 307–24, for a possible reconstruction of the Torah-centered position of Paul's opponents.

39. Or "to pervert" (NRSV).

40. Whether "as I have said and now I say again" refers to a statement made in an earlier (founding?) visit or to v. 8 need not detract us; my reading does not depend on how one comes out on this issue.

41. The most detailed is the study by Seyoon Kim, *The Origin of Paul's Gospel*, WUNT 2/4 (Tübingen, Germany: Mohr, 1981).

42. See, among others, Schlier, *Galater*, 121; Betz, *Galatians*, 132. It is tempting to add baptism to this list, but although Paul's description of the rite in 3:27 ("For as many as you have been baptized, you were clothed in Christ") seems suggestive, it is unclear whether "clothing in Christ" represents an ecstatic experience or a theological formulation regarding identification with Christ.

43. Richard Hays, *The Faith of Jesus Christ: An Investigation of the Narrative Substructure of Galatians 3:1–4:11*, SBLDS (Chico, Calif.: Scholars Press, 1981), has argued that this alludes to a "narrative substructure" of the gospel story that his Galatian converts would readily recall. The visual reference of *kat' ophthalmous*, however, presents a problem to the theory.

44. Virtually all commentators agree on this point; see Betz, *Galatians*, 134; Martyn, *Galatians*, 285.

45. Johnson, *Writings*, 335.

46. For details of this argument, see Sze-kar Wan, "Abraham and the Promise of Spirit: Points of Convergence between Philo and Paul," *Things Revealed: Studies in Early Jewish and Christian Literature in Honor of Michael E. Stone*, eds. Esther G. Chazon, David Satran, and Ruth A. Clements, JSJSup 89 (Leiden, Netherlands: Brill, 2004), 209–20.

47. Elliott, "Evil Eye," 270.

The Beatitudes: Jesus' Recipe for Happiness?

1. Frederick William Danker, ed., *A Greek-English Lexicon of the New Testament and Other Early Christian Literature*, 3rd ed. (BDAG) (Chicago: University of Chicago Press, 2000), 610–11 (s.v. *makarios*).

2. Ibid.

3. Charlton T. Lewis, *An Elementary Latin Dictionary* (Oxford: Clarendon Press, 1891; 1979), 90 (s.v. *beatus*).

4. Charlton T. Lewis and Charles Short, *A Latin Dictionary* (Oxford: Clarendon Press, 1879; 1969), 225 (s.v. *beatitudo*).

5. H. G. Liddell and R. Scott, *Greek-English Lexicon with a Revised Supplement* (Oxford: Clarendon Press, 1843; ninth edition 1940, with new supplement added in 1996), 708 (s.v. *eudaimonia*).

6. Even though this paper honors the scholarly work of my longtime friend and colleague Luke Johnson, who published a popular treatment of the Beatitudes early in his career, its immediate audience is the Pursuit of Happiness working group sponsored by Emory's Center for the Study of Law and Religion. This five-year interdisciplinary project is funded by the John Templeton Foundation and directed by my Emory colleague Philip Reynolds.

7. The three following discourses relate to mission (ch. 10), parables of the kingdom (ch. 13), and community life (ch. 18). The fourth discourse, comprising chs. 23–25, contains three discrete units: a critique of hypocritical behavior (ch. 23), an apocalyptic discourse about the end of time (ch. 24), and parables relating to the final judgment (ch. 25).

8. Benjamin W. Bacon, *Studies in Matthew* (London: Constable, 1930), 81. Similarly, A. H. M'Neile, *The Gospel According to St. Matthew* (London: Macmillan, 1965), xxx. For a critical analysis of Bacon's views, see W. D. Davies, *The Setting of the Sermon on the Mount* (Cambridge, Mass.: Cambridge University Press, 1964), 14–25.

9. See John O. York, *The Last Shall Be First: The Rhetoric of Reversal in Luke*, Journal for the Study of the New Testament Supplement Series 46 (Sheffield, England: JSOT Press, 1991).

10. See C. F. Evans, *Saint Luke*, TPI New Testament Commentaries (London: SCM Press, 1990), 328, noting Deut 28; 30:15-20; Isa 3:9-12; Jer 17:5-8; 1 Enoch 9:8-9.

11. See Luke T. Johnson, *The Writings of the New Testament: An Interpretation*, rev. ed. (Minneapolis: Augsburg Fortress, 1999), 229–31.

12. This aspect of Luke's theological vision has been explored especially by Luke T. Johnson, *The Literary Function of Possessions in Luke-Acts*, Society of Biblical Literature Dissertation Series 39 (Missoula, Mont.: Society of Biblical Literature [Scholars Press], 1977); *Sharing Possessions: Mandate and Symbol of Faith*, Overtures to Biblical Theology (Philadelphia: Fortress Press, 1981).

13. For a discussion of theories relating to the composition of the Gospels, see Carl R. Holladay, *A Critical Introduction to the New Testament: Interpreting the Message and Meaning of Jesus Christ* (Nashville: Abingdon Press, 2005), 39–75.

14. According to the Griesbach hypothesis, Matthew was the first Gospel; Luke used Matthew in composing his Gospel; and at a later stage Mark used both Matthew and Luke in compiling his abbreviated Gospel. See David L. Dungan, "Two-Gospel Hypothesis," *Anchor Bible Dictionary* (New York: Doubleday, 1992), 6.671–79.

15. 1QM 14:7. The obscurity of the Hebrew is complicated by a lacuna in the text. Geza Vermes translates the verse: "Among the poor in spirit [there is power] over the hard of heart" (*The Complete Dead Sea Scrolls in English* [New York: Penguin Books, 1998], 178). Florentino García Martínez displays the lacuna in his translation: "Among the poor in spirit . . . to a hard heart" (*The Dead Sea Scrolls Translated: The Qumran Texts in English*, 2nd ed. [Leiden, Netherlands: Brill, 1996], 109).

16. BDAG, 896 (s.v. *ptōchos* 3).

17. A close parallel is Psalm 34:18: "The LORD is near to the brokenhearted, and saves the crushed in spirit." A more distant parallel is Isaiah 57:15, in which God dwells with "those who are contrite and humble in spirit."

18. This formulation, which is literally rendered "the kingdom of the heavens," is typical of Matthew's Gospel. Here, "the heavens" is a circumlocution for "God." The other Gospels employ the more familiar formulation "kingdom of God" (*hē basileia tou theou*).

19. For a fuller treatment of Matthew's understanding of the kingdom as reflected in the parables, see Holladay, *Critical Introduction*, 149–50.

20. Matthew uses the term "righteousness" (*dikaiosynē*) seven times in his Gospel, five of them in the Sermon on the Mount (5:6, 10, 20; 6:1, 33; also cf. 3:15; 21:32). By contrast, the term does not appear in Mark.

21. BDAG (s.v. *eleos*).

22. The couplet regularly occurs in the opening greetings of Pauline letters (see Rom 1:7; 1 Cor 1:3).

23. My Emory colleague, John H. Hayes, prefers this less-inflated sense.

24. In the NRSV, cognate forms of the verb "persecute" occur seventeen times, mostly in Psalms (10:2; 31:15; 49:5; 69:26; 119:84, 86, 150, 157, 161; 142:6) and Jeremiah (15:15; 17:18; 20:11). Also, see Judg 2:18; Job 19:28; 30:21; Isa 14:6.

25. The verb *diōkō*, "persecute," occurs forty-five times in the NT, almost half of which (eighteen) occur in writings attributed to Paul. The noun *diōgmos*, "persecution," occurs ten times in the NT, five of which are in writings attributed to Paul.

26. BDAG (s.v. *diōkō*) 2.

27. See J. David Pleins, "Poor, Poverty (Old Testament)," *Anchor Bible Dictionary* (New York: Doubleday, 1992), 5.402–14.

28. See Thomas D. Hanks, "Poor, Poverty (New Testament)," *ABD*, 6.414–24.

29. The healing of the crippled beggar in Acts 3 belongs to the same series.

Kerygma and Midrash: A Conversation with Luke Timothy Johnson and C. H. Dodd

1. This essay is offered with congratulations and thanks to Luke Johnson, who has been for me an inspiration, an occasional sparring partner, and a friend in Christ.

2. L. T. Johnson, *Septuagintal Midrash in the Speeches of Acts*, The Père Marquette Lecture in Theology 2002 (Milwaukee: Marquette University Press, 2002).

3. For a recent statement of Johnson's qualms about "New Testament theology," see L. T. Johnson, "Does a Theology of the Canonical Gospels Make Sense?" in C. Rowland and C. Tuckett (eds.), *The Nature of New Testament Theology: Essays in Honour of Robert Morgan* (Oxford: Blackwell, 2006), 93–108.

4. C. H. Dodd, *According to the Scriptures: The Sub-Structure of New Testament Theology* (London: Nisbet & Co., 1952).

5. Dodd's book deals more broadly with OT citations across the range of the NT canon; still, here, as in his earlier work *The Apostolic Preaching and Its Developments* (New York: Harper and Bros., 1936), Dodd places special emphasis on the speeches in Acts as sources for understanding the earliest Christian message.

6. Dodd, *According to the Scriptures*, 11–12.

7. Dodd's description shows some signs of inconsistency: sometimes he seems to treat the OT texts as an integral part of the *kerygma*, while in other formulations he seems to describe it as a secondary layer of interpretation of the *kerygma*. The architectural metaphor seems to suggest the latter option.

8. Ibid., 13. Interestingly, Dodd does not list Luke as one of the authors who constructs a theological building on the substructure of tradition. This striking omission probably reflects his tendency to regard Luke, along with the other synoptic authors, chiefly as a collector and conserver of tradition. See also p. 110, where Dodd counts "Paul, the author to the Hebrews, and the Fourth Evangelist" as the only three "Christian thinkers of the first age known to us" that are "of genuinely creative power."

9. Ibid., 28.

10. Ibid., 32. This example strangely overlooks the fact that the author of Acts certainly knew the Gospel of Mark, so that Acts 13:33 is hardly independent evidence for an earlier usage of the psalm in this way. Nonetheless, the citations in Hebrews might well be treated as independent of the synoptic tradition; this would give Dodd his requisite two witnesses, though not the three that he claims.

11. J. Rendel Harris, *Testimonies* (Cambridge, Mass.: Cambridge University Press, 1916–1920). For an updating of Harris's hypothesis, see M. C. Albl, *'And Scripture Cannot Be Broken': The Form and Function of the Early Christian Testimonia Collections*, NovTSup 96 (Leiden, Netherlands: Brill, 1999).

12. Dodd, *According to the Scriptures*, 57–60. The reference on page 58 to the last of these texts contains a typographical error, citing it as "Acts ii.20."

13. Dodd gives a helpful complete list of the passages on pages 107–08.

14. Ibid., 108–9.

15. Ibid., 110.

16. Ibid., 127.

17. Ibid., 133.

18. Johnson, *Septuagintal Midrash*, 4.

19. Johnson, *Septuagintal Midrash*, 5. Johnson's comment pertains to *The Apostolic Preaching and Its Developments*, but it is necessarily relevant also for *According to the Scriptures*.

20. Johnson, *Septuagintal Midrash*, 10. Dodd was not unaware of Luke's stylistic and redactional shaping of the apostolic speeches, but he argued that they were nonetheless based, at least in their general outlines, on accounts or reminiscences of actual speeches delivered by the apostles.

21. Johnson, *Septuagintal Midrash*, 10.

22. On the strategies of biblical interpretation in Pseudo-Philo, see B. N. Fisk, *Do You Not Remember? Scripture, Story and Exegesis in the Rewritten Bible of Pseudo-Philo*, JSPSup 37 (Sheffield, England: Sheffield Academic, 2001).

23. Johnson, *Septuagintal Midrash*, 29.

24. Ibid., 29–35.

25. Ibid., 42.

26. Ibid., 46.

27. Dodd writes: "It appears then that the whole psalm [Psalm 2] was regarded as a description of messiahship, fulfilled in the mission and destiny of Jesus" (*According to the Scriptures*, 105).

28. Johnson, *Septuagintal Midrash*, 47.

29. Ibid.

30. Ibid., 48.

31. Ibid., 50.

32. Ibid., 51.

33. Ibid., 52.

34. Dodd, *According to the Scriptures*, 11.

35. Ibid., 111.

36. Ibid., 108.

37. This is a longstanding methodological stance for Johnson. For his wariness also about reconstructions of the specific historical circumstances of Luke's readers, see his essay "On Finding the Lukan Community: A Cautious Cautionary Essay," *1979 SBL Seminar Papers*, ed. P. J. Achtemeier (Missoula, Mont.: Scholars Press, 1979), 87–100.

38. See particularly *The Real Jesus: The Misguided Quest for the Historical Jesus and the Truth of the Traditional Gospels* (San Francisco: HarperSanFrancisco, 1996) and *Living Jesus: Learning the Heart of the Gospel* (San Francisco: HarperSanFrancisco, 1999).

39. In his essay "Does a Theology of the Canonical Gospels Make Sense?" Johnson eschews the attempt to find a theology *in* the Gospels collectively and proposes to ask instead what sort of theologies they might enable or preclude (see especially pages 106–8). This indicates that the four canonical Gospels have some sort of coherence or family resemblance, which Johnson cautiously spells out in his essay.

40. Dodd, *According to the Scriptures*, 40.

41. Ibid., 40–41.

42. Johnson, *Septuagintal Midrash*, 24.

43. Ibid., 39.

44. Ibid., 33–34.

45. Dodd, *According to the Scriptures*, 106.

46. Ibid., 107.

47. This theme does not receive significant emphasis in *Septuagintal Midrash* (10, 58n39). For fuller explication of this motif, see L. T. Johnson, *The Gospel of Luke*, Sacra Pagina (Collegeville, Minn.: Liturgical Press, 1991), 17–21. For the significance of Mosaic typology also in other major NT witnesses, see W. A. Meeks, *The Prophet-King: Moses Traditions and the Johannine Christology*, NovTSup 14 (Leiden, Netherlands: Brill, 1967); D. C. Allison, Jr., *The New Moses: A Matthean Typology* (Minneapolis: Augsburg Fortress, 1993).

48. Dodd, *According to the Scriptures*, 113.

49. Dodd's judgment here also overlooks Paul's emphatic argument in Romans 9–11 against precisely the position that Dodd articulates. This oversight is perhaps not surprising in light of Dodd's dismissive treatment of these chapters in his commentary on Romans. He regards this section of the letter as a previously composed sermon only tangentially related to the letter's main themes and even remarks that "the epistle could be read without any sense of a gap if these chapters were omitted" (C. H. Dodd, *The Epistle of Paul to the Romans*, MNTC [New York: Harper and Bros., 1932], 149).

50. On these issues, see further R. B. Hays, *The Moral Vision of the New Testament: Community, Cross, New Creation* (San Francisco: HarperSanFrancisco, 1996), 407–43, and the literature cited there.

51. See Hays, *Moral Vision*, 417–21.

52. It should be noted that Johnson's case for the LXX as Christian scripture is based, at least in this essay, only on Luke's preference for citing Scripture in its Greek-language form. This argument does not directly address the question of whether the Apocrypha (books included in the LXX but not in the MT) should

be canonical for Christians. Since Luke's scriptural quotations in the speeches of Acts do not quote from these books, the question never arises. Clearly, however, if one decides that the Greek textual tradition should be deemed canonical the question of the extent and boundaries of the canon would logically follow.

53. For example, *According to the Scriptures*, 42n1, 69n1.

54. Johnson, *Septuagintal Midrash*, 50.

55. Ibid., 50, 51. For further reflections on this topic, with regard to Lukan and Pauline Christology, see C. K. Rowe, *Early Narrative Christology: The Lord in the Gospel of Luke*, BZNW 139 (Berlin: de Gruyter, 2006), 219–26.

56. See, for example, his introduction to *The Writings of the New Testament: An Interpretation*, rev. ed. (Minneapolis: Augsburg Fortress, 1999), 10–16.

57. Johnson, *Septuagintal Midrash*, 52.

58. These works are in fact cited by Johnson in a footnote to this concluding paragraph: L. T. Johnson, *Scripture and Discernment: Decision Making in the Church* (Nashville: Abingdon, 1996); *Faith's Freedom: A Classic Spirituality for Contemporary Christians* (Minneapolis: Augsburg Fortress, 1990).

59. See Johnson's essay, "Imagining the World That Scripture Imagines," in L. T. Johnson and W. S. Kurz, S.J., *The Future of Catholic Biblical Scholarship: A Constructive Conversation* (Grand Rapids, Mich.: Eerdmans, 2002), 119–42.

60. Dodd, *According to the Scriptures*, 134–35.

61. In any case, we can all be grateful for the substantial help Luke Johnson has given us in thinking more clearly about these matters.

Jesus Made Real in Music: La Pasión según San Marcos *and* Luke Timothy Johnson's Experience/Interpretation Model

1. Luke Timothy Johnson, *The Real Jesus: The Misguided Quest for the Historical Jesus and the Truth of the Traditional Gospels* (San Francisco: HarperSanFranciso, 1996).

2. The passion of this book (needless to say) evoked similar passionate responses by those who disagreed with Johnson. See, for example, Robert J. Miller, "The Jesus of Orthodoxy and the Jesuses of the Gospels: A Critique of Luke Timothy Johnson's *The Real Jesus*," *JSNT* 68 (1997): 101–20.

3. Johnson, *The Real Jesus*, chapter 5 (see especially 121–22).

4. Ibid., 133.

5. Ibid., 141: "Although the Christian creed contains a number of historical assertions about Jesus, Christian faith as a living religious response is simply not

directed at those historical facts about Jesus, or at a historical reconstruction of Jesus. Christian faith is directed to a living person."

6. Ibid., 142.

7. See, for example, the April 8, 1996 *Time* cover story, "The Gospel Truth?" (Vol. 147, Issue 15): 52–60.

8. Johnson, *The Real Jesus*, 167–77.

9. Ibid., 174.

10. Ibid., 175–76.

11. Ibid., 174–75.

12. A recording of *Water Passion* is available from Sony Classic Recordings; of *La Pasión* from Hänssler Classic. Both are live recordings from the Stuttgart premieres. The other two passions have not received the same attention, although they have had many repeat performances in Europe.

13. See, for example, this review of its U.S. premiere: "Osvaldo Golijov's *La Pasión según San Marcos* is a work of genius. As such it is both assimilative and profoundly original. The piece grabs you by the throat from the first moments and doesn't let you go until it sets you down, changed, an hour and a half later, with the Hebrew prayer for the dead quietly intoned" (Richard Dyer, *The Boston Globe*, February 9, 2001, Arts Section, C1); "When the Bach Academy of Stuttgart commissioned four new settings of the Passion, . . . the roaring success was the score by the Argentine composer Osvaldo Golijov" (Paul Griffiths, "Writing Music that Sings, Cries, Screams, and Prays, *The New York Times*, October 27, 2002, Sunday, Arts and Leisure, 1).

14. Martin Kähler, *The So-Called Historical Jesus and the Historic Biblical Christ* (Philadelphia: Fortress Press, 1988), 80n11.

15. This, too, distinguishes *La Pasión* from the other passions commissioned by Rilling.

16. For this aspect of Bach, see Paul S. Minear, "Matthew, Evangelist, and Johann, Composer," *Theology Today* 30 (1973): 243–55, especially 244.

17. Conversation between Osvaldo Golijov and David Harrington, http://www.osvaldogolijov.com/wd1n.htm (accessed August 2007). This conversation provided the basis for the concert notes at the Stuttgart premiere.

18. Concert notes from Robert Kirzinger/Boston Symphony Orchestra http://www.osvaldogolijov.com/wd1n.htm (accessed August 2007). For Reynolds Price on Mark, see *A Palpable God* (New York: Athenaeum, 1978) and *The Three Gospels* (New York: Scribner, 1996).

19. Ibid.

20. Conversation between Osvaldo Golijov and David Harrington, http://www.osvaldogolijov.com/wd1n.htm (accessed August 2007).

21. The word *immediately* punctuates four key moments in the passion narrative—when Judas arrives in the garden, when Judas kisses Jesus to identify him to the soldiers, when the cock crows after Peter's betrayal, and when the chief priests gather and lead Jesus to his trial before Pilate.

22. Conversation between Osvaldo Golijov and David Harrington, http://www.osvaldogolijov.com/wd1n.htm (accessed August 2007).

23. The libretto to *La Pasión según San Marcos* is included with the recording and also is available for download in PDF form at http://www.osvaldogolijov.com/wd1n.htm.

24. *La Pasión*, CD 1, tracks 8 and 9.

25. Ibid., CD 1, track 9.

26. Ibid., CD 1, tracks 11 and 12.

27. Ibid., CD 1, track 13.

28. Ibid., CD 1, track 14.

29. Minear, "Matthew, Evangelist, and Johann, Composer," 247.

30. Conversation between Osvaldo Golijov and David Harrington, http://www.osvaldogolijov.com/wd1n.htm (accessed August 2007).

31. See, for example, the comments by Michael Linton, "Furthermore, by having sopranos and altos usually sing Jesus' words . . . Golijov makes the Son of God weirdly androgynous. When Jesus tells the Sanhedrin that they will see the Son of Man 'coming in clouds of heaven' (Mark 14:26), Golijov extends Mark's text by a long passage of nonsense syllables to which he sets the *Passion's* most contorted and chromatic melody. Sung by a mezzo-soprano, doubled by trumpets, this passage of scat singing not only makes Jesus appear feminine, but dangerously deranged," in "Passion Stomp," *First Things* 118 (2001): 20–21. Sadly, Linton's broadside against *La Pasión* is the only article on this work listed in the ATLA database.

32. Johnson, *The Real Jesus*, 149.

33. "I cannot finish with his last scream—I just cannot do it—so I need a moment of transcendence," conversation between Osvaldo Golijov and David Harrington, http://www.osvaldogolijov.com/wd1n.htm (accessed August 2007).

34. *La Pasión*, CD 2, track 11.

35. Ibid., CD 2, track 12. The Kaddish is sung in Aramaic. This translation is not Golijov's translation, but that from the Jewish prayer book.

36. Alex Ross, "Resurrection: The Passion according to Osvaldo Golijov," *The New Yorker* (March 5, 2001): 100.

37. Philip McCarthy, "Cross Purposes; Music Composing Passion," *Sydney Morning Herald* (Australia) (December 23, 2002): Metropolitan Section, 6. McCarthy includes parts of his interview with Golijov in his article. See also Paul Griffiths, "Writing Music that Sings, Cries, Screams, and Prays."

38. Ibid.

39. Conversation between Osvaldo Golijov and David Harrington, http://www.osvaldogolijov.com/wd1n.htm (accessed August 2007).

"Watch How You Hear": The Healing of kōphoi ["Deaf-mute"] Persons in Luke

1. This is especially evident in Johnson's commentaries on Luke's two-volume work, *The Gospel of Luke* (Sacra Pagina Series, vol. 3; Collegeville, Minn.: Liturgical Press, 1991); *The Acts of the Apostles*, Sacra Pagina Series, vol. 5 (Collegeville, Minn.: Liturgical Press, 1992).

2. Johnson, *Gospel of Luke*, 180–84.

3. Ibid., 183.

4. Given as the primary meaning in BDAG, 580.

5. Here BDAG cites Hab 2:18; 3 Macc 4:16; JosAs 13:1.

6. Johnson is aware of the various meanings of *kōphos* (*Gospel of Luke*, 181), but does not explore the possibilities pursued in the present study.

7. The instances apart from Isaiah are LXX Exodus 4:11; LXX Leviticus 19:14 (the mandate against abusing the deaf and the blind); LXX Psalm 37 (38):13; LXX 57 (58):4; LXX Wisdom 10:21 (wisdom opened the mouth of the dumb); and LXX Habakkuk 2:18 (dumb idols, implying both deafness and muteness).

8. It is interesting, in the context of this study, that the verb *pachynō*, which appears in the NT only in the quotation of Isaiah 6:10 (Matt 13:15 and Acts 28:27), when used figuratively means "make impervious, gross, dull" (BDAG); so the past particple *epachynthē* is very close in meaning to *kōphos*.

9. Luke omits the first healing entirely (the deaf-mute of Decapolis); it falls within his Big Omission of Mark 6:45–8:26. As for the demonized boy that the disciples could not heal, Luke ascribes no functional disability to him (Luke 9:39, 42).

10. See Dennis Hamm, "What the Samaritan Leper Sees: The Narrative Christology of Luke 17:11-19," *Catholic Biblical Quarterly* 56.2 (1994): 273–87.

11. See m. *Tamid* 6.3–7.3.

12. The phrase, "while he was speaking these things," indicates that Luke wants the exchange with the woman to be understood in continuity with the Beelzebul controversy and the healing of the deaf-mute.

13. The blind see (7:21; 18:35-43), the lame walk (Luke 5:17-25, the paralytic), lepers are cleansed (5:12-16; 17:11-19), dead are raised (Luke 7:11-17, widow of Nain's son; 8:40-56, Jairus' daughter; Acts 9:36-43, Tabitha). The *kōphoi* who hear would seem to be Zechariah and the *kōphos* demoniac of 11:14.

14. That *dialogismoi* of the heart constitute a block to hearing and responding properly is deeply thematic in the Third Gospel. Simeon had prophesied to Mary that a sword should pierce her heart "so that the thoughts of many hearts [*ek pollōn kardiōn dialogismoi*] should be revealed" (2:35). When Jesus claims authority to forgive the sins of the paralytic, the scribes and the Pharisees begin to ask themselves [*dialogizesthai*], "Who is this who speaks blasphemies? Who but God alone can forgive sins?" Jesus knew their thoughts [*dialogismous*] and said to them in reply, "What are you thinking in your hearts [*ti dialogizesthē en tais kardiais hymōn*]?" (5:21-22). The verbal form of this pondering of the heart is in Luke always sinister; see also 12:17, where it describes the acquisitive planning of the rich fool, and 20:14, where it describes the murderous strategizing of the wicked vineyard tenants. Luke's final example of *dialogismoi* in the heart that can inhibit proper response to Jesus occurs during the appearance of the risen Lord to the disciples. Seeing him and hearing his greeting of peace, they are terrified and think they see a ghost. Jesus says "Why are you troubled? And why do questions [*dialogismoi*] arise in your hearts?" (24:38).

15. This saying is not to be confused with an analogous saying from the triple tradition, the one about receiving *a child* as receiving both Jesus and the one who sent him (Mark 9:37; Matt 18:5; and Luke 9:37).

16. Johnson's commentary (*Gospel of Luke*, 173–76) catches nicely the thematic import of this episode.

From the Servant in Isaiah to Jesus and the Apostles in Luke-Acts to Christians Today: Spirit-Filled Witness to the Ends of the Earth

1. Luke Timothy Johnson and William S. Kurz, *The Future of Catholic Biblical Scholarship: A Constructive Conversation* (Grand Rapids, Mich.: Eerdmans, 2002).

2. For arguments on how Luke used the Septuagint, see Luke Timothy Johnson, *Septuagintal Midrash in the Speeches of Acts*, Père Marquette Lecture in

Theology (Milwaukee: Marquette University Press, 2002), *passim*. Compare H. Van de Sandt, "The Quotations in Acts 13:32-52 as a Reflection of Luke's LXX Interpretation," *Biblica* 75.1 (1994): 26–58; Stanley E. Porter, "Scripture Justifies Mission: The Use of the Old Testament in Luke-Acts," *Hearing the Old Testament in the New Testament*, McMaster New Testament Studies, ed. Stanley E. Porter (Grand Rapids, Mich.: Eerdmans, 2006), 104–26.

3. Compare Jacques Ménard, "Un titre messianique propre au libre des Actes: le paij qeou," *Studia Montis Regii* 1.2 (1958): 213–24.

4. Witness to God to all nations even to the end of the earth finds its biblical grounding in the mission given to the Lord's servants. The prime early paradigm for servant of the Lord in the Jewish Scriptures is Moses in the exodus. Several times Scripture refers to God's "servant Moses." Note esp. Exodus 14:31, "Israel saw the great work that the LORD did against the Egyptians. So the people feared the LORD and believed in the LORD and in his servant Moses."

Most latter references to Moses as God's servant derive from this basic description of Moses and his relationship to God. Numbers 12:7-8 contrasts "my servant Moses," with whom God speaks face to face, to other prophets who are addressed in dreams and visions. God announces to Joshua, "My servant Moses is dead," and orders him to lead the people into the land and keep the law of Moses (Jos 1:2, 7). Joshua is repeatedly subordinated to Moses (Jos 11:15). See also 1 Kings 8:56; Joshua 9:24; 2 Kings 21:8; Nehemiah 1:7-8; 9:14; Psalms 105:26; Malachi 4:4.

Expectation of the prophet like Moses is grounded especially in the prophecy, "The LORD your God will raise up for you a prophet like me from among your own people; you shall heed such a prophet" (Deut 18:15; see Acts 3:22; 7:37; but contrast Deut 34:10, that the Lord knew only Moses face to face). Later, Elijah is a wonderworking prophet like Moses. Though Moses probably also influenced portrayals of other prophets as the Lord's servants (see Isaiah 20:3), it is Jesus who is described most insistently as the prophet like Moses and as God's servant, but this is a New Testament phenomenon. Paul often begins his letters as the servant (*doulos*) of Christ (Rom 1:1; Phil 1:1; cf. Titus 1:1, "Paul, a servant of God and an apostle of Jesus Christ"; 1 Cor 3:5, 9; 4:1; 2 Cor 6:4; Gal 1:10).

5. Contrast Richard I. Pervo, *Profit with Delight: The Literary Genre of the Acts of the Apostles* (Philadelphia: Fortress Press, 1987). Richard Clifford points to a similar use of humor and irony in passages mocking idols and their makers in the preaching of Second Isaiah to make serious contrast between powerless idols and the one living and saving God: "The Function of Idol Passages in Second Isaiah," *CBQ* 42.4 (1980): 450–64.

6. Thomas Moore argues that Luke distinguished between terms for *servant* as applied to Jesus and those referring to those he commissioned. He reserved *pais* as a christological title for Jesus alone, and used *doulos* or other titles for Jesus' followers. See Thomas S. Moore, "The Lucan Great Commission and the Isaianic Servant," *Bibliotheca Sacra* 154 (January–March 1997): 47–60.

For diverse views concerning collective and individual senses of *servant*, see Christopher R. Seitz, "'You are my Servant, You are the Israel in whom I will be glorified': The Servant Songs and the Effect of Literary Context in Isaiah," *Calvin Theological Journal* 39 (2004): 117–34; W. J. Dumbrell, "The Role of the Servant in Isaiah 40–55," *Reformed Theological Review* 48 (September–December 1989): 105–13; Torleif Elgvin, "The Individual Interpretation of the Servant," *Mishkan* 43 (2005) 25–33; Michael A. Grisanti, "Israel's Mission to the Nations in Isaiah 40–55: An Update," *The Masters Seminary Journal* 9/1 (Spring 1998): 39–61.

7. Compare David F. Payne, "The Meaning of Mission in Isaiah 40–55," *Mission and Meaning: Essays Presented to Peter Cotterell*, ed. Antony Billington, Tony Lane, Max Turner (Carlisle, England: Paternoster Press, 1995): 3–11.

8. Compare Bart J. Koet, "Isaiah in Luke-Acts," *Isaiah in the New Testament*, ed. Steve Moyise and Maarten J. J. Menken, The New Testament and the Scriptures of Israel (New York: T & T Clark International, 2005): 79–100. Vittorio Fusco ("'Point of View' and 'Implicit Reader' in Two Eschatological Texts: Lk 19,11-28; Acts 1,6-8," *The Four Gospels 1992: Festschrift Frans Neirynck*, eds. F. Van Segbroeck, C. M. Tuckett, et al., Vol. 2 [Leuven, Belgium: University Press, 1992]: 1677–96) argues that for Luke the witness to the ends of the earth has fundamentally been completed and the conditions for the parousia have almost been fulfilled.

9. Compare H. H. Rowley, "The Servant Mission: The Servant Songs and Evangelism," *Interpretation* 8.3 (July 1954): 259–72.

10. Unless stated otherwise, biblical quotations will be from the NRSV. Compare David L. Tiede, "The Exaltation of Jesus and the Restoration of Israel in Acts 1," *Christians among Jews and Gentiles: Essays in Honor of Krister Stendahl on His Sixty-Fifth Birthday*, ed. George W. E. Nickelsburg with George W. MacRae, S.J. (Philadelphia: Fortress Press, 1986), 280–86.

11. Luke Timothy Johnson, *The Acts of the Apostles*, Sacra Pagina Series (Collegeville, Minn.: Liturgical Press, 2006), 26–27; C. K. Barrett, *A Critical and Exegetical Commentary on the Acts of the Apostles*, The International Critical Commentary on the Holy Scriptures of the Old and New Testaments

(Edinburgh, Scotland: T & T Clark, 1994), 78–81; Joseph A. Fitzmyer, *The Acts of the Apostles*, trans. Joseph A. Fitzmyer (New York: Doubleday, 1998), 205–8; W. C. van Unnik, "Der Ausdruck 'EŌS 'ESCHATOU TĒS GĒS (Apostelgeschichte 1:8) und sein alttestamentlicher Hintergrund," *Studia Biblica et Semitica Theodoro Christiano Vriezen* (Wageningen, H. Veenman, 1966 [1967]): 335–49. Especially confirming of my positions is Thomas S. Moore, "'To the End of the Earth': The Geographical and Ethnic Universalism of Acts 1:8 in Light of Isaianic Influence on Luke," *JETS* 40.3 (September 1997): 389–99.

12. Even when the other occurrences in LXX Isaiah of the precise phrase "to the end of the earth" accentuate its geographical sense, their contexts also refer to the Gentiles or all other nations. Isaiah 8:9 uses the same phrase (literally "listen to the end of the earth" from *epakousate heōs eschatou tēs gēs*) to warn the nations (especially Gentiles) that any plots against God's people will be frustrated, because "God is with us" (in Hebrew, a play on the name *Immanuel*, as in Isa 7:14). Compare Isaiah 48:20; 62:11. In LXX Isaiah, other passages use *ap' akrou tēs gēs* with the same sense, "from [or to] the end of the earth": Isaiah 5:26; 24:16; 40:28; 41:5, 9; 42:10; 43:6; 52:10.

13. Regarding implications of the term in "New Testament echoes" of a Septuagint text, see Kenneth Duncan Litwak, *Echoes of Scripture in Luke-Acts Telling the History of God's People Intertextually*, Journal for the Study of the New Testament (London; New York: T & T Clark International, 2005). For the influence of Isaiah 49:6, see also Moore, "To the End of the Earth," 392–95.

14. Compare the collection of essays, *Witness to the Gospel: The Theology of Acts*, ed. I. Howard Marshall and David Peterson (Grand Rapids, Mich.: Eerdmans, 1998).

15. Compare Edward Fudge, "Paul's Apostolic Self-Consciousness at Athens," *Journal of the Evangelical Theological Society* 14.3 (Summer 1971): 193–98.

16. There are no references to *pais* after Isaiah 55. Before Isaiah 40 it appears only a few times. In Isaiah 20:3, *pais* refers to the prophet himself as "my servant Isaiah" who walked naked and barefoot as a prophetic sign portending the fate of Egyptians and Ethiopians before Assyria. It applies to "my servant Eliakim" who will replace the threatened steward Shebna in Isaiah 22:20. In Isaiah 24:2 it is used in parallelisms to predict that everyone will suffer: "as with the slave, so with his master." In narrative, it is a formal self-designation: "Please speak to your servants in Aramaic" (Isa 36:11). Later in the same passage it is used for "the servants of King Hezekiah" (37:5). Hezekiah is reassured, "For I will defend this city to save it, for my own sake and for the sake of my servant David" (37:35).

The only occurrence of *doulos* before Isaiah 40–55 is the promise that Israel will enslave nations who had enslaved them (Isa 14:2). This same term occurs only three times after Isaiah 40–55 for groups of God's servants: in Isaiah 56:6 (foreigners); in 63:17 and 65:9 (Israelites). W. A. M. Beuken, "The Main Theme of Trito-Isaiah: The Servants of YHWH," *JSOT* 47 (1990): 67–87, argues that the servant of YHWH in Second Isaiah is succeeded by servants of YHWH in Trito-Isaiah, portrayed as "offspring" of the servant (compare the promise in Isa 53:10, "he shall see his offspring").

17. Compare Dennis E. Johnson, "Jesus against the Idols: The Use of the Isaianic Servant Songs in the Missiology of Acts," *WTJ* 52 (1990): 343–53.

18. Ibid., 350–51.

19. Compare Francis Cardinal George, "A new apologetics for a new evangelization," *TD* 47:4 (Winter 2000): 341–50; Roch Kereszty, "Why a new evangelization? A study of its theological rationale," *Communio: International Catholic Review* 21 (Winter, 1994): 594–611; Avery Dulles, "John Paul II and the New Evangelization—What Does It Mean?" *John Paul II and the New Evangelization: How You Can Bring the Good News to Others*, eds. Ralph Martin and Peter Williamson (San Francisco: Ignatius Press, 1995): 25–39, 170–72.

20. Compare Reinhard Gregor Kratz, "Cyru, Messie de Dieu," *Foi et Vie* 93.4 (1994): 51–65. G. I. Davies notes that the closest parallel to traditionally Davidic dominion transferred to a foreign ruler is to Nebuchadrezzar in Jeremiah ("The Destiny of the Nations in the Book of Isaiah," *The Book of Isaiah, Le Livre d'Isaïe: Les oracles et leurs relectures, unité et complexité de l'ouvrage par Jacques Vermeylen*, Bibliotheca Ephemeridum Theologicarum Lovaniensium 81 [Leuven, Belgium: University Press, 1989], 116).

21. Compare Walter C. Kaiser, *Mission in the Old Testament: Israel as a Light to the Nations* (Grand Rapids, Mich.: Baker Books, 2000), especially chapter 4, "God's Call to Israel to Be a Light to the Nations" (51–63).

22. *The Septuagint Version of the Old Testament and Apocrypha with an English Translation*, trans. Charles Lee Brenton (Grand Rapids, Mich.: Zondervan, 5th reprint 1978 of London: Samuel Bagster & Sons, 1851), 886.

23. Compare G. P. Hugenberger, "The Servant of the Lord in the 'Servant Songs' of Isaiah: A Second Moses Figure," *The Lord's Anointed: Interpretation of Old Testament Messianic Texts*, eds. Philip E. Satterthwaite, Richard S. Hess, and Gordon J. Wenham (Grand Rapids, Mich.: Baker Book House, 1995), 105–40.

24. On the court setting of the Isaianic witness motif, compare Moore, "Lucan Great Commission and Isaianic Servant," 55–56.

25. On the commission to be witnesses in Luke and Isaiah, compare Moore, "Lucan Great Commission and Isaianic Servant," 53–56, 58.

26. See Kereszty, "Why a new evangelization?" 610–11; *Salvation to the ends of the earth: A biblical theology of mission*, New Studies in Biblical Theology 11, eds. Andreas J. Köstenberger and Peter T. O'Brien (Downers Grove, Ill.: InterVarsity Press [Apollos], 2001).

27. See Beverly Roberts Gaventa, "'You Will Be My Witnesses': Aspects of Mission in the Acts of the Apostles," *Missiology: An International Review* 10.4 (October 1982): 413–25, especially pages 422–23, "The Mission and the Cultures."

28. Compare Kereszty, "Why a new evangelization?" 608; *Jesus and the Suffering Servant: Isaiah 53 and Christian Origins*, eds. William H. Bellinger, Jr. and William R. Farmer (Harrisburg, Pa.: Trinity Press, 1998).

29. Dulles, "New Evangelization—What Does It Mean?" 25–39.

30. Compare also John Paul II, *Redemptoris Missio* [RM], no. 3, cited on page 28.

31. Avery Dulles, "John Paul II and the New Evangelization," *New Evangelization in the Third Millenium*, Studia Missionalia 48 (Rome: Editrice Pontificia Università Gregoriana, 1999): 178.

32. Dulles, "John Paul II, New Evangelization," 169–77.

33. Ibid.

34. A thorough argument is provided in the same collection by Earl Muller, "The Holy Spirit, the Principal Agent of Evangelization," *New Evangelization in the Third Millenium*, Studia Missionalia 48 (Rome: Editrice Pontificia Università Gregoriana, 1999): 123–163.

35. Keretszty, "Why a new evangelization?": the list is on pages 606–11, this point on pages 607–8.

36. George, "A new apologetics": 341–50.

37. Benedict XVI, *Deus Caritas Est* ("God is Love"), § 19.

Swallowing Jonah: Scripture and Identity in Early Christianity

1. For example, in Luke T. Johnson, "Fragments of an Untidy Conversation: Theology and the Literary Diversity of the New Testament," in *Biblical Theology: Problems and Perspectives*, eds. Steven J. Kraftchick, Charles D. Myers, Jr., and Ben C. Ollenburger (Nashville: Abingdon, 1995), 276–89; *Scripture and Discernment: Decision Making in the Church* (Nashville: Abingdon Press, 1996);

and in his dialogue with William S. Kurz, S.J., *The Future of Catholic Biblical Scholarship: A Constructive Conversation* (Grand Rapids, Mich.: Eerdmans, 2002).

2. On the visuality of Greco-Roman culture, see the stimulating essays by Ja Elsner, *Roman Eyes: Visuality and Subjectivity in Art and Text* (Princeton, N.J.: Princeton University Press, 2007). As one example of an attempt to interpret a New Testament text (the Apocalypse) by evoking the Roman love of spectacle, see Christopher A. Frilingos, *Spectacles of Empire: Monsters, Martyrs, and the Book of Revelation* (Philadelphia: University of Pennsylvania Press, 2004).

3. From the third century, the period of the earliest catacomb evidence, the only significant set of decorations discovered in a Christian meeting place was in the remodeled house unearthed in 1931–32 in the long-buried Roman garrison town of Dura Europos, on the banks of the Euphrates. There we see three different modes of early Christian visual identification—a scene from the Bible: Adam, Eve, and the snake; a representation of Christ in the Greco-Roman figure of the *Kriophorus*, the shepherd of souls; and three scenes from the Gospels: Jesus walking on water and saving the impetuous Peter, his healing the paralytic, and, most impressively presented, the procession of women to the tomb on Easter morning. For many years this portion of the Christian baptismal room from Dura was reconstructed in the Yale University Art Gallery, but unfortunately the exhibit was dismantled some three decades ago, and the remaining portions of the original paintings are poorly preserved and presently inaccessible.

4. E. J. Bickerman, *Four Strange Books of the Bible: Jonah, Daniel, Koheleth, Esther* (New York: Schocken Books, 1968).

5. See the included picture of the Jonah Sarcophagus; also Wolfgang Wischmeyer, "Zur Entstehung und Bedeutung des Jonasbildes," *Actes du Xe Congrès international d'archéologie chrétienne: Thessalonique, 28 Septembre–4 Octobre, 1980*, Studi di antichità cristiana (Vatican City: Pontificio istituto di archeologia cristiana; Thessaloniki: Hetaireia Makedonikōn Spoudōn, 1984), 717.

6. On the form of this "paradigm prayer," later adopted in the Christian tradition of *commendationes animae*, see Wolfgang Wischmeyer, "Das Beispiel Jonas: Zur kirchengeschichtlichen Bedeutung von Denkmälern fruhchristlicher Grabeskunst zwischen Theologie und Frommigkeit," *Zeitschrift für Kirchengeschichte* 92 (1981): 175f. Jonah also appears as a paradigm in a comment of the Mishnah on the sixth benediction of the daily prayer: "He who answered Jonah in the belly of the fish will answer you and hear the sound of your cry this day. Blessed are You, O Lord, who answers prayer in a time of trouble" (*m. Ta'an.* 2.4,

quoted in Roger David Aus, *The Stilling of the Storm: Studies in Early Palestinian Judaic Traditions*, International Studies in Formative Christianity and Judaism (Binghamton, N.Y.: Global Publications, Binghamton University [SUNY], 2000), 5n16.

7. This sociological implication is well observed by Wischmeyer, "Beispiel," 172; see also Wolfgang Wischmeyer, "The Sociology of Pre-Constantine Christianity: Approach from the Visible," *Origins of Christendom in the West*, ed. Alan Kreider (Edinburgh, Scotland: T & T Clark, 2001), 121–52.

8. Marion Lawrence, "Ships, Monsters and Jonah," *American Journal of Archaeology* 66 (1962): 295.

9. On a red-figured cup in the Vatican; Lawrence, "Ships, Monsters and Jonah," 294 and Pl. 78, fig. 7.

10. Marion Lawrence, "Three Pagan Themes in Christian Art," *De Artibus Opuscula XL: Essays in Honor of Erwin Panofsky*, ed. Millard Meiss (New York: NYU Press, 1961), 323–34. Wischmeyer, "Beispiel," lists much of the older literature. The classic is still Otto Mitius, *Jonas auf den Denkmälern des christlichen Altertums*, Archäologische Studien zum christlichen Altertum und Mittelalter (Freiburg i.B.: Mohr, 1897). An excellent example of an Endymion sarcophagus is in the Metropolitan Museum in New York (Rogers Fund, 1947 [47.100.4]).

11. The essays cited in the previous note provide rich evidence.

12. Aus, *Stilling of the Storm*, 3–55, with an excellent account of the variations of ancient Jewish midrash on Jonah.

13. Yves-Marie Duval, *Le Livre de Jonas dans la littérature chrétienne grecque et latine: Sources et influence du Commentaire sur Jonas de saint Jérôme* (Paris: Études augustiniennes, 1973), 29n84.

14. This is the principal point argued so persuasively by Wischmeyer, "Beispiel." On the liturgical reading of Jonah, for which scant evidence survives, see Duval, *Le Livre de Jonas*, 39–51. He finds great variety from one region to another; in Milan it was habitually read in Holy Week in the fourth century (Ambrose, *Ep.* 20. 25–26), on Holy Thursday according to a text in the Hexameron (Duval 41); in Antioch Chrysostom attests the use of Jonah during Lent; Cyril of Jerusalem connects it with the general resurrection and 1 Corinthians 15 (Duval 42–44).

15. Theodore's discussion of Jonah is part of his commentary on the Dodekapropheton (*PG* 66, cols. 124–632), comprising cols. 319–45. Quotations below are from Theodore of Mopsuestia, *Commentary on the Twelve Prophets*, trans. Robert C. Hill (Washington, D.C.: Catholic University of America Press,

2004); the text is cited by the columns of PG. For Jerome, I have used the critical edition by Yves-Marie Duval: Jérôme, *Commentaire sur Jonas*, Sources chrétiennes (Paris: Editions du Cerf, 1985), which is reprinted with minor corrections and a German translation in Jerome, *Commentarius in Ionam prophetam = Kommentar zu dem Propheten Jona*, trans. and ed. Siegfried Risse, Fontes Christiani (Turnhout, Belgium: Brepols, 2003). When the text is cited below, I give page numbers from both Duval's and Risse's editions. I have made use of the English translation by Timothy Michael Hegedus, "Jerome's Commentary on Jonah: Translation with Introduction and Critical Notes," ed. M. A. Thesis (Waterloo, Ont.: Wilfrid Laurier University, 1991). Evidence for possible antecedents of Jerome's commentary is exhaustively treated by Duval, *Le Livre de Jonas*, cited above, with a sketch of Jerome's influence on subsequent commentaries down to the twelfth century.

16. Col. 336, trans. Hill, 199. In a Hellenistic Jewish homily that has come down to us among the works of Philo in an Armenian translation, the *kētos* appears as "a new ship" to save Jonah from the sea. Its belly becomes a house for him, "its eyes a mirror of things without" (§§63f., Folker Siegert, *Drei hellenistisch-jüdische Predigten: Ps.-Philon, "Über Jona," "Über Simson" und "Über die Gottesbezeichnung 'wohltätig verzehrendes Feuer'"* [Tübingen, Germany: Mohr, 1980], 19). The underwater trip is elaborated in terms worthy of Jules Verne in §§65f., in a first-person addition of Jonah's prayer, §§79–81, and again in Jonah's complaint after Nineveh's salvation, §§163–81, in which he admits that the ultimate purpose of his flight has been to make him to be a witness of this miraculous voyage. The rabbinic midrash on Jonah has come down in several variations; the most useful recension is conveniently available in the collection of Adolph Jellinek, *Bet ha-midrash. Sammlung kleiner Midraschim und vermischter abhandlungen aus der ältern jüdischen literatur. Nach handschriften und druckwerken gesammelt und nebst einleitungen hrsg. von Adolph Jellinek*, 2nd ed. (Jerusalem: Bamberger & Wahrmann, 1938), 2:96–105; a German translation in August Wünsche, ed. and trans., *Aus Israels Lehrhallen. Zum ersten Male übersetzt von Aug. Wünsche* (Leipzig, Germany: E. Pfeiffer, 1907–10), 2:39–56. It also emphasizes Jonah's luxurious accommodation within the fish and his marvelous journey. Jonah went into the mouth of the fish as one goes into the great house of assembly. The fish's eyes were like two windows, providing light for Jonah (Ps. 97:11) and through which he could see everything in the depths. For the motif of Jonah's *Unversehrtheit* in Christian iconography, see Wischmeier, "Entstehung," 714.

17. Further on Jerome's interest in the etymology of the names, see Risse, 389.

18. Uwe Steffen, *Die Jona-Geschichte: ihre Auslegung und Darstellung im Judentum, Christentum und Islam* (Neukirchen-Vluyn, Germany: Neukirchener, 1994), 75–83. The use of the example of Nineveh in preaching about repentance in Antioch and Milan leads Duval to ask whether it was part of preparation of catechumens for baptism; later in the western church (fifth and sixth centuries) it was drawn into the liturgy of rogation days, beginning with the report that Mamertus of Vienne used the example of the Ninevites in calling for penitential fasting on the occasion of an earthquake (Duval, *Livre de Jonas*, 44–47). On the absence of the motif of conversion of the Gentiles from early Christian art, against the interpretation by Yves Congar, see Duval (*Livre de Jonas*, 22).

19. Jellinek, 1:102; my trans.; cf. Wünsche, 50. The tension between God's two "powers" was well known in Greek Jewish tradition, as attested by Philo, for example *Cher.* 27–29; *QE* 2.68; see the classic work by A[rthur] Marmorstein, "Philo and the Names of God," *Jewish Quarterly Review* 22 (1932): 295–306.

20. Comment on Jonah 1:3a, Duval 172, Risse 98. Cf. Risse's discussion in his introduction, 57–60.

21. Perhaps the most vigorous and consistent advocate for a renewed canonical norm was my late and much lamented teacher and colleague, Brevard S. Childs, for example, *Introduction to the Old Testament as Scripture* (Philadelphia: Fortress Press, 1979); *The New Testament as Canon: An Introduction* (Philadelphia: Fortress Press, 1985); *Biblical Theology of the Old and New Testaments: Theological Reflection on the Christian Bible* (Minneapolis: Augsburg Fortress, 1993). Cf. also the important work of James A. Sanders; for example, *From Sacred Story to Sacred Text: Canon as Paradigm* (Philadelphia: Fortress Press, 1987), and *Canon and Community: A Guide to Canonical Criticism* (Philadelphia: Fortress Press, 1984).

22. Luke Timothy Johnson, "Fragments of an Untidy Conversation: Theology and the Literary Diversity of the New Testament," *Biblical Theology: Problems and Perspectives*, eds. Steven J. Kraftchick, Charles D. Myers, Jr., and Ben C. Ollenburger (Nashville: Abingdon Press, 1995), 285f.

23. Johnson and Kurz, *The Future of Catholic Biblical Scholarship*, 135.

24. I echo Richard B. Hays, *Echoes of Scripture in the Letters of Paul* (New Haven, Conn.; London: Yale University Press, 1989), who borrows from the poet and critic John Hollander the figure *metalepsis*, an apt term for the kind of resonance found through many parts of Jewish scripture and the New Testament.

25. Timothy Radcliffe, O.P., *Talking to Strangers*, Woodward Lecture, Yale University, October 8, 1996 (N.p.: Privately printed, 1996), 10.

26. Luke Timothy Johnson, *Religious Experience in Earliest Christianity: A Missing Dimension in New Testament Studies* (Minneapolis: Augsburg Fortress, 1998).

27. Johnson, "Fragments," 283, 284; italics original. The process of "discernment" described here is strikingly like that advocated by Dale Martin in several of his recent essays, in which he attacks "the myth of textual agency" or "Christian textual foundationalism." Like Johnson, he emphasizes the diversity of scripture and the necessity for the reading community to exercise its freedom, surmounting "the anxiety of uncertainty." He also takes up the community's experience as ingredient of the interpretive practice, using the model of Paul's moves in Galatians 3–4 and 1 Corinthians 10: "It is certainly not true that Paul *simply* inscribes them [the Corinthian Christians] into the world of the text. It is truer that Paul interprets the text by means of their experiences as new Christians." See Dale B. Martin, *Sex and the Single Savior: Gender and Sexuality in Biblical Interpretation* (Louisville; London: Westminster John Knox Press, 2006), especially chapters 1, 10, and 11; quotations from pages 2, 3, 156, italics original. The convergence of hermeneutical stances by Martin and Johnson is the more remarkable, as their own religious experiences and biographies would seem, from without, almost opposite in so many respects.

28. See Johnson, *Scripture and Discernment*.

29. Johnson and Kurz, *The Future of Catholic Biblical Scholarship*, 135.

30. Martin, 16.

31. Johnson, "Fragments" 284.

32. Bernard Williams, *Ethics and the Limits of Philosophy* (Cambridge, Mass.: Harvard University Press, 1985). But see also the important critique of Williams's recommendations by Hilary Putnam, "Bernard Williams and the Absolute Conception of the World," *Renewing Philosophy* (Cambridge, Mass.: Harvard University Press, 1992), 80–107.

33. Garrett Green, *Theology, Hermeneutics, and Imagination: The Crisis of Interpretation at the End of Modernity* (Cambridge, Mass.; New York: Cambridge University Press, 2000), 14f.

34. Ibid.

35. See Green's earlier essay, "'The Bible as . . .': Fictional Narrative and Scriptural Truth," *Scriptural Authority and Narrative Interpretation*, ed. Garrett Green (Philadelphia: Fortress Press, 1987), 79–96.

36. For further discussion of the rhetorical shape of Jonah beyond the standard commentaries, see especially Jonathan Magonet, *Form and Meaning: Studies in Literary Techniques in the Book of Jonah*, Bible and Literature Series (Sheffield, England: Almond Press, 1983); Phyllis Trible, *Rhetorical Criticism: Context, Method, and the Book of Jonah*, Guides to Biblical Scholarship (Minneapolis: Augsburg Fortress, 1994); and Kenneth M. Craig, *A Poetics of Jonah: Art in the Service of Ideology*, 2nd ed. (Macon, Ga.: Mercer University Press, 1999).

37. Rabbinic midrash ties Jonah firmly to Elijah, even identifying Jonah with the widow's child that Elijah raised to life: see the citations collected by Aus (3n10).

SELECT BIBLIOGRAPHY OF WORKS BY LUKE TIMOTHY JOHNSON

Books

Ed., *Teaching Religion to Undergraduates: Some Approaches and Ideas from Teachers to Teachers*. Society for Religion in Higher Education, 1973.

The Literary Function of Possessions in Luke-Acts. Society for Biblical Literature Dissertation Series 39. Missoula: Scholars Press, 1977.

Invitation to the Letters of Paul III: Ephesians, Colossians, Pastorals. Invitation to the New Testament. Garden City: Doubleday, 1980.

Sharing Possessions: Mandate and Symbol of Faith. Overtures to Biblical Theology. Philadelphia: Fortress Press, 1981. London: SCM Press, 1986.

Some Hard Blessings: Meditations on the Beatitudes in Matthew. Niles, Ill.: Argus Communications, 1981.

Decision Making in the Church: A Biblical Model. Philadelphia: Fortress Press, 1983.

The Writings of the New Testament: An Interpretation. Philadelphia: Fortress Press, 1986. London: SCM Press, 1986; trans. into Korean, 2000; 2nd revised and enlarged English edition with the assistance of Todd Penner, 1999.

First Timothy, Second Timothy, Titus. John Knox Preaching Guides. Atlanta: John Knox Press, 1987; trans. into Korean, 1999.

Faith's Freedom: A Classic Spirituality for Contemporary Christians. Philadelphia: Fortress Press, 1990.

A Commentary on the Gospel of Luke. Sacra Pagina. Collegeville, Minn.: Liturgical Press, 1991. Italian ed., 2004.

A Commentary on the Acts of the Apostles. Sacra Pagina. Collegeville, Minn.: Liturgical Press, 1992.

Proclamation 5: Interpreting the Lessons of the Church Year (Pentecost 3). Minneapolis: Augsburg Fortress, 1993.

The Letter of James. The Anchor Bible 37A; New York: Doubleday, 1995.

Letters to Paul's Delegates: A Commentary on 1 Timothy, 2 Timothy and Titus. Valley Forge: Trinity Press International, 1996.

The Real Jesus: The Misguided Quest for the Historical Jesus and the Truth of the Traditional Gospels. San Francisco: HarperSanFrancisco, 1996. Korean trans. by Hae Sook Son [Seoul, Korea: Christian Literature Crusade, 2003].

Scripture and Discernment: Decision Making in the Church. Nashville: Abingdon Press, 1996.

Reading Romans: A Literary and Theological Commentary. New York: Crossroad, 1997; reissued by Smyth and Helwys, 2001.

Living Jesus: Learning the Heart of the Gospels. San Francisco: HarperSanFrancisco, 1998.

Religious Experience: A Missing Dimension in New Testament Studies. Minneapolis: Augsburg Fortress, 1998.

The First and Second Letter to Timothy. The Anchor Bible 35A; New York: Doubleday, 2001.

With William Kurz. *The Future of Catholic Biblical Scholarship: A Constructive Conversation.* Grand Rapids, Mich.: Eerdmans, 2002.

Septuagintal Midrash in the Speeches of Acts. Père Marquette Lectures 33; Milwaukee: Marquette University Press, 2002.

The Creed: What Christians Believe and Why It Matters. New York: Doubleday, 2003. In U.K., published by Darton, Longman, and Todd.

Brother of Jesus, Friend of God: Studies in the Letter of James. Grand Rapids, Mich.: Eerdmans, 2004.

The Living Gospel. London: Continuum, 2004.

Hebrews: A Commentary. The New Testament Library. Louisville: Westminster John Knox Press, 2006.

Light among Gentiles: Greco-Roman Religion and the Ways of Being Christian. [Forthcoming].

Scholarly Articles

"Gnosticism in the Rabbinic Tradition," *Resonance* 4 (1969): 5–17.

"The Natural Knowledge of God according to Vatican I's Dei Filius," *Resonance* 5 (1970): 9–17.

"Norms for True and False Prophecy in 1 Corinthians 12–14," *American Benedictine Review* 22 (1971): 29–45.

"2 Timothy and the Polemic Against False Teachers: A Re-Examination," *Journal of Religious Studies* 6/7 (1978–79): 1–26.

"On Finding the Lukan Community: A Cautious Cautionary Essay," 1979 SBL Seminar Papers ed. P. Achtemeier (Missoula, Mont.: Scholars Press, 1979), 87–100.

"The Lukan Kingship Parable (Lk 19:11-27)," *Novum Testamentum* 24 (1982): 139–59. Reprinted in *The Composition of Luke's Gospel*, Brill's Readers in Biblical Studies 1, ed. D. Orton (Leiden, Netherlands: Brill, 1999): 69–89.

"Romans 3:21-26 and the Faith of Jesus," *Catholic Biblical Quarterly* 44 (1982): 77–90.

"The Use of Leviticus 19 in the Letter of James," *Journal of Biblical Literature* 101 (1982): 391–401.

"James 3:13–4:10 and the *Topos* PERI PHTHONOU," *Novum Testamentum* 25 (1983): 327–47.

"Friendship with the World and Friendship with God: A Study of Discipleship in James," *Discipleship in the New Testament*, ed. F. Segovia (Philadelphia: Fortress Press, 1985), 166–83.

"The Mirror of Remembrance (James 1:22-25)," *Catholic Biblical Quarterly* 50 (1988): 632–45.

"The New Testament's Anti-Jewish Slander and the Conventions of Ancient Polemic," *Journal of Biblical Literature* 108 (1989): 419–41.

"The Authority of the New Testament in the Church: a Theological Reflection," *Conservative, Moderate, Liberal: The Biblical Authority Debate*, ed. C. R. Blaisdell (St. Louis: CPB Press, 1990), 87–99.

"Taciturnity and True Religion (James 1:26-27)," *Greeks, Romans, and Christians: Essays in Honor of Abraham J. Malherbe*, eds. D. Balch, et al. (Minneapolis: Augsburg Fortress, 1990), 329–39.

"The Social Dimensions of *Soteria* in Luke-Acts and Paul," *Society of Biblical Literature Seminar Papers*, ed. E. H. Lovering (Atlanta: Scholars Press, 1993), 520–36.

"Fragments of an Untidy Conversation: Theology and the Literary Diversity of the New Testament," *Biblical Theology: Problems and Perspectives; in Honor of J. Christiaan Beker*, eds. S. J. Kraftchick, C. D. Myers, and B. C. Ollenburger (Nashville: Abingdon Press, 1995), 276–89.

"Religious Rights and Christian Texts," *Religious Human Rights in Global Perspective*, Vol 1: *Religious Perspectives*, eds. J. Witte Jr., and J. van der Vyver (Dordrecht, Netherlands: Martinus Nijhoff, 1995), 65–96.

"The Social World of James: Literary Analysis and Historical Reconstruction," *The Social World of the First Christians: Essays in Honor of Wayne A. Meeks*, eds. L. Michael White and O. Larry Yarbrough (Minneapolis: Augsburg Fortress, 1995), 178–97.

"Glossolalia and the Embarrassments of Experience," *The Princeton Seminary Bulletin* 18 (1997), 113–34.

"Imagining the World Scripture Imagines," *Modern Theology* 14/2 (1998), 165–80; appearing also in *Theology and Scriptural Imagination*, Directions in Modern Theology, eds. L. G. Jones and J. J. Buckley (Oxford, England: Blackwell, 1998), 3–18.

"The Christology of Luke-Acts," *Who Do You Say That I Am? Essays in Christology in Honor of Jack Dean Kingsbury*, eds. M. A. Powell and D. R. Bauer (Louisville: Westminster John Knox Press, 1999), 49–65.

"A Historiographical Response to Wright's Jesus," *Jesus and the Restoration of Israel: A Critical Assessment of N. T. Wright's* Jesus and the Victory of God, ed. C. N. Newman (Downer's Grove, Ill,: InterVarsity Press, 1999), 206–24.

"The Humanity of Jesus: What's At Stake in the Quest for the Historical Jesus," *The Jesus Controversy: Perspectives in Conflict* (with John Dominic Crossan and Werner Kelber) [Rockwell Lecture Series, ed. G. P. McKenny] (Harrisburg, Penn.: Trinity Press International, 1999), 48–74; trans. into Korean, 2006.

"Koinonia: Diversity and Unity in Early Christianity," *Theology Digest* 46 (1999): 303–13.

"*Oikonomia Theou*: The Theological Voice of 1 Timothy from the Perspective of Pauline Authorship," and "Response to Margaret Mitchell," *Horizons in Biblical Theology* 21/2 (1999): 87–104, 140–44.

"Proselytism and Witness in Earliest Christianity: A Study in Origins," *Sharing the Book: Religious Perspectives on the Rights and Wrongs of Proselytism*, Religion and Human Rights 4, eds. J. Witte, Jr., and R. C. Martin (Maryknoll, N.Y.: Orbis Books, 1999), 145–57, 376–84.

With Wesley Wachob, "The Sayings of Jesus in the Letter of James," *Authenticating the Words of Jesus*, New Testament Tools and Studies 28,1, eds. B. Chilton and C. A. Evans (Leiden, Netherlands: Brill, 1999), 431–50.

"God Ever New, Ever the Same: The Witness of James and Peter," *The Forgotten God: Perspectives in Biblical Theology*, eds. A. D. Das and F. J. Matera (Louisville: Westminster John Knox Press, 2002), 211–27.

"The Jewish Bible after the Holocaust: A Response to Emile Fackenheim," *A Shadow of Glory: Reading the New Testament after the Holocaust*, ed. Tod Linafelt (New York: Routledge, 2002), 216–31.

"Reading Wisdom Wisely," *Louvain Studies* 28 (2003): 99–112.

"The Revelatory Body: Notes toward a Somatic Theology," in *The Phenomenology of the Body*, ed. D. J. Martino (Pittsburgh: Simon Silverman Phenomenology Center at the University of Duquesne, 2003), 69–85.

"The Scriptural World of Hebrews," *Interpretation* 57 (2003): 237–50.

"Transformation of the Mind and Moral Discernment in Paul," in *Early Christianity and Classical Culture: Comparative Studies in Honor of Abraham J. Malherbe*, ed. J. T. Fitzgerald, et. al. (NovTSupp 110; Leiden, Netherlands: Brill, 2003), 215–36.

"Gender in the Letter of James: A Surprising Witness," *A Feminist Companion to the Catholic Epistles and Hebrews*, ed. A. J. Levine (Feminist Companion to the New Testament and Early Christian Writings 8; New York: T & T Clark International, 2004), 103–13.

"The Material Expression of Friendship in the New Testament," *Interpretation* 58 (2004): 158-71.

"Literary Criticism of Luke-Acts: Is Reception History Pertinent?" *Journal for the Study of the New Testament* 28 (2005): 159–62.

"Conversation, Conversion, and Construction," *Nova et Vetera* 4/1 (2006), 172–85.

"Does a Theology of the Canonical Gospels Make Sense?" in *The Nature of New Testament Theology: Essays in Honor of Robert Morgan*, edited by C. Rowland and C. Tuckett (Oxford: Blackwell, 2006), 93–108.

"Anti-Judaism and the New Testament," *The Handbook for the Study of the Historical Jesus* (Forthcoming).

"1 Timothy 1:1-20: The Shape of the Struggle," *Colloquium Paulinum Papers* (Forthcoming).

"John and Thomas in Context: An Exercise in Canonical Criticism" *Richard Hays Festschrift* (Forthcoming).

"Narrative Criticism and Translation: The Case of the NRSV," *Holladay Festschrift* (Forthcoming).

Encyclopedia and Anthology Articles

"Hans Kung," "John the Baptist," "Joseph, Saint," "Jude, Letter of," "Justification," "Kingdom of God," "Last Supper," "Mary, Saint," "Mary Magdalene, Saint," "Palm Sunday," "Passion," "Pentecost," "Peter, Letters of," "Peter, Saint," and "Philemon, Letter to," *The Encyclopedia Americana* (Danbury, Conn.: Grolier, 1981–82).

"James," *Harper's Bible Commentary*, ed. James L. Mays (San Francisco: HarperCollins, 1988) 1272–78.

"The General Letters and Revelation," *The Catholic Study Bible* (Oxford University Press, 1990; revised edition, 2006): 496–525.

"Luke-Acts, Book of" and "Tongues, Gift of," *The Anchor Bible Dictionary*, ed. David Noel Freedman, (New York: Doubleday, 1992), 4:403–20, 6:596–600.

"The Letter of James," *New Interpreter's Bible*, vol. XII (Nashville: Abingdon Press, 1998), 175–225.

"James, Letter of," *Dictionary of Biblical Interpretation*, ed. J. Hayes (Nashville: Abingdon Press, 1999), 560–62.

"Worship in the New Testament," and "James the Son of Zebedee," *Religion in Geschichte und Gegenwart*, 4th ed. (Leiden, Netherlands, Brill, 1999).

"Cross and Crucifixion" and "Sermon on the Mount," *The Oxford Companion to Christian Thought*, eds. A. Hastings, A. Mason, and H. Pyper (Oxford, England: Oxford University Press, 2000), 146–47, 654–56.

"Paul's Ecclesiology," *The Cambridge Companion to Saint Paul*, ed. J. D. G. Dunn, (Cambridge, Mass.: Cambridge University Press, 2003), 199–211.

With Mark Jordan, "Christianity," *Sex, Marriage, & Family in World Religions*, eds. D. S. Browning, M. Christian Green, and J. Witte (New York: Columbia University Press, 2006), 77–149.

"The Bible's Authority for and in the Church" *Engaging Biblical Authority: Perspectives on the Bible as Scripture*, ed. W. P. Brown (Louisville: Westminster John Knox Press, 2007), 62–72.

"The Jesus of the Gospels and Philosophy," *Jesus and Philosophy: New Essays*, ed. Paul Moser (Cambridge University Press, Forthcoming).

"The Law in Early Christianity," *Cambridge Companion to Law and Christianity*, (Cambridge University Press, Forthcoming).

"The Letter of James," *Theological Commentary on the Bible*, eds. G. O'Day and D. Peterson (Forthcoming).

"The New Testament," *The Blackwell Companion to Catholicism*, ed. J. Buckley (Forthcoming).

Popular Articles

"Theology and the Spiritual Life," *Reflection* (1981): 9–11.

Luke-Acts: A Story of Prophet and People [Pamphlet]. New York: Franciscan Herald Press, 1982.

Select Bibliography of Works by Luke Timothy Johnson

"Conflict and Christian Self-Definition," *The Bible Today* 25 (1987): 215–19.

"The Bible and the Poor," *Biblical Literacy Today* 3 (1989): 8–9.

"Shattering the Closure of Unbelief," in "Living by the Word," *The Christian Century* 107 (7/11-18/90): 668.

"Discerning What Is Right," in "Living by the Word," *The Christian Century* 107 (7/25-8/1/90): 699.

"Participating in Revelation," in "Living by the Word," *The Christian Century* 107 (8/8-15/90): 731.

"Two Divine Promises," in "Living by the Word," *The Christian Century* 107 (8/22-29/90): 763.

"Obedience in Context," in "Living by the Word," *The Christian Century* 107 (9/5-12/90): 795.

"Seeking God While God is Near," in "Living by the Word," *The Christian Century* 107 (9/19-26/90): 828.

"How Saint Luke Affirms the World," *Priests and People* 6 (1992): 202–6.

"How Saint Luke Challenges the World," *Priests and People* 6 (1992): 280–84.

"Luke 24:1-11: The Not-So-Empty Tomb," *Interpretation* 46 (1992): 57–61.

"In the Catholic Tradition: G. K. Chesterton," *Priests and People* 7 (1993): 67–71.

"Debate and Discernment/Scripture and the Spirit," in "Disputed Questions: Homosexuality," *Commonweal* 121:2 (1994): 11–13. Reprinted in *Virtues and Practices in the Christian Tradition*, eds. N. Murphy, B. Kallenberg, and M. T. Nation (Harrisburg, Penn.: Trinity Press International, 1997), 215–20.

"Preaching the Resurrection," *Priests and People* 8 (1994): 133–35.

"Discerning God's Word," *Priests and People* 9 (1995): 137–40.

"The New Testament and the Examined Life: Thoughts on Teaching," *The Christian Century* 112/4 (1995): 108–11.

"The Search for the (Wrong) Jesus," *Bible Review* 11/6 (December, 1995): 20–25, 44.

"Who Is Jesus? The Academy vs. the Gospels," *Commonweal* 122 (1995): 12–14.

"Decision-Making as a Theological Process: The Necessity and Difficulty of Discernment," *Sewanee Review* 39:4 (1996): 353–61.

"Edification as a Formal Criterion for Discernment in the Church," *Sewanee Review* 39:4 (1996): 362–72.

"Holiness as a Material Criterion for Discernment in the Church," *Sewanee Review* 39:4 (1996): 373–84.

"The Holy Spirit in the New Testament," *Priests and People* 10 (1996): 138–42.

"The Jesus Seminar's Misguided Quest for the Historical Jesus," *The Christian Century* 113 (1996): 16–22.

"John the Baptist: Prophet of the Great Reversal," *The Bible Today* 34 (1996): 295–99.

"Sickness and the Stoic Sage," *Voices in Our Midst: Spiritual Resources*, ed. G. R. Gary (Atlanta: Scholars Press, 1996), 9–11.

"Current Publishing in the Field of New Testament: A Not Disinterested Review," *Nexus Libri* (Spring/Summer, 1997): 1–3.

"How Does Jesus Save Us: The New Testament Witness," *Priests and People* 11 (1997): 129–33.

"A Message from Caravaggio: A Symposium on Revelation" (with Kathleen Norris, Sandra Schneiders, Donald Senior, Susan Ross), *Commonweal* 124 (1997/12): 14–18.

"Response to Criticism of *The Real Jesus*," *Bulletin for Biblical Research* 7 (1997): 249–54.

"A Scholar's Life in the Church: Raymond E. Brown," *Commonweal* 125 (1998): 7.

"Wealth and Property in the New Testament," *Priests and People* 12 (1998): 181–84.

"What Is a Seminar? Two Views of the Same Course" (with Carl Holladay), *Teaching Theology and Religion* 1 (1998): 27–30.

"So What's Catholic About It?" *Commonweal* (Jan. 16, 1998): 11–15.

"Atlanta, Georgia" in "Liturgical Reports," *Commonweal* (Jan. 30, 1998): 10.

"Learning Jesus," *The Christian Century* 115 (Dec. 2, 1998): 1142–46.

"Is History Essential for Christians to Understand the Real Jesus?" *The CQ Researcher* 8/46 (Dec. 11, 1998): 1089.

"Suffering, Sin, and Scripture," *Priests and People* 13 (1999): 87–90.

"Learning Jesus in Liturgy," *Theology, News, and Notes* (Fuller Theological Seminary) 46/2 (June, 1999): 20–23.

"The Mystery that Is Christmas," *Beliefnet.com* (December, 1999).

"Shaping a Citizen Faculty," *Academic Exchange* (Emory University, December, 1999): 10.

"An Introduction to the Letter of James," *Review and Expositor* 97 (2000): 155–67.

"A Jesus to Ponder," *The Christian Century* 117 (2000): 626–29.

"Knowing Jesus through the Gospels: A Theological Approach," *The World of the Bible* 3 (2000): 19–23.

"The Real Jesus: The Challenge of Contemporary Scholarship and the Truth of the Gospels," *The Historical Jesus through Catholic and Jewish Eyes*, eds. B. F. LeBeau, L. Greenspoon, D. Hamm (Harrisburg, Penn.: Trinity Press International, 2000), 51–65.

"Teaching Theology in Context" (with Charlotte McDaniel), *The Christian Century* 117/4 (2000): 118–22.

"Why We Must Practice Our Faith," *Priests and People* 14/6 (2000): 213–17.

"Minding Our Business: Conflicting Construals of Faculty Citizenship," *Emory Academic Exchange* (February, 2000), http://www.emory.edu/ACAD_EXCHANGE/2000/aprmay/johnson.html (accessed July 7, 2008).

"Leaving Priesthood," *BeliefNet.com* (October, 2000).

"A Disembodied 'Theology of the Body': John Paul II on Love, Sex, and Pleasure," *Commonweal* (128/2; 2001): 11–17.

"The Eucharist and the Identity of Jesus," *Priests and People* 15 (2001): 230–35.

"Isaiah the Evangelist," *Milltown Studies* 48 (2001), 88–105.

"The Church as the House/Household of God," *The Bible Today* 40/4 (2002): 224–28.

"Forward" to Richard B. Hays, *The Faith of Jesus Christ*, 2nd edition (Grand Rapids, Mich.: Eerdmans, 2002), xi–xv.

"Jesus, [Flyer] (Chicago: Claretian Press, 2002).

"The Last Word: A Way Forward," *Commonweal* 129/10 (2002): 31.

"Sacrifice Is the Body-Language of Love," *Priests and People* 16:3 (March 2002): 87–91.

"Continuing the Conversation: The Church and Daniel Goldhagen," *Commonweal* 129 (March 8, 2002): 7–8.

"Renewing Catholic Biblical Scholarship," *Priests and People* 16 (August/September, 2002): 297–301.

"The Biblical Foundations for Matrimony," *The Bible Today* 41/2 (2003): 113–16.

"Hebrews' Challenge to Christians: Christology and Discipleship," *Preaching Hebrews*, Rochester College Lectures on Preaching 4, eds. D. Fleer and D. Bland (Abilene, Tex.: ACU Press, 2003), 11–28.

"Jesus and the Little Children," *Priests and People* 17/3 (2003): 102–5.

"Christians and Jews: Starting Over," *Commonweal* 130:2 (Jan 31, 2003): 15–19.

"Sex, Women, and the Church," *Commonweal* 130 (June 20, 2003): 11–17. Also appears as "Abortion, Sexuality, and Catholicism's Public Presence," *American Catholics, American Culture: Tradition and Resistance*, ed. Margaret O'Brien Steinfels (New York: Rowman and Littlefield, 2004), 27–38.

"Building the Church in Love," *Priests and People* 18 (2004): 305–9.

"Reconciliation in the New Testament," *Priests and People* 18 (2004): 87–91.

"The Things that Make for Peace," *The Sign of Peace* Journal of the Catholic Peace Fellowship 3 (2004): 7–9.

"The New Gnosticism: An Old Threat to the Church," *Commonweal* 131/19 (Nov. 5, 2004): 28–31.

"Caring for the Earth: Why Environmentalism Needs Theology," *Commonweal* 132/13 (July 15, 2005): 16–20.

"The Church Is Creedal," in *The Many Marks of the Church*, ed. W. Madges and M. J. Daley (New London, Conn.: Twenty-Third Publications, 2006), 100–103.

"On Taking the Creed Seriously," *Handing on the Faith*, ed. R. P. Imbelli (New York: Herder and Herder, 2006), 63–76, 229–30.

"After the Big Chill: Intellectual Freedom and Catholic Theologians," *Commonweal* 133/1 (Jan. 27, 2006): 10–14.

"The Good Word: Signs of Hope," *Commonweal* 133/4 (Feb. 24, 2006): 38.

"The Good Word: Trust the Laity," *Commonweal* 133/6 (Mar. 24, 2006): 31.

"The Good Word: With Thankfulness and Praise," *Commonweal* 133/8 (April 21, 2006): 31.

"The Good Word: A Larger Sense of Church," *Commonweal* 133/10 (May 19, 2006): 31.

"The Good Word: The Chosen," *Commonweal* 133/12 (June 16, 2006): 30.

"The Examined Life: Use Only as Directed," *US Catholic* 71/8 (August 2006): 50.

"The Good Word: You Say Potato, I Say…" *Commonweal* 133/14 (Aug. 11, 2006), 30.

"The Good Word: Thank You, Sister," *Commonweal* 133/16 (Sept. 22, 2006): 38.

"The Good Word: The Catholic Presence," *Commonweal* 133/18 (October, 2006): 38.

"Creation," *Perspectives on Science and Christian Faith* 59/1 (2007).

"Irenaeus of Lyons, Teacher of the Church," *Liguorian* 95/4 (2007): 20–23.

"Onward," *Take Heart: Catholic Writers on Hope in Our Time*, ed. B. Birnbaum (New York: Crossroad, 2007), 137–41.

"Homosexuality and the Church: Scripture and Experience," *Commonweal* 134/12 (June 15, 2007): 14–17.

"Stanley or Matthew: Pick One," Symposium on Hauerwas' *Gospel of Matthew*, *Pro Ecclesia* (July 2007).

"Did Jesus Have Faith?" *Commonweal* 135/2 (January 31, 2008).

www.ingramcontent.com/pod-product-compliance
Lightning Source LLC
Chambersburg PA
CBHW010717300426
44114CB00021B/2878